IMAGES of America

SACRAMENTO'S OAK PARK

Edited by Lee M.A. Simpson

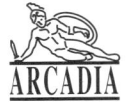

ARCADIA

Copyright © 2004 by Lee M.A. Simpson
ISBN 0-7385-2932-X

Published by Arcadia Publishing
Charleston SC, Chicago IL, Portsmouth NH, San Francisco CA

Printed in Great Britain

Library of Congress Catalog Card Number: 2004109467

For all general information contact Arcadia Publishing at:
Telephone 843-853-2070
Fax 843-853-0044
E-mail sales@arcadiapublishing.com
For customer service and orders:
Toll-Free 1-888-313-2665

Visit us on the internet at http://www.arcadiapublishing.com

Contents

Acknowledgments		6
Introduction		7
1.	The Eden of California By Kevin Leonard	9
2.	A Place Called Home By Lawrence Adams	17
3.	The Here and There of It By Jennifer Hartzell	29
4.	People of the Park By Casey Wendt	41
5.	Making Ends Meet By Gabe Aeschliman	53
6.	A Walk in the Park By Michael Farda	67
7.	Education is Golden By Pattie Bastian	81
8.	Ministers and Ministries By Marcelo Zamarripa	95
9.	In Case of Emergency By Lawrence Adams	107
10.	Revitalization and Rebirth By Gabe Aeschliman	119

Thank you David!

Acknowledgments

This project is the result of a unique collaborative effort between the history department at California State University, Sacramento, and the Sacramento Archives and Museum Collections Center (SAMCC). The book is the end result of a semester-long research project conducted by students in a senior research seminar. The staff at SAMCC graciously opened their collections to us in exchange for receiving all royalties from the sale of this book. Unless otherwise noted, all photos are courtesy of SAMCC. Special thanks are due to staff members Sally Stephenson, Pat Johnson, and James Henley who patiently answered student questions, tirelessly hunted down missing photographs, and scanned the images for publication.

In addition to the staff and volunteers at SAMCC, several Oak Park residents opened their family photo albums and shared their memories of life in the community. Specifically, we would like to thank Steven Ballew for permission to reprint several family photographs. Jerry Drobny of the First English Evangelical Lutheran Church provided information on that church's history. Georgia West, Alex Nivet, and the staff of St. HOPE gave us a tour of Oak Park's redevelopment and provided pictures. Randy Wooten opened the collection of the Pioneer Mutual Hook & Ladder Society. The Sacramento Police Department granted us access to their collection. Clarence Caesar of the California Office of Historic Preservation provided photographs of historic structures in Oak Park.

The text of this book relies heavily on several published and unpublished research projects. The work of Steven Avella, Ken Owens, and Robert Dunn has helped us establish both the local historical context for the photographs and a broader national context.

INTRODUCTION

The history of American cities is a history of suburbs. It is a history of moving out and settling in, of technological innovation, of rearrangements of space, and of the creation and erosion of community. The community of Oak Park, Sacramento's first suburb, reflects this national history. In the microcosm of this local community, history readers can see the impact of national trends on everyday people and on a middle-American community. The images of Oak Park show us who were and who we are as we redefine ourselves in the way we live, work, play, study, worship, and contend with our environment.

Located just south of downtown Sacramento, and bounded roughly by Stockton Boulevard, Franklin Boulevard, Fourteenth Avenue, and Broadway, Oak Park evolved from an independent farming village into a modern inner-city ghetto. Platted in 1887, its development marked Sacramento's first attempt to push beyond the original boundaries of the city established in 1848. Sacramentans celebrated the first auction of Oak Park subdivisions as an indication that the city had finally arrived as a destination city for western immigrants, not merely a way station to opportunities elsewhere.

In typical American suburban fashion, Oak Park retained its own identity separate from Sacramento through its first 20 years of existence. Indeed, the goal of developers was to create an independent city in which residents would be unencumbered by the expenses of city services. Developers helped the new city establish a separate newspaper, separate law enforcement, and—perhaps the biggest selling point of all—a separate amusement park. Independence, however, would be somewhat elusive for Oak Park due to its proximity to downtown and its inability to establish an economy separate from its parent city. Early Oak Park residents included a large number of farmers, who were soon replaced by a burgeoning working class primarily employed in Sacramento. Thus, Oak Park emerged not as a separate city, but as a bedroom community or commuter suburb of Sacramento. Annexation in 1911 fully integrated the suburb into the city.

As a commuter suburb, changes in transportation technology have radically altered the face of Oak Park. Streetcars, with their 5¢ fares, created a financial environment in which laborers could afford to buy property in the suburbs and work in the main city. In addition, streetcars brought outsiders into the community to enjoy the Sacramento area's only amusement park, Joyland. The closure of Joyland in 1927 marked the beginning of the end to the streetcar system. By the mid-1940s, all of Sacramento's streetcar lines were abandoned in favor of bus and automobile transit. The California car culture of the 1950s left the blackest mark on Oak Park's physical layout. While providing Oak Park residents with the freedom to travel when and where they wanted, the car also brought about the freeway. Construction of Highway 99 through Oak Park split the community in half and virtually guaranteed the urban blight that would follow in the 1960s and 1970s.

Although a commuter suburb, Oak Park has also been a traditional working class suburb. Unlike the more elite suburban developments of Land Park and East Sacramento, residential development in Oak Park reflected this working class background in smaller and less pretentious homes. In the early 20th century, Oak Park residents worked predominantly at the Southern Pacific Railroad shops in the northeast corner of the city as carpenters, clerks, painters, and blacksmiths. As time passed, carpentry and other construction trades surpassed railroad laborer as the most common occupations of Oak Parkers.

Ethnically, the original settlers in Oak Park were primarily of Northern European descent, a trend that also reflected the overall ethnicity of immigrants to the United States at the turn of the 20th century. During the 1910s and 1920s, Southern and Eastern Europeans entered the suburb, including a large number of Italians. By the middle of the 20th century, the predominantly white neighborhood had shifted to a mostly black neighborhood, in part due to redevelopment projects elsewhere in the city and forced relocation.

Today Oak Park is in the midst of rediscovering its history and rebuilding itself as a distinct community. Thanks in large part to native son Kevin Johnson's St. HOPE Development Company, Oak Park is witnessing the revitalization of its historic structures. On August 2, 2001, St. HOPE unveiled an immaculate Victorian home, beautifully restored as the company's headquarters. Perhaps St. HOPE's biggest success is its creation of a new charter school at Sacramento High School. Like similar inner city high schools, Sacramento High experienced poor student performance and was scheduled to close in 2003. Instead of giving up on the students and the school, thus adding to inner-city blight and disaffection, St. HOPE proposed a radical reorganization of the school and its curriculum. Encountering strong resistance from the California Teachers Union, the proposal landed in the courts only to be resolved in St. HOPE's favor a mere hours before classes were scheduled to begin. In the brief first year of this experiment, Sacramento High School has experienced a profound turnaround. No longer do students walk to school dejected and unmotivated. While the jury is perhaps still out on the long-term success of this charter, the initial results are remarkable.

This book will chronicle the history of Oak Park from working-class streetcar suburb to slum to revitalized urban center. It will explore the variety of ethnic groups that have found a home in the community and the patterns of ethnic dispersion characteristic of cities across the nation. Additionally, it will consider the impact of annexation, transportation modes, and jobs on the independent community. Finally, it will explore the effect of both the State Fair Grounds (initially built on Upper Stockton Road) and the U.C. Davis Medical Center on the vitality of the neighborhood.

One

THE EDEN OF CALIFORNIA

By Kevin Leonard

With a title as daunting and impressive as the "Eden of California," Oak Park has seen much development and growth as a community in the past 100 years. What started as the small vision of developer Edwin K. Alsip and the Oak Park Association, grew into Sacramento's first full-fledged suburb. Beginning in 1887, with an initial division of 56 whole or partial lots, Oak Park gained a reputation as a community built by hard-working citizens. At what was billed as "The Greatest Auction Sale Ever Held in California," 200 lots were purchased in the Oak Park area, with more than 500 people attending the event. This early sale of real estate started Oak Park's transition from farm to city.

Edwin Alsip and the Oak Park Association sold this rural area by advertising its quality land and exceptional growing conditions. The main selling points, however, were the promises of no city taxes, graded avenues, and a common belief that a real-estate boom had finally reached Northern California. Buyers from all over the state purchased lots, as many thought the value of the lots would easily double upon purchase. Most remained vacant for at least four years after the auction, and major development of the area did not take place until the early 1900s. Between 1900 and 1950, the area developed as a traditional working-class suburb.

In the 1940s and 1950s, Oak Park experienced the early signs of urban blight. In response, the Sacramento city council and city planning commission decided to develop a community plan for Oak Park and make a few changes to its appearance. The concept of single-family residences growing to multiple-family residences, future developments within the Oak Park Business District, and the influence of South Sacramento and future freeways, led the city to adopt a plan of updating certain areas. Widening of streets to accommodate traffic, as well as construction of underpasses were some of the changes that affected quality of life in Oak Park. The business district of Oak Park also was updated in an attempt to enhance the classic appearance and draw future patrons. Unfortunately, most of these "improvements" only enhanced the problems of the community, particularly problems associated with absentee landlords and sub-standard multi-family housing. Residents increasingly felt removed from the decision-making process and developed an antagonistic relationship with both the police and city government.

Presently, Oak Park holds the reputation of a working class community, albeit with a recent stigma as a neighborhood in need of redevelopment. St. HOPE Corporation is leading the way in this new phase of Oak Park development. A weathered city with a vast history, Oak Park has the potential to emerge from neglect, to recapture the title of Eden of California.

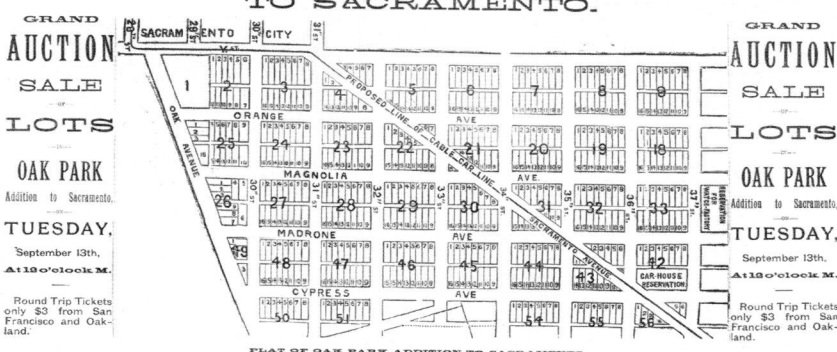

An advertisement in the Sacramento *Daily Record Union* in 1887 announced Oak Park's addition to Sacramento with the "Greatest Auction Sale Ever Held in California." This full-page ad signified the beginning of Oak Park, as lots were sold and investors from all over the state flocked to purchase land in Northern California.

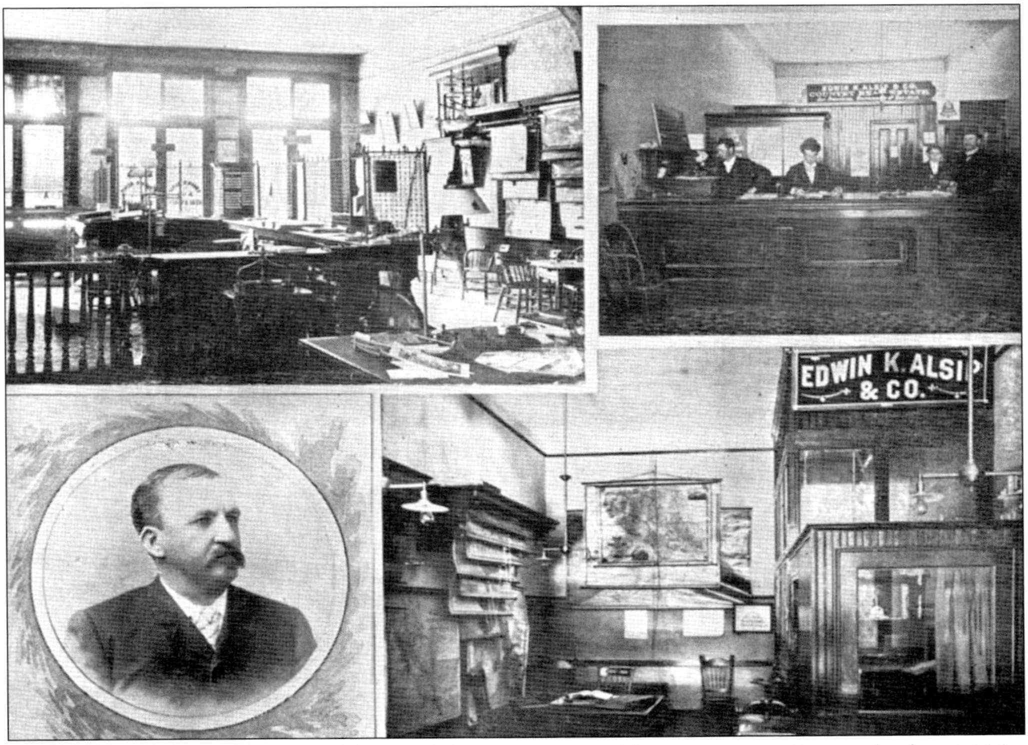

This photograph of Edwin K. Alsip and his real-estate office was taken during the late 1890s. Alsip was the primary developer of Oak Park and the coordinator of an auction of real estate that began the start of this Sacramento community.

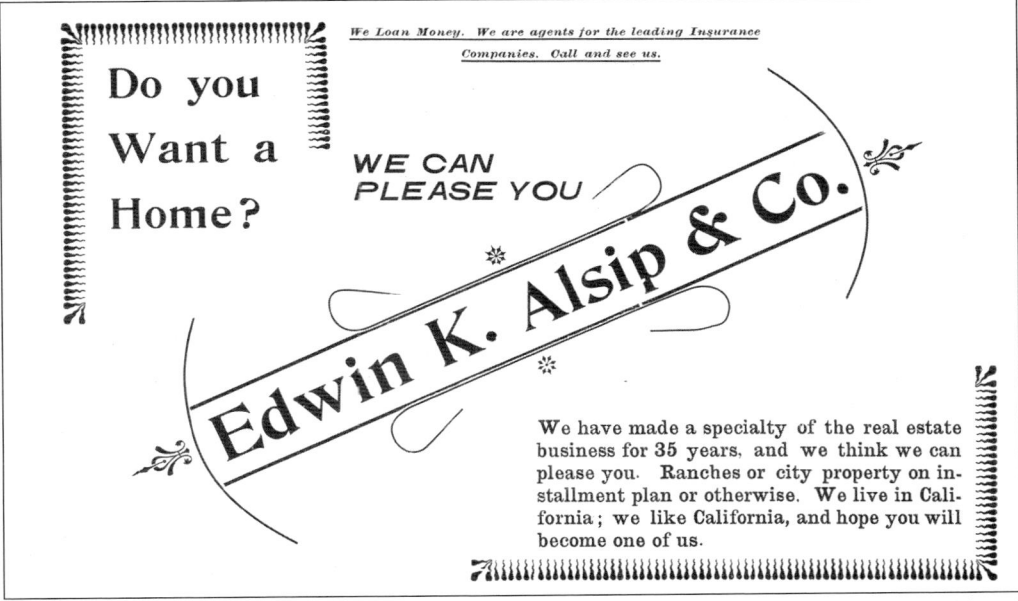

As well as developing property in the Oak Park area, the Edwin K. Alsip Company sold real estate. This advertisement from the late 1800s explains some of the services offered.

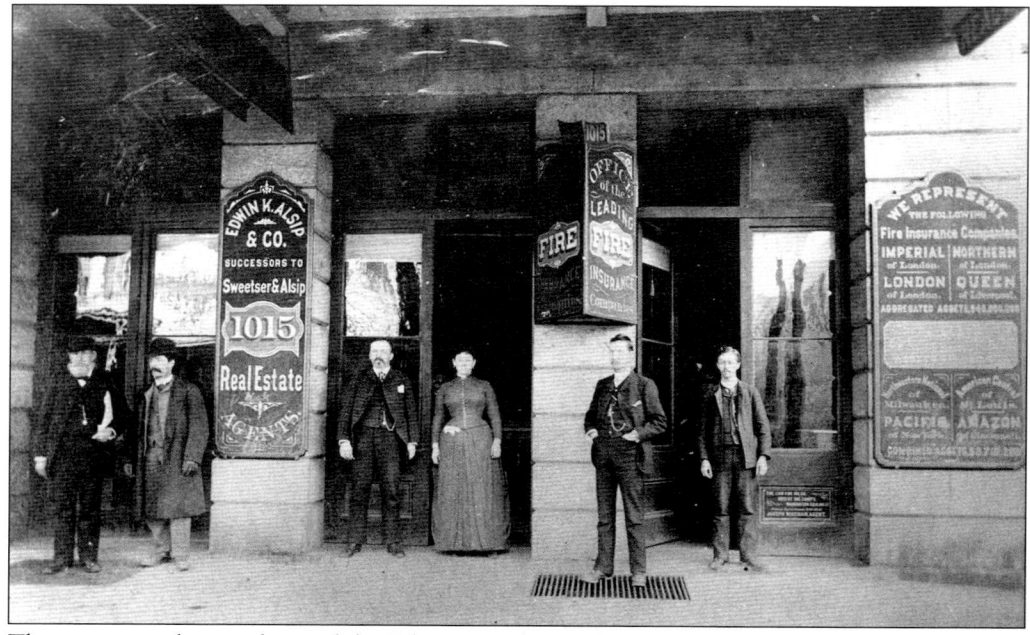

This picture, taken in front of the Edwin K. Alsip real-estate office in the early 1900s, shows some of Alsip's employees. Alsip is shown third from the left.

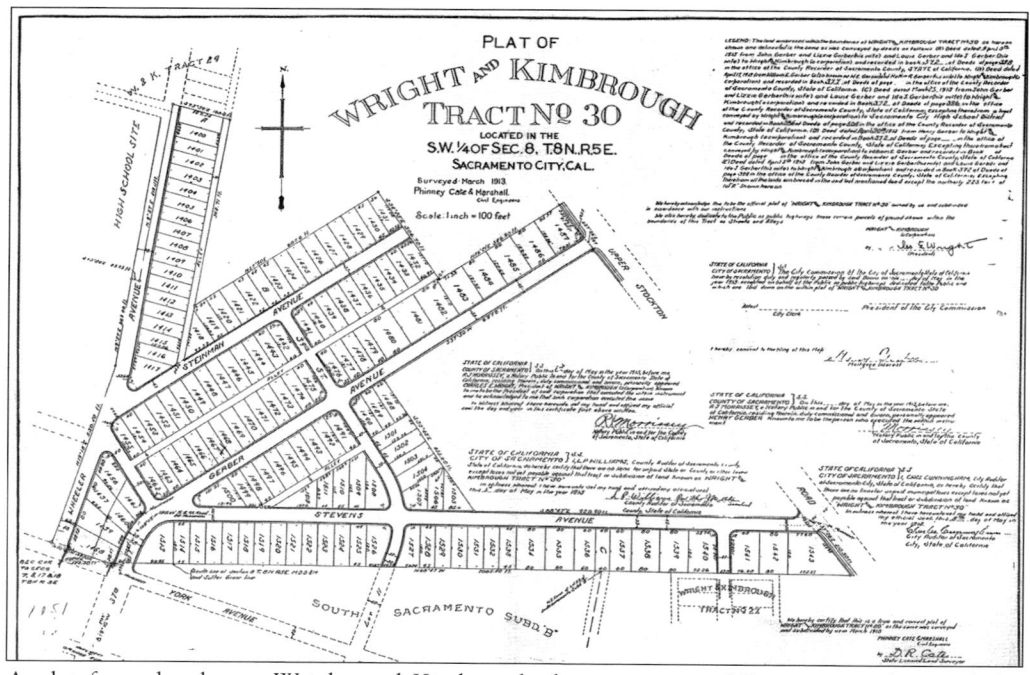

A plat from developers Wright and Kimbrough shows an area of Sacramento that includes part of Oak Park. The plat was surveyed in 1913 and shows the future high-school site off Wheeler Avenue.

In this written proposal from 1915, addressed to the attention of Alden Campbell, C.J. Guth agrees to construct the Oak Park post office station for $4,794. The new station was funded by Judge John McMahon.

> OFFICE AND RESIDENCE: 1516 27TH ST.   TELEPHONE: 1517-R
>
> ## C. J. GUTH
> ### GENERAL CONTRACTOR AND BUILDER
> #### JOBBING A SPECIALTY
>
> SACRAMENTO, CAL. August, 14, 1915,
>
> Mr Alden Campbell
> Architect
> Dear Sir – I propose to build the Oak Park Post Office Station for Judge MacMahon according to plans & specifications for same prepared by you for the sum of $4794.00 Four Thousand Seven hundred ninety four dollars
>
> Respectfully Submitted
> C. J. Guth
> Gen. Contractor
>
> THE RELIABLE BUILDER WITH THE BEST OF REFERENCES

H.W. Baker worked as a residential real-estate agent in Oak Park for the Royal Insurance Company. This advertisement from 1920 illustrates the typical relationship between realtors and insurance companies.

> # WE HOLD YOU SAFE
> # H. W. BAKER
> ## RESIDENT AGENT
> ## ROYAL INSURANCE CO., LTD.
> ## NOTARY PUBLIC   REAL ESTATE
> ### 3452 Third Ave & 35th St.,
> Phone Capital 601W
>
> Oak Park, Sacramento, Cal.

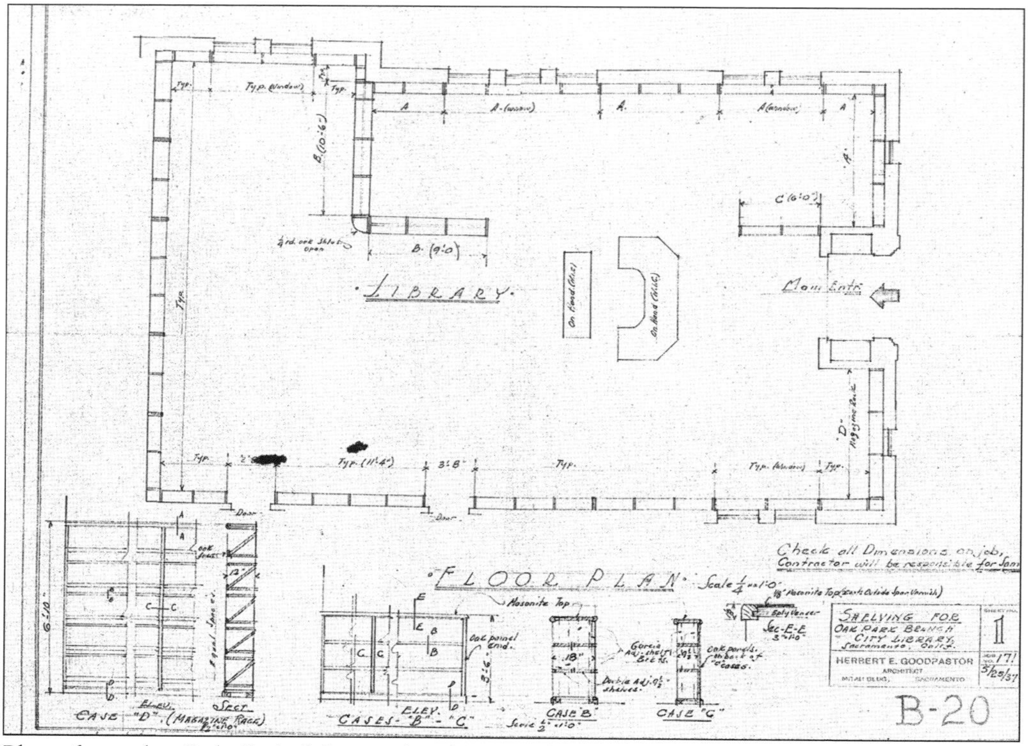

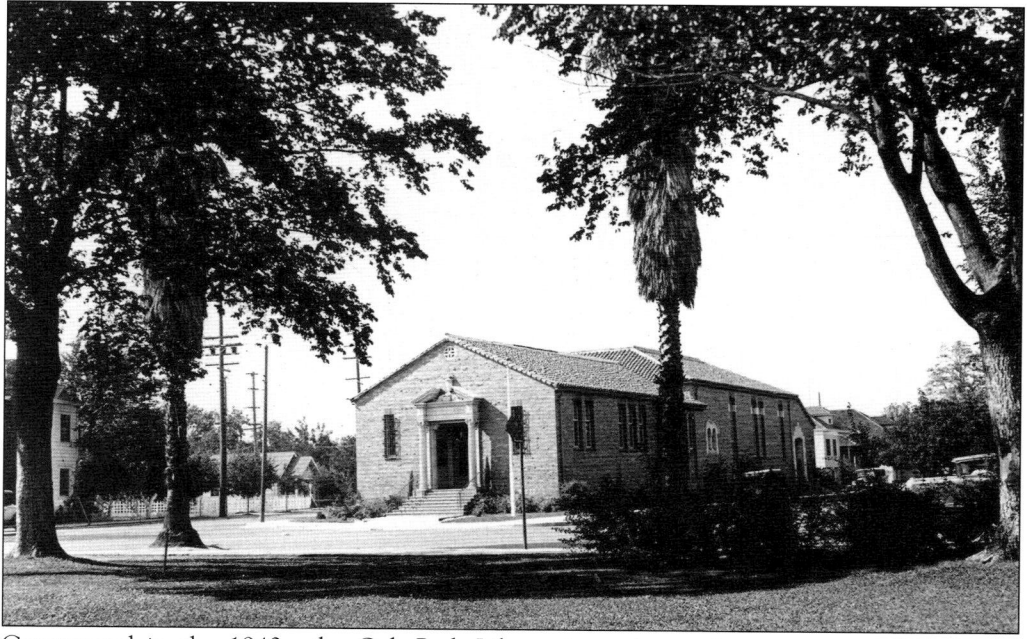

Plans from the Oak Park Library, dated May 25, 1937, show the early specifications and blueprints of a very important structure in Oak Park.

Constructed in the 1940s, the Oak Park Library is an impressive structure with beautiful masonry detailing.

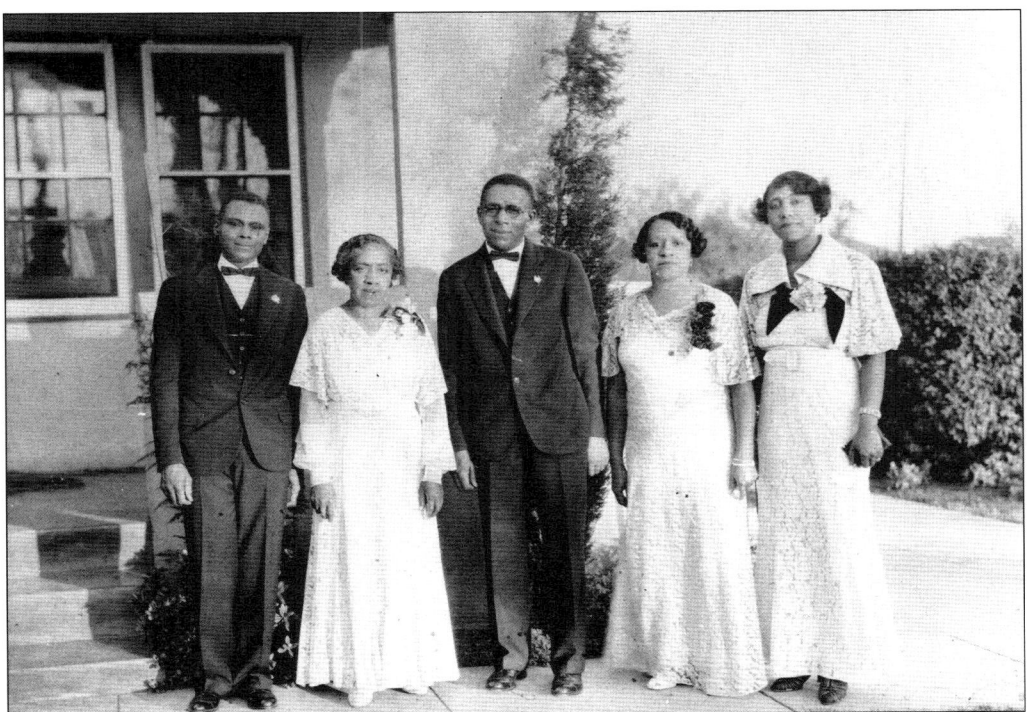

L.N. Crawford was Sacramento's first black realtor. Shown in this c. 1940 photo with his wife, brother, sister-in-law, and friend, Crawford is the man on the far left.

An estimate for improvements to the Oak Park Recreation Center in 1982 projected the cost at $1,640,307.06 and included the acquisition of land, landscaping, automatic irrigation, and the construction of a basketball court and parking lot.

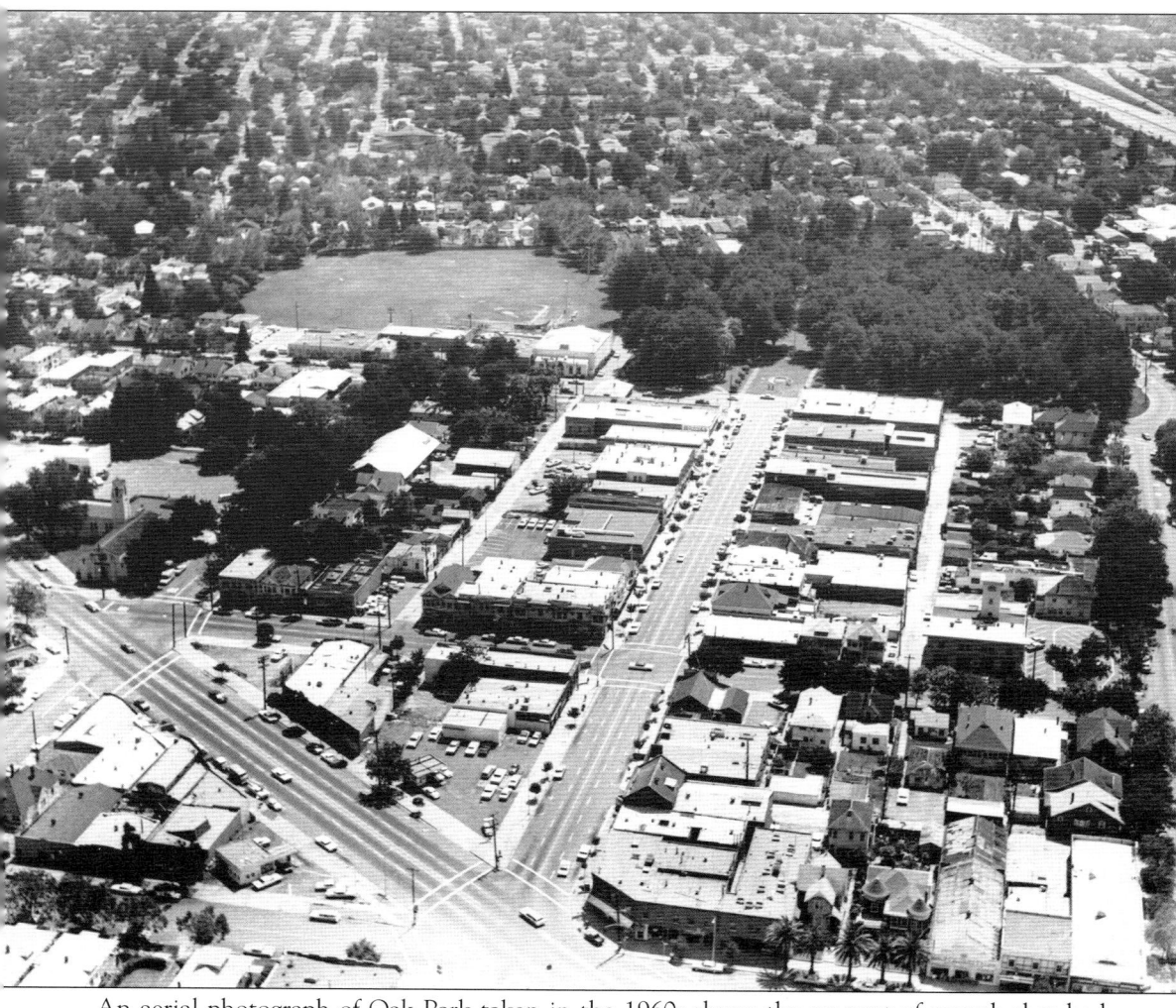

An aerial photograph of Oak Park taken in the 1960s shows the amount of growth that had occurred in the area by the mid-20th century. The picture displays some of Oak Park's well known streets, particularly Broadway and Alhambra Boulevard.

Two

A Place Called Home
By Lawrence Adams

The architectural style of the homes of Oak Park demonstrate the intentions of the early developers to move away from early vernacular farm dwellings to a more elaborate architectural style that would be more suitable for the people they envisioned living in the new community. One of the more popular and higher-priced styles was the Queen Anne, predominantly built for upper-middle-class residents. Many of the inhabitants in these types of homes tended to be well-to-do businessmen or doctors in the community. Working- and middle-class homes consisted of the craftsman, vernacular, or bungalow-style homes.

During the early years of Oak Park development, although a majority of the residents were white, a few African-American families did make their homes in the community. One of the first black residents of Oak Park, Isaiah Dunlap, established residency in 1906. During the Depression his son George Dunlap opened a small restaurant out of his dining room, where he specialized in Southern cooking. The Dunlap restaurant quickly became an Oak Park landmark for discriminating Sunday diners from all over the city.

The revolving door of ethnic change in Oak Park continued for several decades. As one ethnic group moved into the area in an attempt to reach middle-class status, the previous groups of residents relocated elsewhere. Never more evident was that the case as when African Americans began to move into Oak Park in large numbers in the mid to late 1950s. Many longtime residents moved to newer developments throughout the city. But as these residents left the area, they took with them the economic infrastructure that made Oak Park flourish during its earlier years.

During the 1960s the neighborhood became predominantly an African-American inner-city ghetto. Beginning in the 1980s and 1990s, the ethnic make-up of the community underwent great changes again. It is now a microcosm of all different types of cultural ethnicity. Today Oak Park is in the midst of an economic redevelopment and is making a strong attempt to dispel the negative reputation and stereotypes that have plagued the neighborhood and its residents for several years. As longtime Sacramento residents have rediscovered the history and architectural style of the homes in the neighborhood, property values have skyrocketed, which has raised the issue of gentrification for lower-income residents. Many of these residents feel they are being pushed out of their neighborhood in order to increase property value. Oak Park is a neighborhood that is trying to overcome the reputation of an inner city ghetto. When investors and residents come together in the revitalization of Oak Park, Oak Park will once again become an enticing place to live.

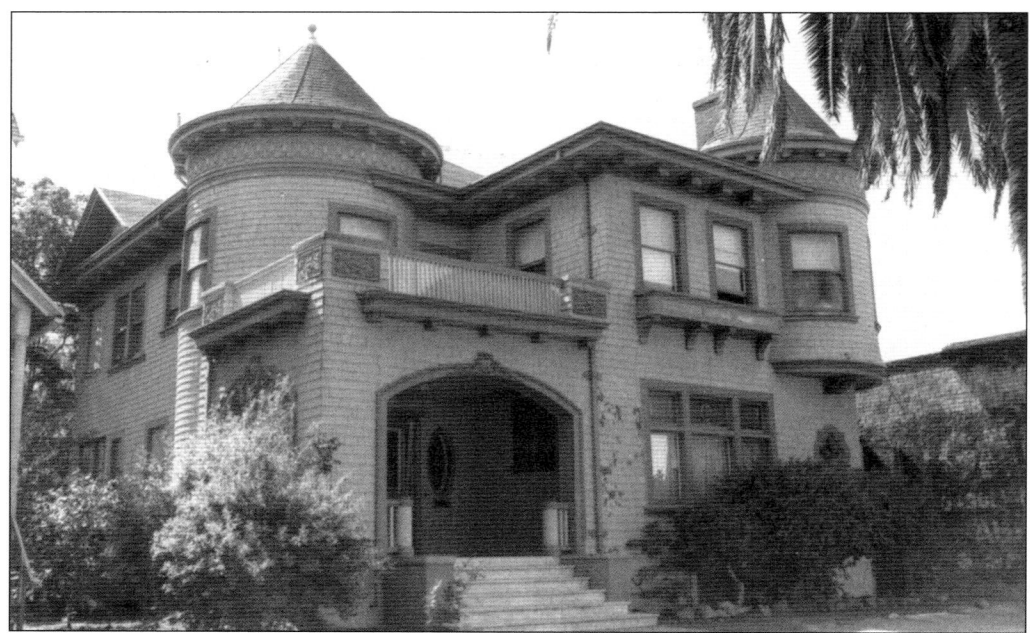

This 1984 photo shows a Queen Anne–Classical Revival house with Georgian influences that was constructed in 1909. The first owner of the house, Joseph L. Lewis, owned a downtown Sacramento saloon. This house is one of the architectural jewels of Oak Park. (Photo courtesy of the California State Office of Historic Preservation [OHP].)

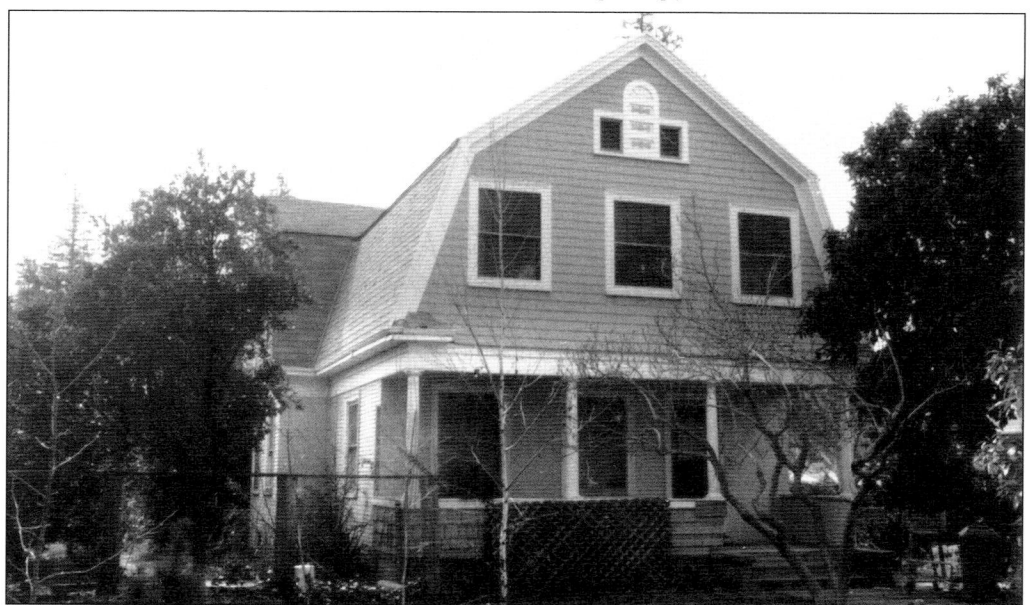

This Colonial Revival–home at 3730 First Avenue was built in 1912, and its original owners were Wellington Baker and Walter T. Foster. Baker was a carpenter, while Foster was a prominent Oak Park realtor. In 1919 the house was purchased by Calvin Berry, a police officer for the City of Sacramento, and he lived in the home until 1938. The home is pictured here in 1984. (Photo courtesy of OHP.)

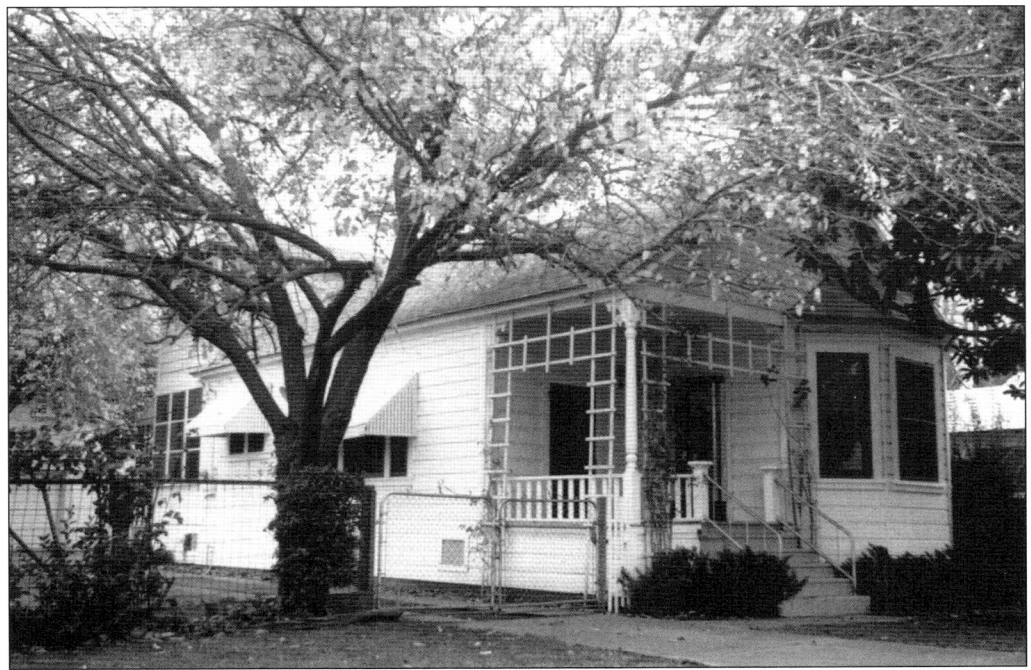

Peter C. Krogh, along with friends and relatives, built this house in 1897. This 1984 photo shows the architectural style of the house to be a modest vernacular structure typical around the turn of the century. (Photo courtesy of OHP.)

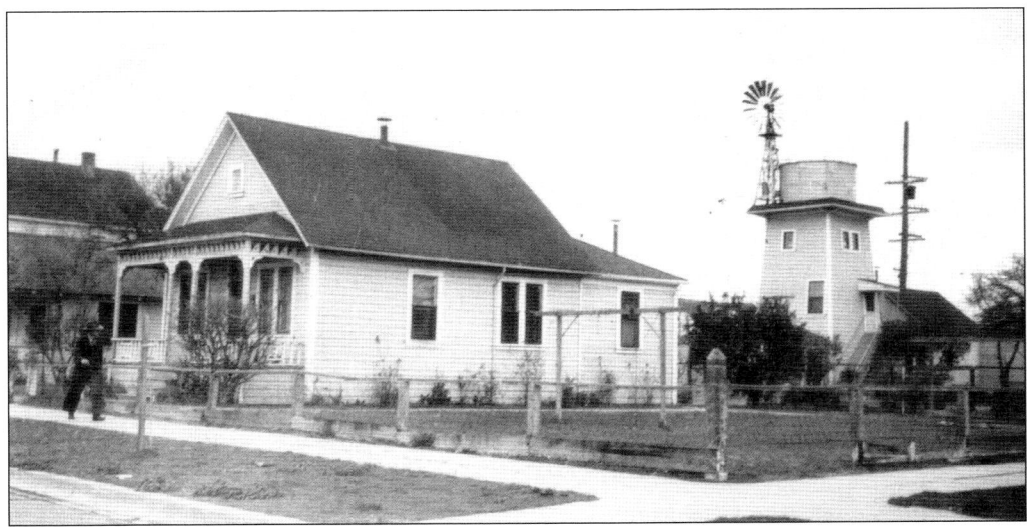

The house in this photo is a modest bungalow-style home situated on the northwest corner of Thirtieth and First Avenue. Note the windmill in the background. It was one of only a few remaining windmills in Sacramento in 1944.

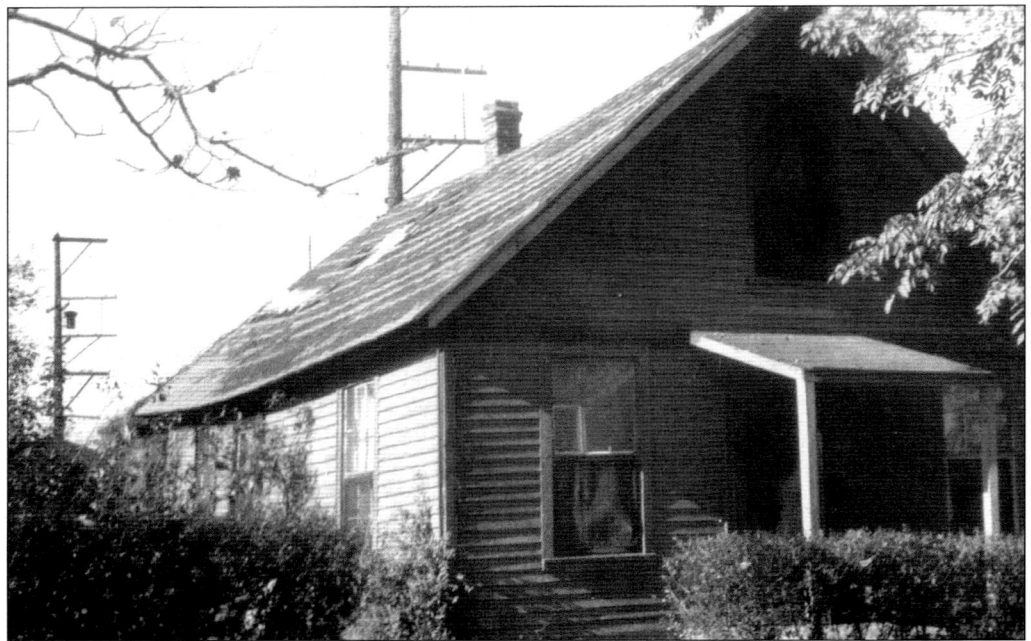

The house in this 1984 photo is perhaps one of the first in Oak Park. Although the construction date is unknown, it is typical of the early A-frame farmhouses of the 1880s. Originally on Thirty-first Avenue, the street was renamed Alhambra Boulevard in 1917. (Photo courtesy of OHP.)

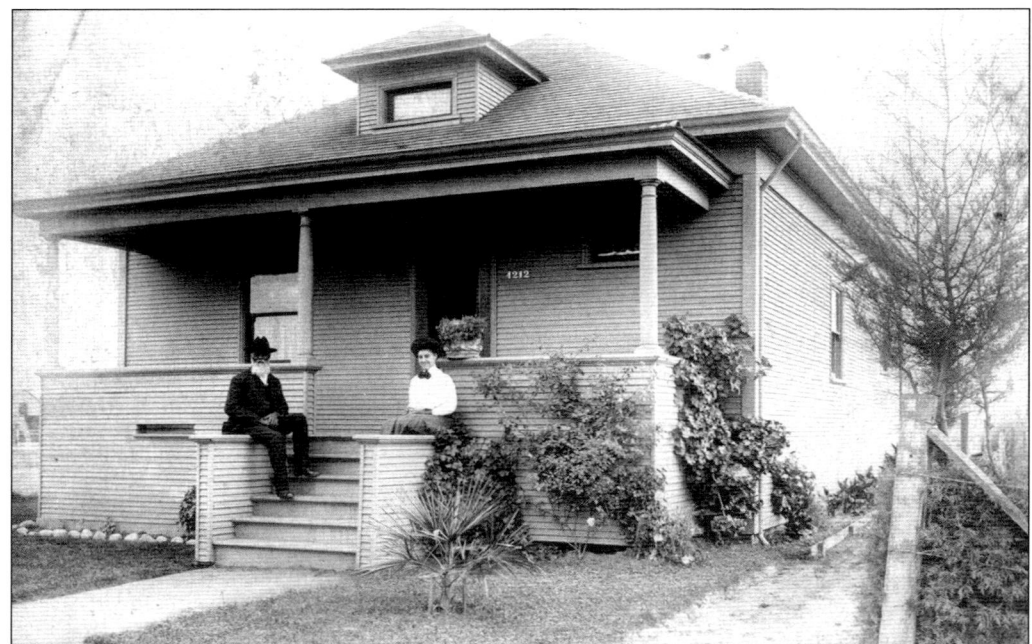

In this 1908 photo, Isaiah Dunlap and his wife Adel, sit, in front of the home they built in 1907. They were one of the first African-American families to live in Oak Park. Their son George achieved great success as an entrepreneur by converting his dining room into a restaurant.

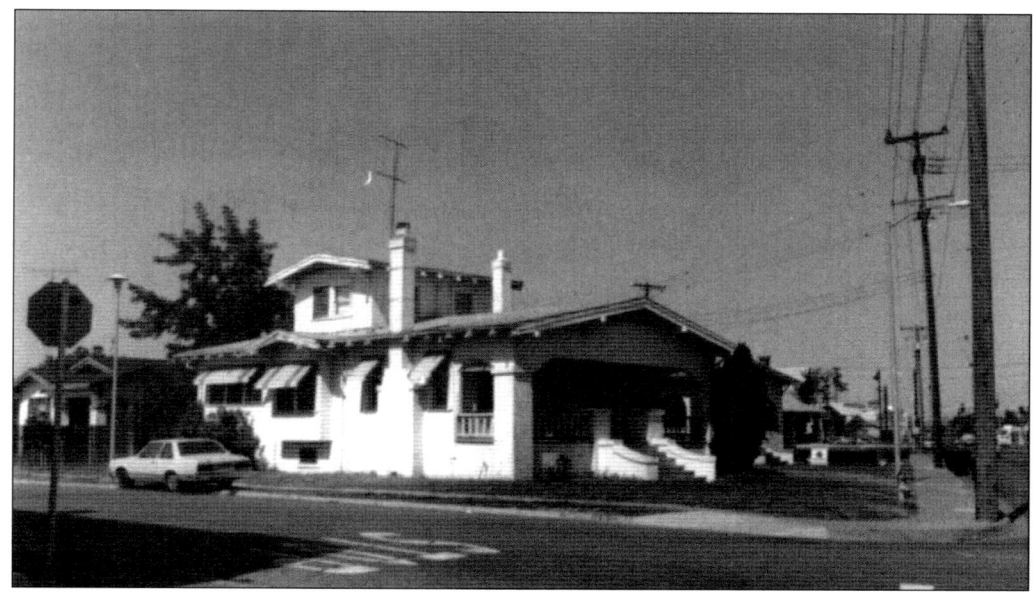

The architectural style of the house in this 1984 photo is consistent with the vernacular style with Craftsman influences. This house was built for Louis and Mary Augustine, a couple who had strong ties to the agricultural community. Although the construction date is unknown, it is estimated to have been built in 1915. The house is situated at the corner of Stockton Boulevard and Sixteenth Avenue. (Photo courtesy of OHP.)

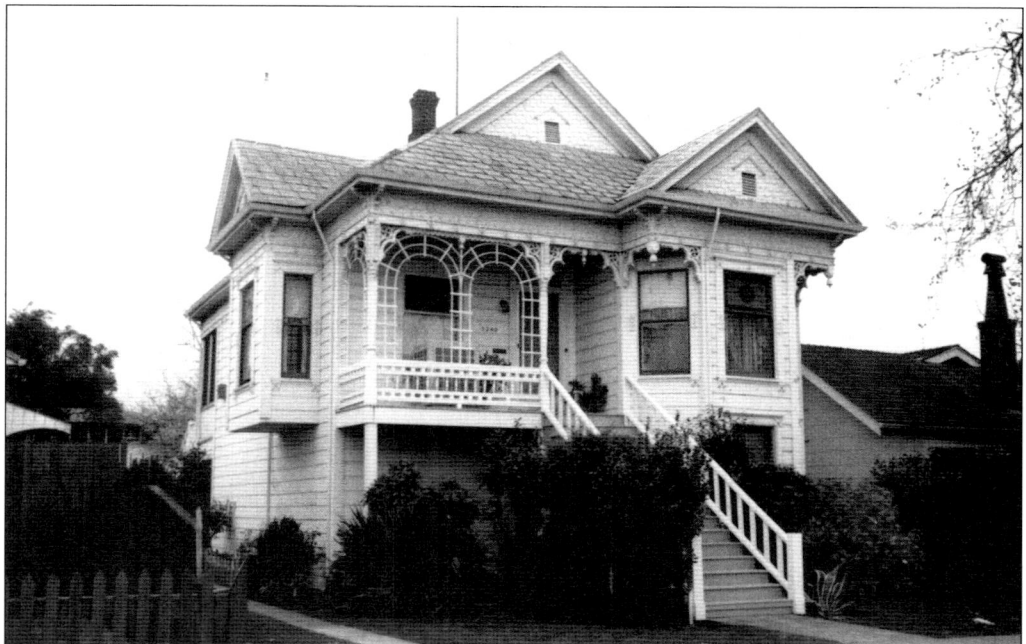

This 1984 photo shows a Queen Anne–style house constructed between 1890 and 1900 for Anderson Pryor. By 1910 C.E. Kleinsager and Otto Hielbronn, two prominent realtors in Sacramento, were owners of the property. They eventually sold it to E.T. & P.F. Rumen. (Photo courtesy of OHP.)

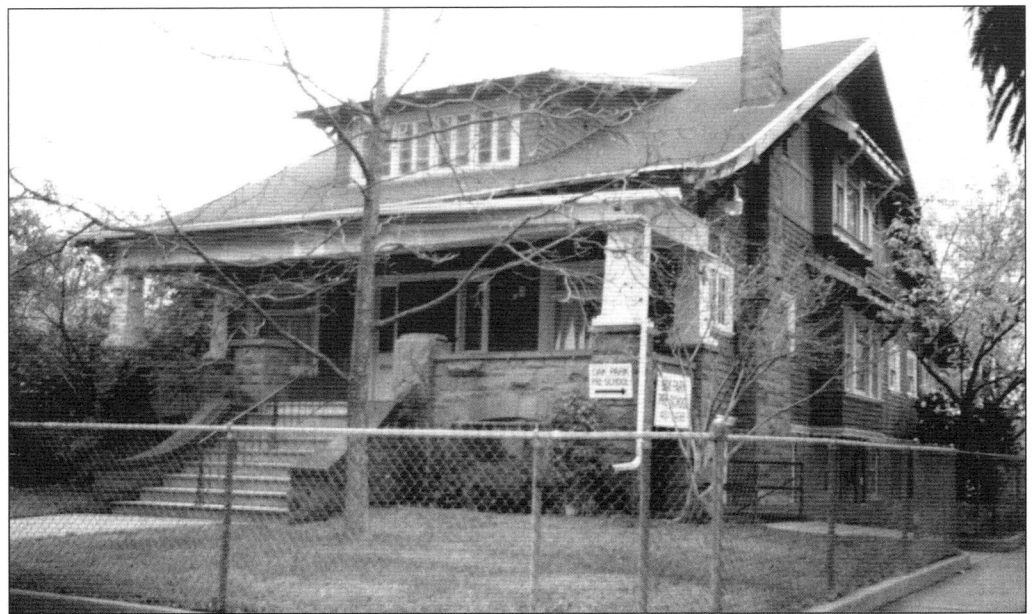

The Craftsman-style residence in this 1984 photo was constructed in 1901 for Dr. John T. Culver, a prominent Oak Park physician, and his wife, Stella. Dr. Culver played an active roll in the annexation of Oak Park into the city of Sacramento. In 1973 the house was used for the Schule Jumamose, a school emphasizing African-American culture and history, opened by James and Cheryl Fisher. In 1975 the Eta Gamma Omega chapter of Alpha Kappa Sorority purchased the home and used it for a daycare facility, which remains today. (Photo courtesy of OHP.)

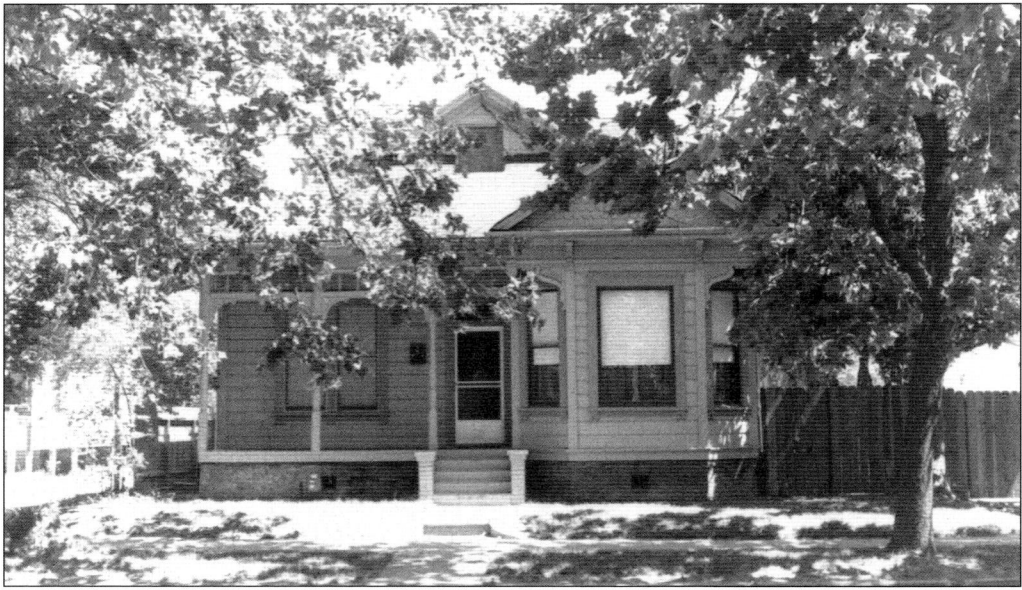

The house in this 1984 photo is a modest one-story Queen Anne cottage built in 1898. The first owner of the home was Charles A. Fical. Mr. Fical lived in the house until his death in 1924. The title of the house passed to Howard and Bertha Fical. Howard Fical was a repairman for the Standard Oil Company. (Photo courtesy of OHP.)

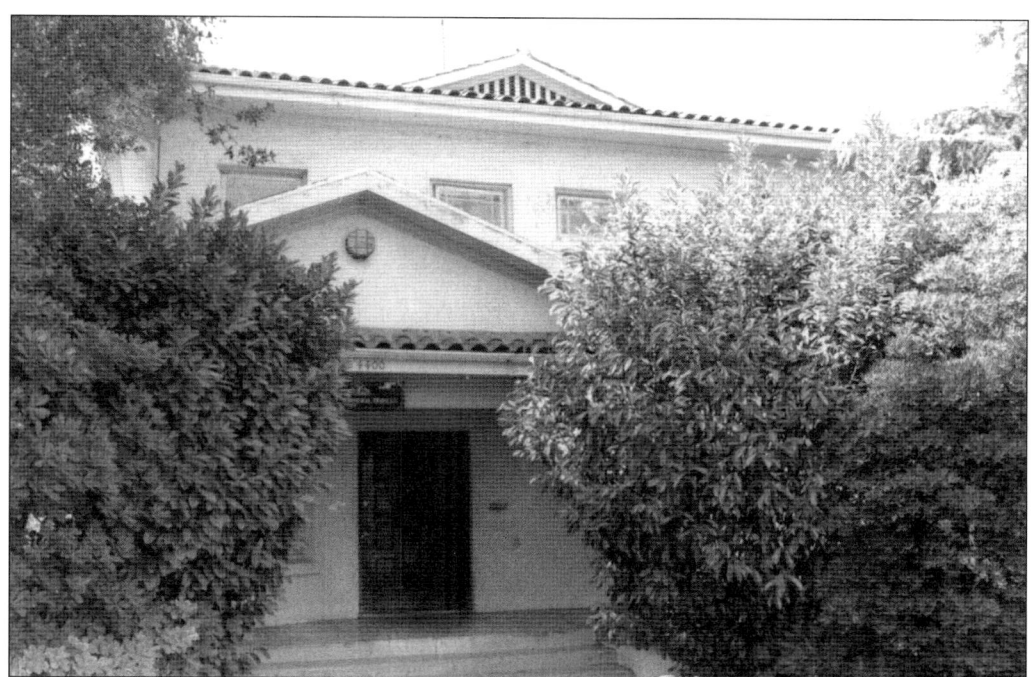

This Mediterranean Revival two-story house, shown in a 1984 photo, is estimated to have been built in 1921 for Archie W. Clifton, a prominent Oak Park businessman who owned the Oak Park Furniture Company and the Clifton Hotel. Clifton also was an active participant in the Oak Park Businessmen's Association. (Photo courtesy of OHP.)

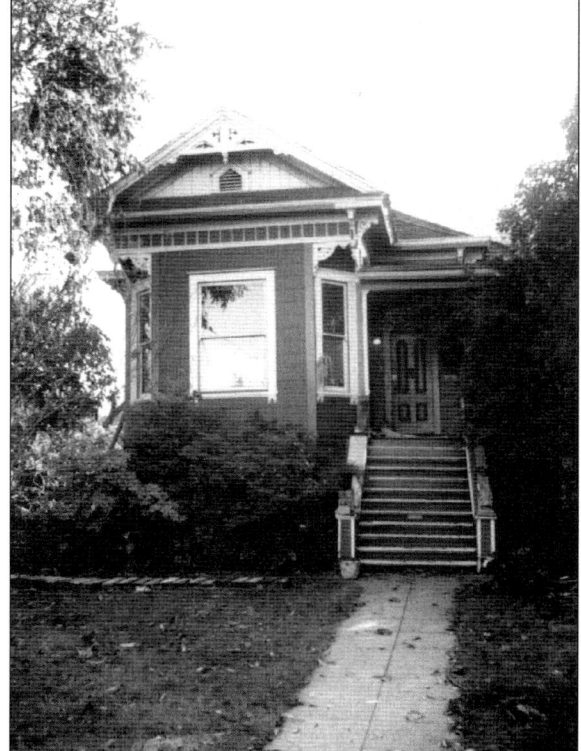

The 1984 photo shows a one-story Queen Anne home. It was built in 1907 for Adolph A. Ostrum after purchasing the lot in 1906. Ostrum was a painter for the Southern Pacific Railroad Company. He lived in the house for 50 years and witnessed the rapid growth of Oak Park as well as Sacramento. (Photo courtesy of OHP.)

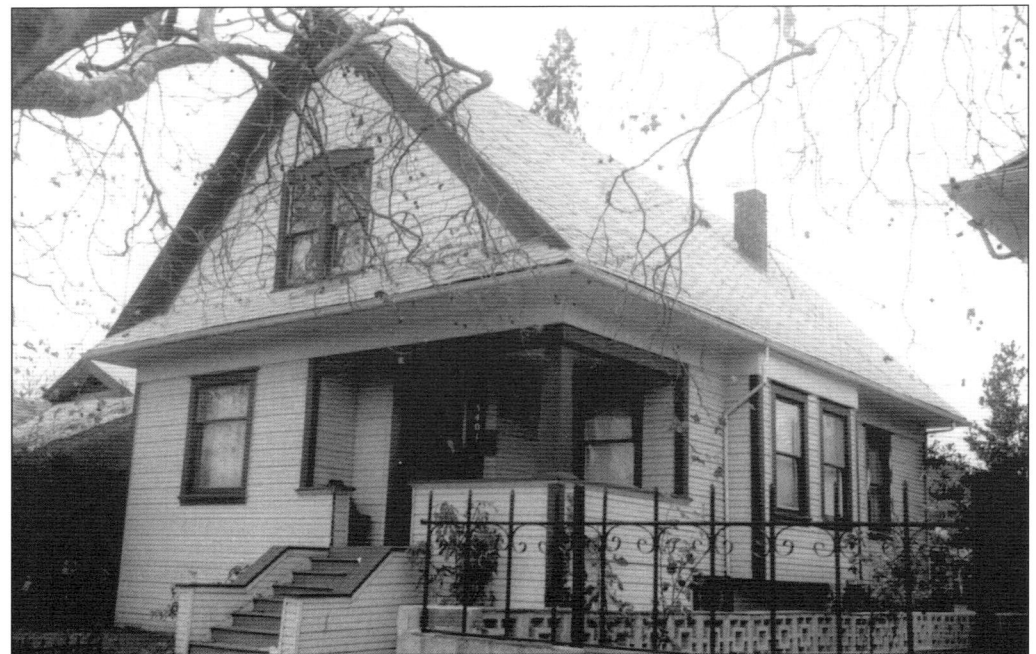

The house shown in this 1984 photo is estimated to have been completed in 1918 for a widow named Mrs. Julia Crenshaw. In 1934 the ownership of the home passed to family members James and Ancel Crenshaw. Mr. Crenshaw was a pipefitter for the Western Pacific Railroad Company. (Photo courtesy of OHP.)

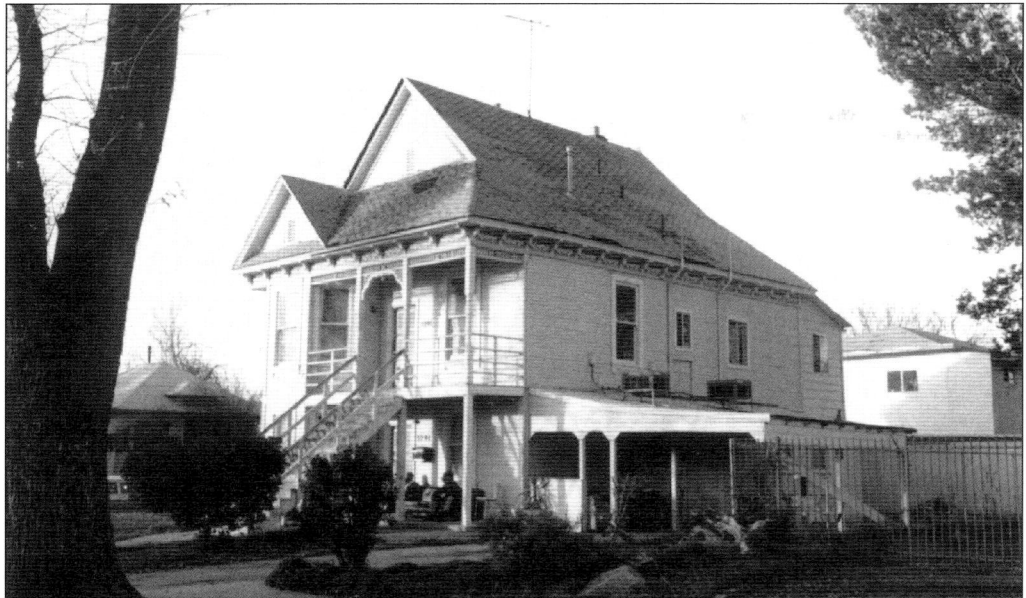

This 1984 photo shows a two-story rectangular Queen Anne cottage that was built in 1901 and was first occupied by Dr. Alex Orr, who used the residence as both home and doctor's office. The house continued to be used as a clinic until 1928, when Lucretia Orr started Orr's Maternity Home, a home for unmarried expecting mothers. (Photo courtesy of OHP.)

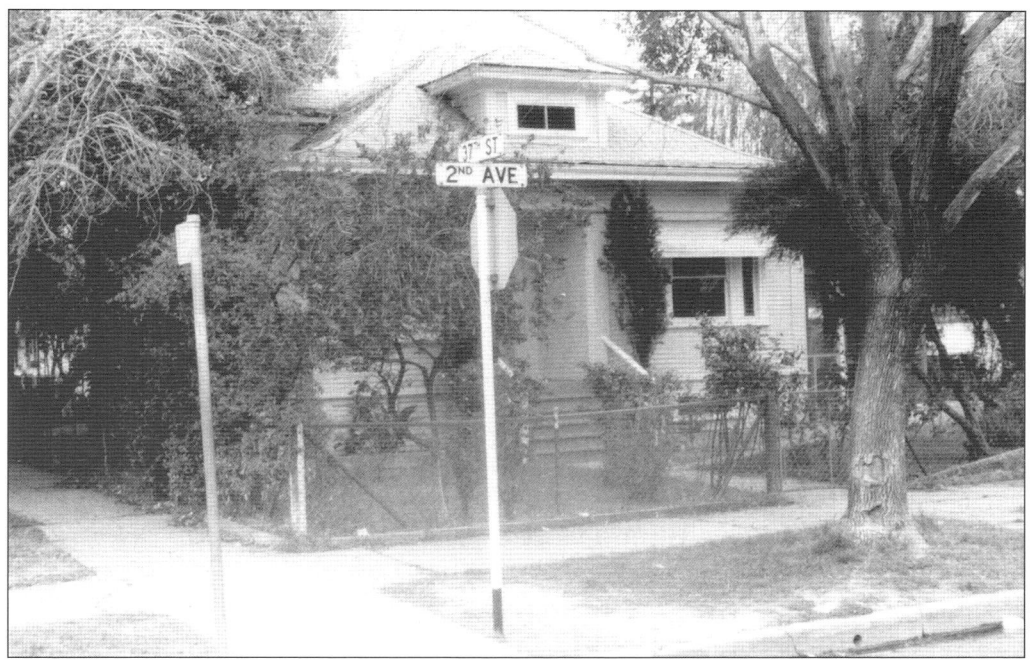

The Craftsman-style house in this 1984 photo is located on the corner of Second Avenue and Thirty-seventh Street. The actual completion date of the house is unknown, but it is estimated to have been built in the early 1900s. (Photo courtesy of OHP.)

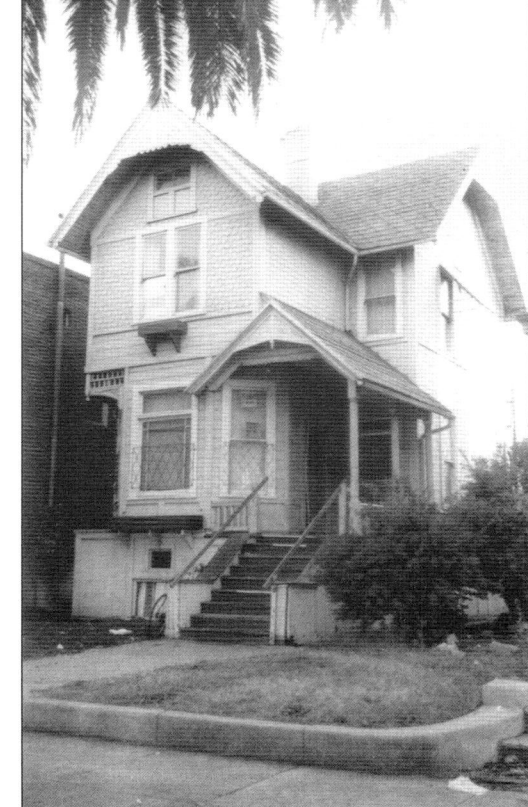

This two-and-a-half-story wood-frame Stick-Eastlake–style residence was estimated to have been built between 1885 and 1895. The earliest known inhabitant of this house was Alfred Berry, a framer who lived in the home from 1910 to 913. This photo was taken in 1984. (Photo courtesy of OHP.)

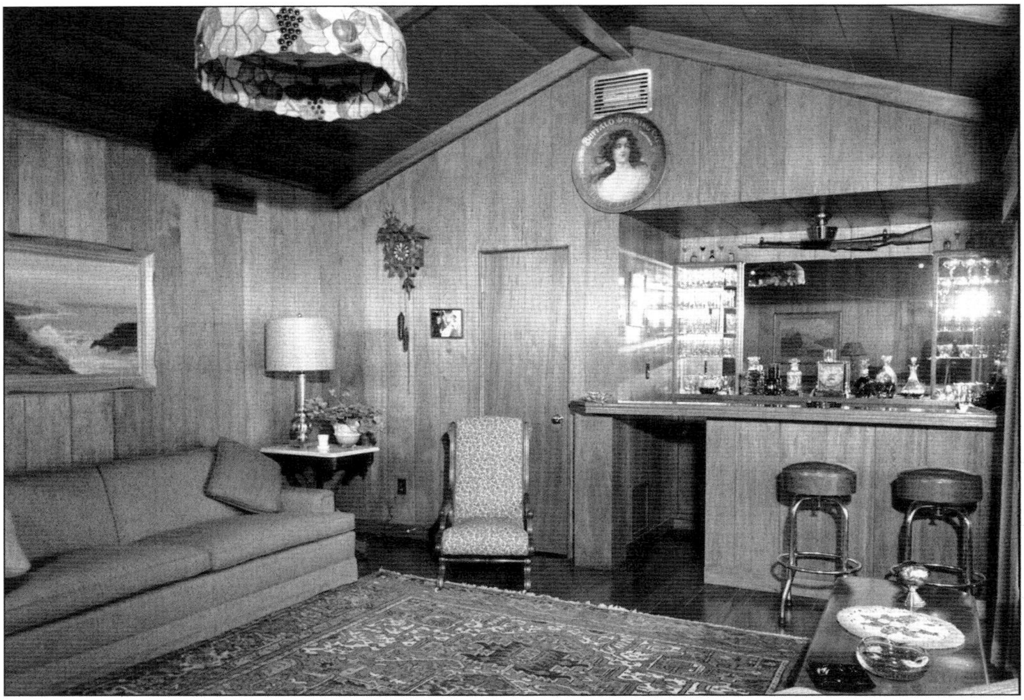

The four images on these pages are views of the interior of the home of John and Audrie McClintock, 1675 Eighth Avenue.

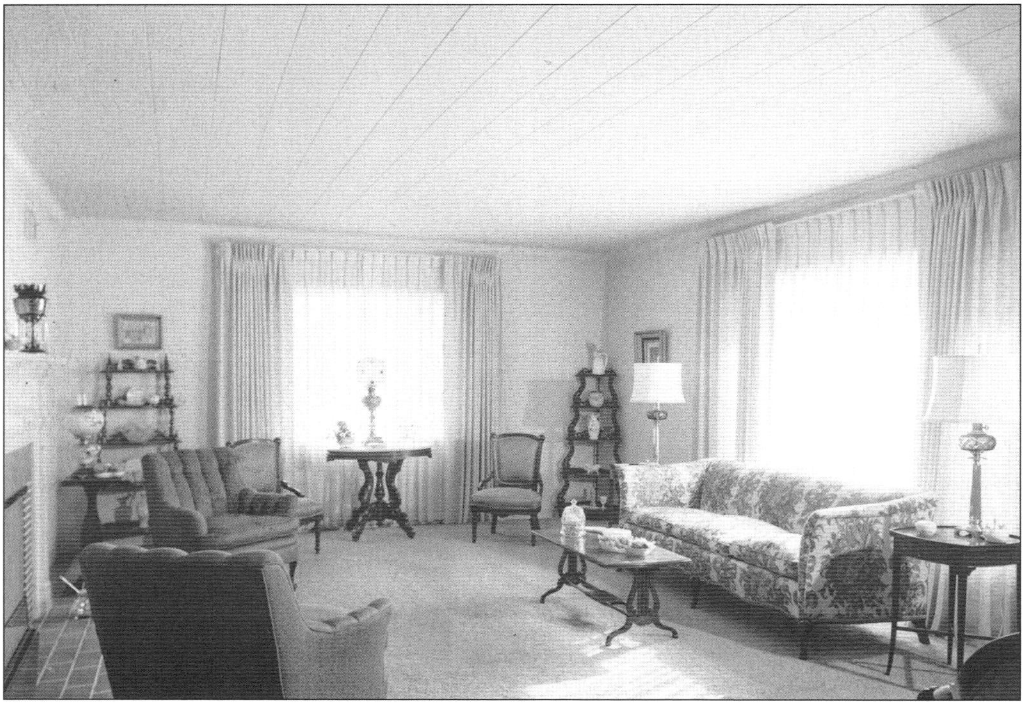

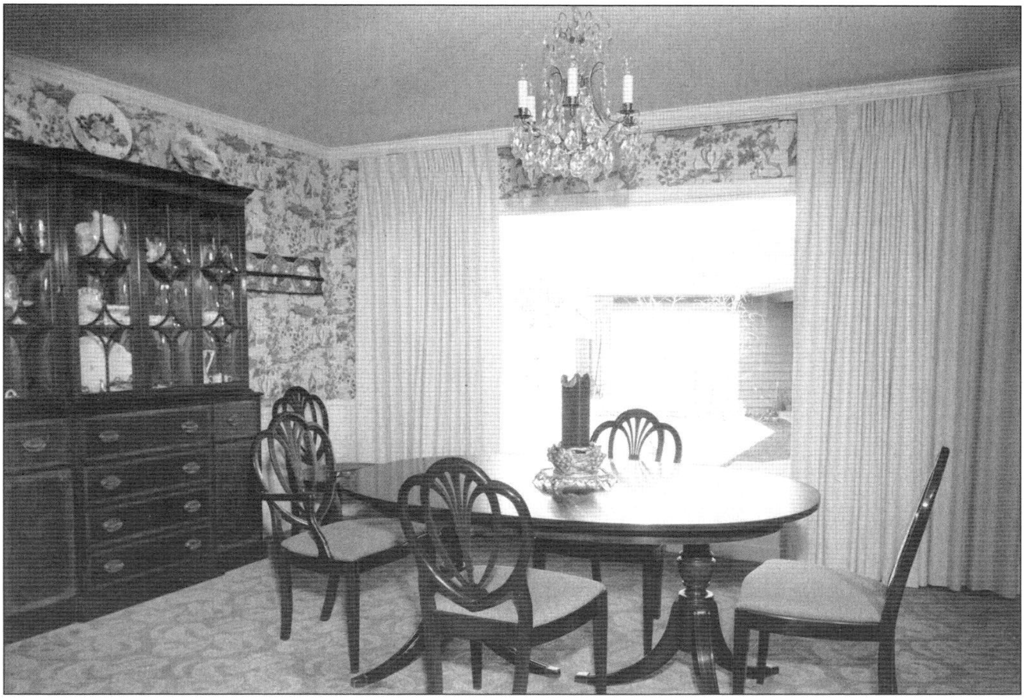

The photos, dated February 24, 1955, show the dining room, the living room, the master bedroom, and the den.

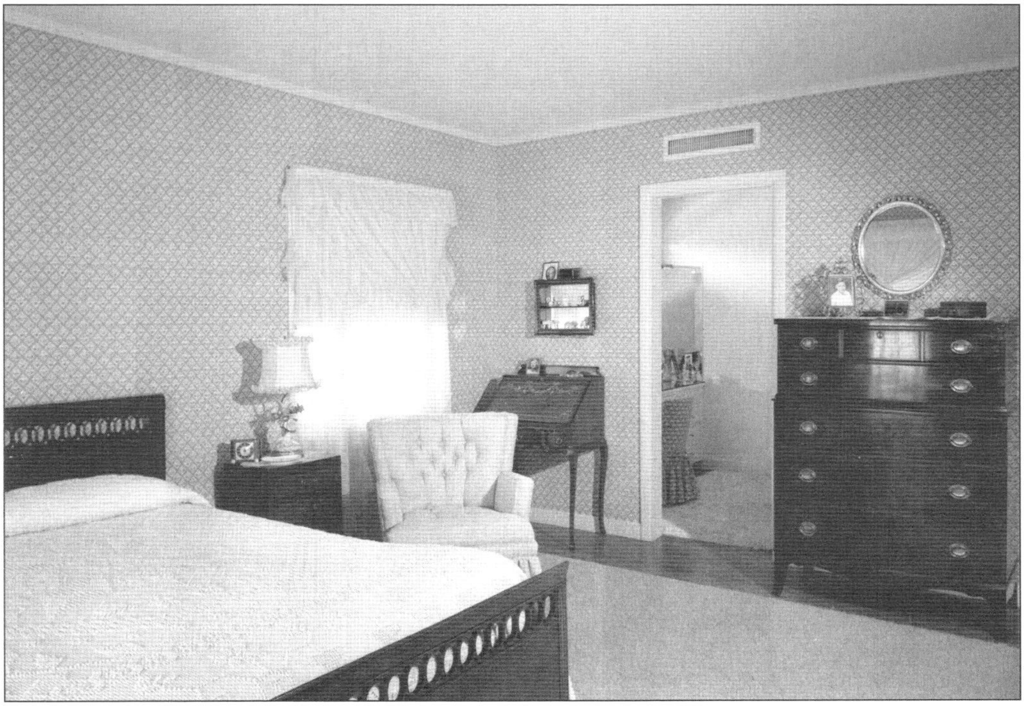

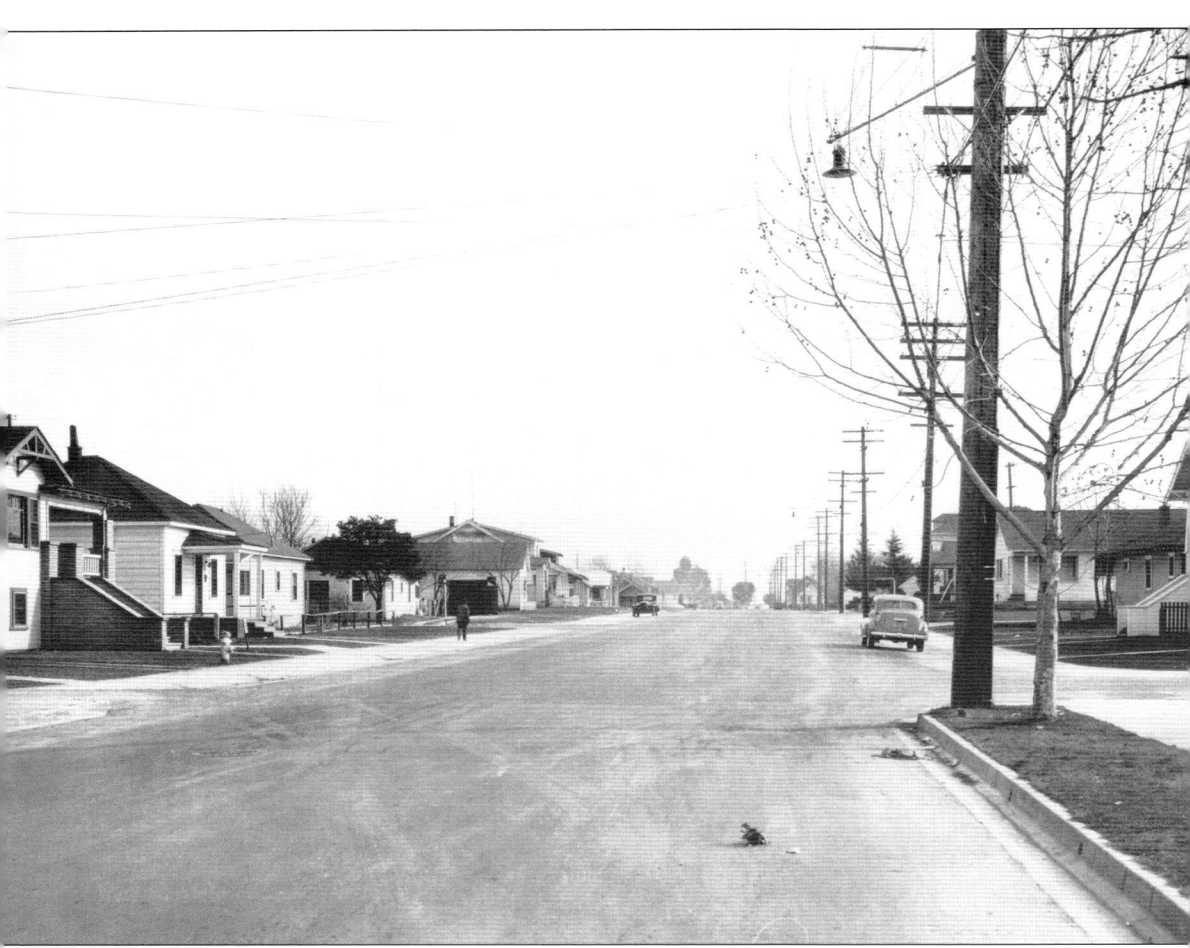
This photo shows a row of houses in 1938. The view is looking east on Fifth Avenue from Fortieth Street.

Three

THE HERE AND THERE OF IT
BY JENNIFER HARTZELL

Transportation has always been an important part of planning a city. From horse-drawn carriages to the automobile, from dirt roads to freeways, people have always needed a way to get around. Oak Park began as a small town with dirt roads but soon grew into a major suburb of Sacramento with trolley lines and bustling traffic. With its annexation into the city in 1911, Oak Park transportation grew and changed with the times. Today Oak Park is well integrated into the overall Sacramento transportation system.

Before the 1880s, Oak Park was a rural area focusing primarily on farming. Roads and city planning were still a decade away. As real estate began to be divided and sold in tracts, the need for platted and paved streets became more prevalent, and Edwin K. Alsip saw to it that this need was met. Trolleys, however, made growth a reality in Oak Park. They were the first true link between Sacramento and Oak Park. Streetcars ran daily from downtown to Oak Park, primarily because of a popular weekend destination, the Joyland amusement park.

The next great advance in transportation for Oak Park came with its annexation into Sacramento. This event brought about many changes for the roads in the area. Beginning in 1912, roads were widened and improved, and by 1917 they were renamed to fit the street numbering scheme of the larger city. By the mid-20th century, trolleys were being replaced by bus and automobile transportation. Buses expanded the land capable of being developed, and routes through Oak Park reflected this growth. To this day, buses remain an integral part of the Sacramento transit system.

The final major change to transportation in Oak Park came with the construction of State Highway 99. Before its construction in the mid-1950s, Oak Park residents relied on boats, trains, and local roads for long-distance travel. With the construction of the freeway, residents gained the freedom to drive themselves. The construction of the freeway, however, brought about many changes for the surrounding area. For construction to begin, many existing homes and businesses were demolished. In addition, the community was split in two with the freeway running down the middle. Although the construction had many benefits to local transportation, the original topography of Oak Park would never be the same.

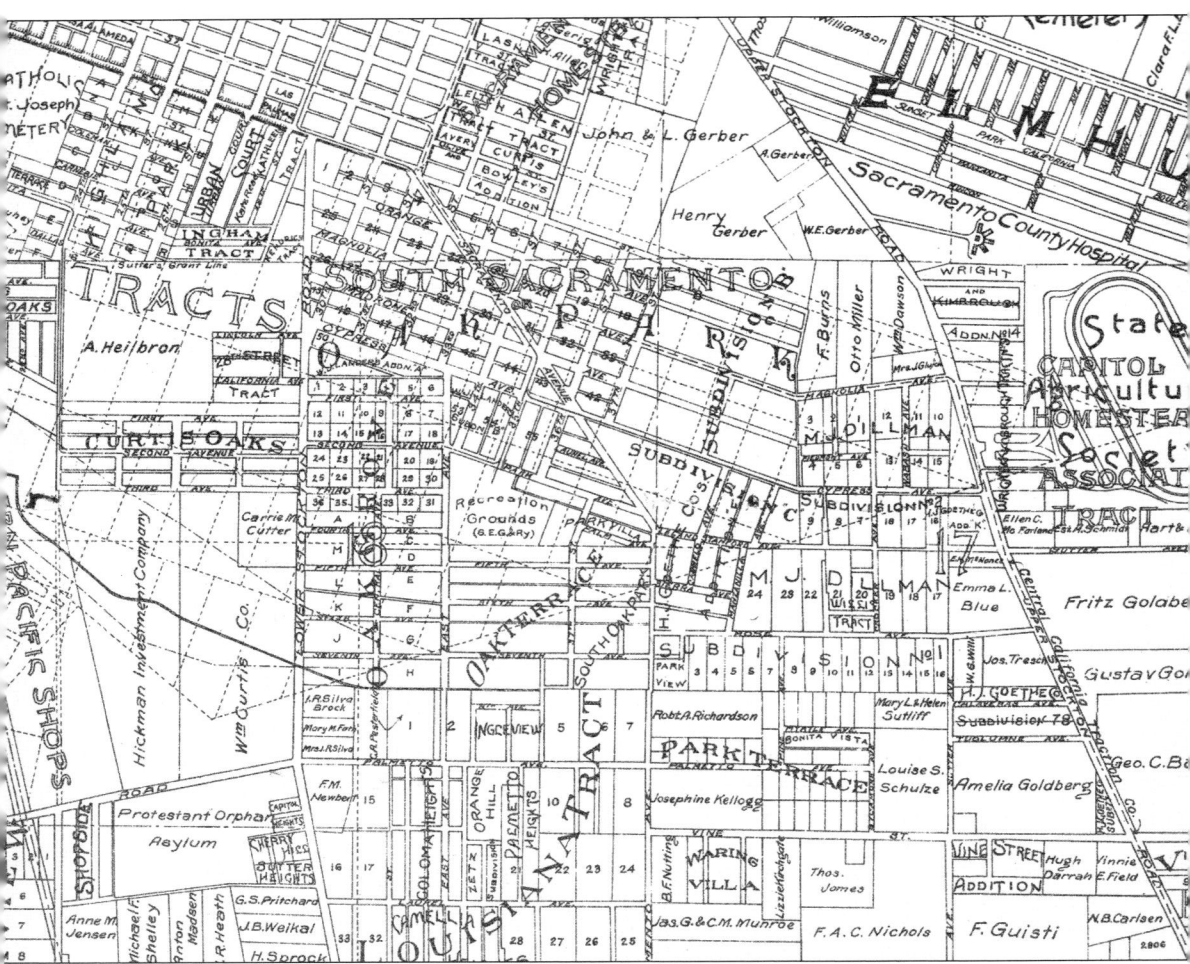

This particular map of Sacramento and the surrounding suburbs was drawn in 1910, prior to the annexation of Oak Park. After annexation in 1911, these street names were changed to correspond with the rest of the city of Sacramento.

On July 30, 1912, this article appeared in the *Sacramento Bee*. The widening of the street and the thought of constructing a streetcar line illustrate the anticipated growth and development of Oak Park. Rose Avenue was later renamed Eighth Avenue after annexation. See the map on the previous page.

PETITION CITY TO WIDEN ROSE AVE.

Oak Park Residents Hope to Secure Loop of the Traction Line

OAK PARK, July 30.—A petition has been signed by the majority of property owners of Rose Avenue requesting the City Commission to order the widening of that thoroughfare by sixteen feet. The plan is to take eight feet on each side off the lots facing the avenue for a sidewalk, thereby giving the forty-foot wildth forming the street between the property lines, exclusively for traffic purposes.

The petition was circulated by W. G. Willi, one of the pargest property owners in the street. It is said that several fine buildings and business blocks are being contemplated by property owners as soon as the new street lines are set.

After Car Line.

It is also reported that when the street is widened the property owners intend to request the Central California Traction Company to build a line from its tracks on Upper Stockton Road to the terminal of its new line to be constructed into the business section of Oak Park at Park Avenue and Thirty-sixth Street. It is pointed out that this would give the Traction Company a loop line through a populated district which has no car service at present.

Willi says he is certain that the large majority of property owners and residents favor both the widening of Rose Avenue and the invitation to the Traction Company to build a loop car line.

On a lovely afternoon c. 1900, Clarissa Wildy, age five, poses for a photo in her goat cart, an example of a child's mode of transportation and a popular photo opportunity of the time period.

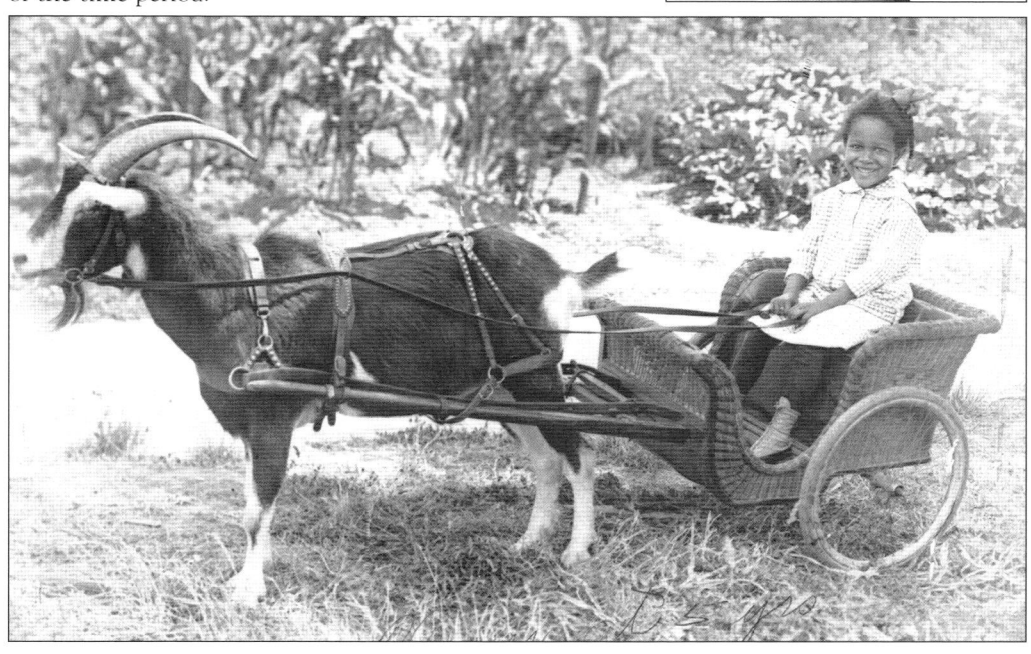

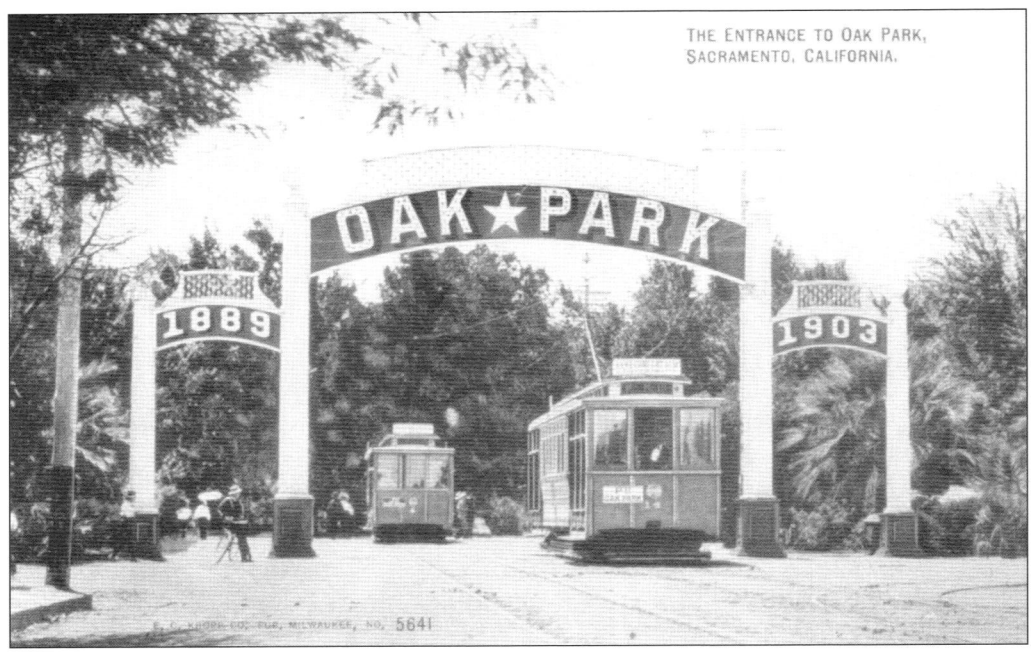

This postcard of the entrance to Oak Park shows one of the more popular ways to get around during the early 1910s. The trolley remained a major part of transportation up through the 1940s. The back, dated 1916, contains a wonderful letter describing an outing in an automobile. Ironically, the rise of automobiles would soon lead to the demise of the streetcar system.

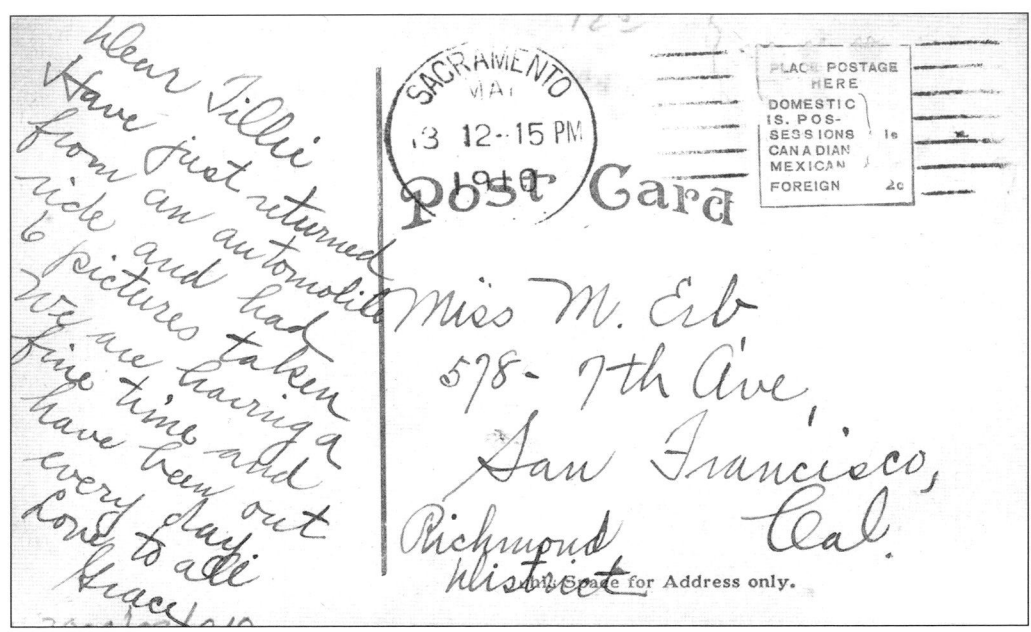

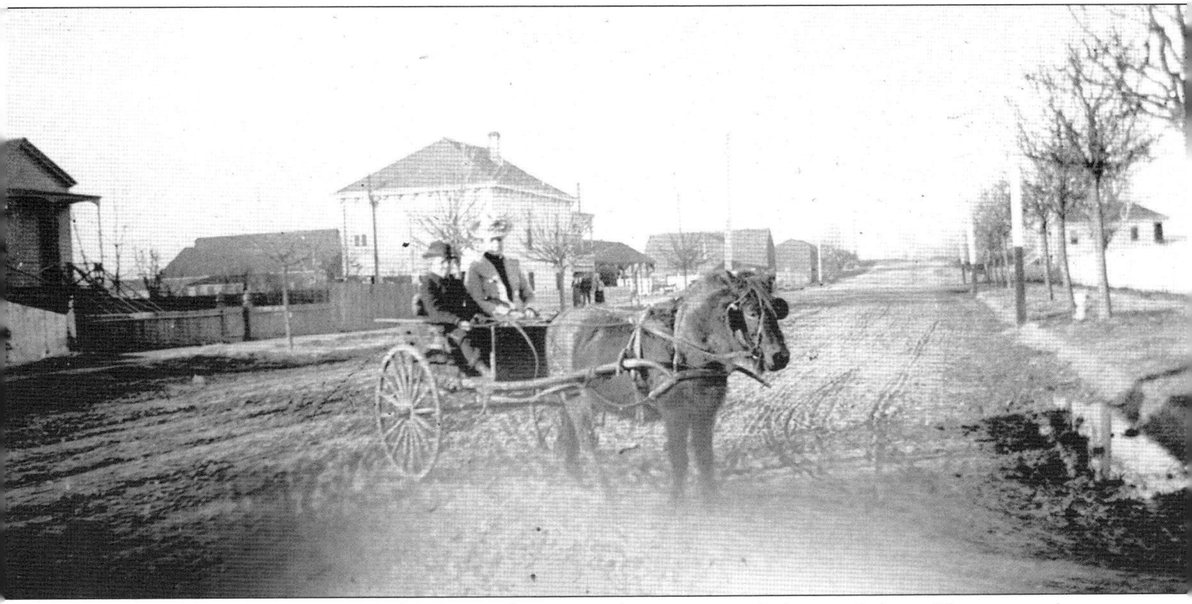

In the late 1890s, Upper Stockton Road remained an unpaved thoroughfare. However, the street shows signs of the increasing development of the area, with its newly constructed power and phone lines.

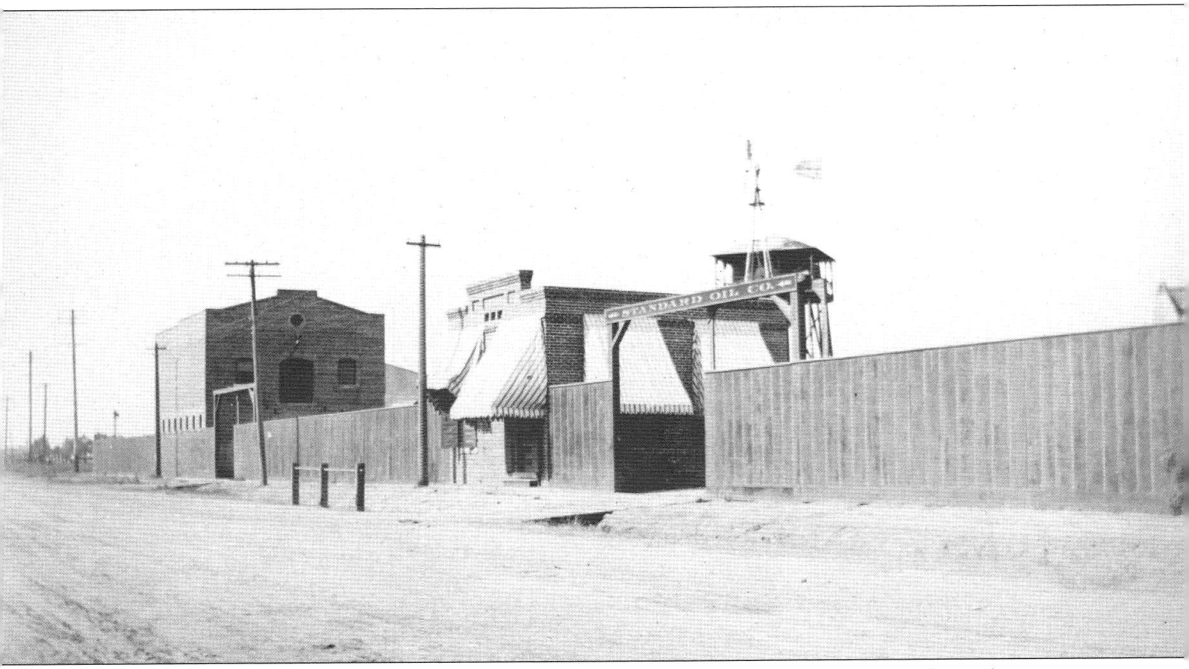

Shown in this c. 1900 photo, Standard Oil Company, located on Stockton Boulevard, was an important contributor to the growth of transportation of Oak Park and its surrounding area.

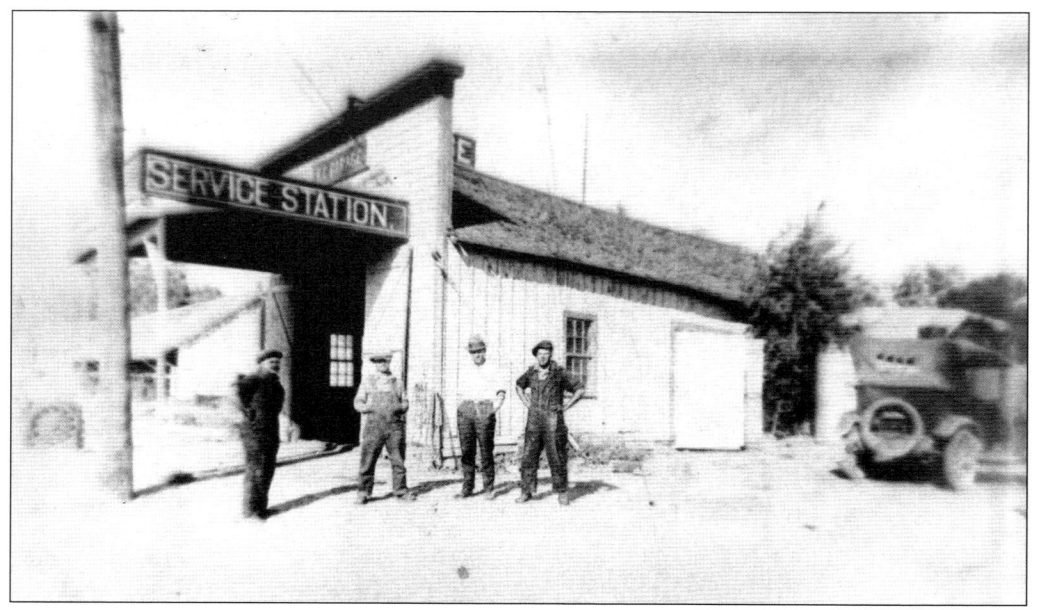

As transportation progressed and the car became more prevalent, service and gas stations became a popular sight in Oak Park. A group of German workers pose c. 1920 outside the garage.

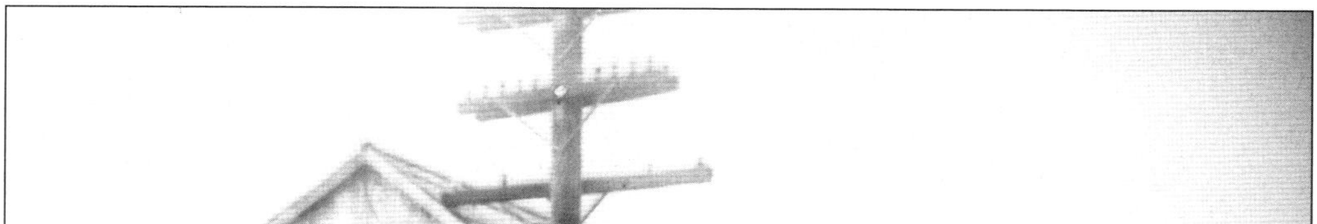

Seven Mile House, located in Oak Park, was a way station for weary travelers on their way out of town. Way stations such as this one were common all over the Sacramento area as well as throughout the Sierra foothills. The particular one in this c. 1890 photo advertised Ruhstaller's Beer to entice travelers.

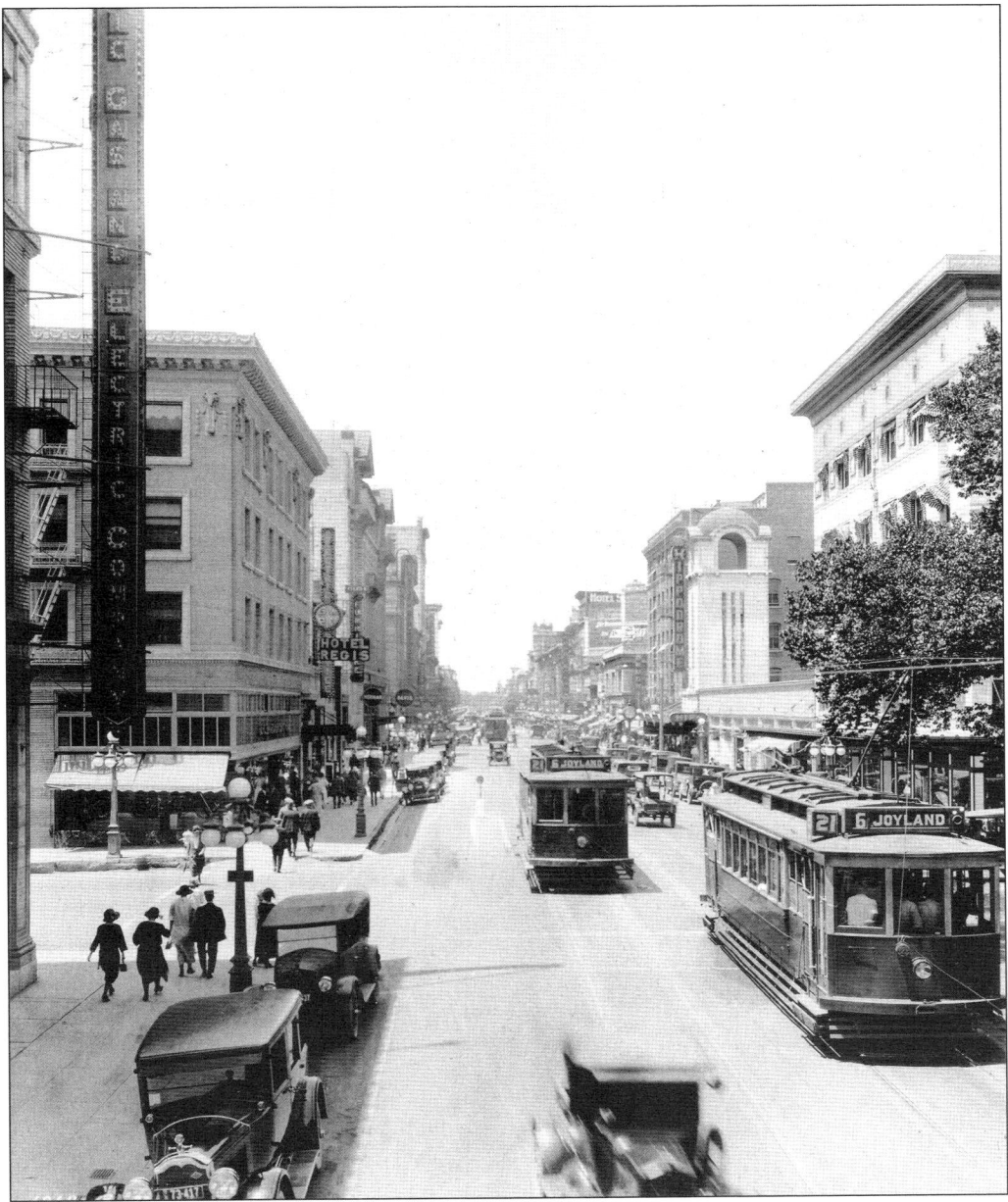

This c. 1910 photo was taken on K Street in Sacramento. The two trolleys in the foreground display their destination as being "Joyland," a popular amusement park located in Oak Park. Trolleys such as these ran daily from Oak Park to downtown Sacramento.

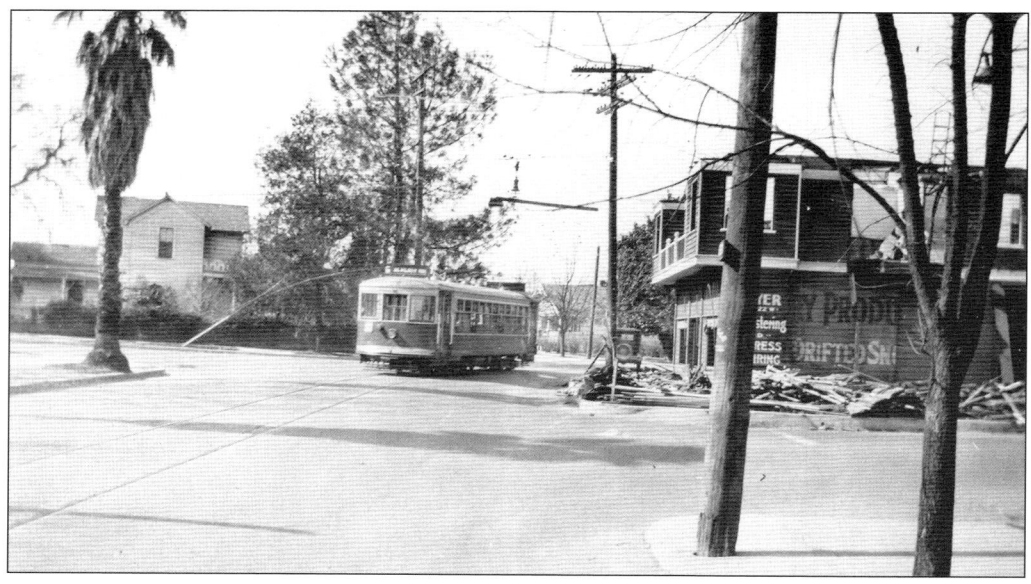

These two photos show the streetcars busy at work. The cars have been modified from their predecessors as seen on the previous pages. After the annexation of Oak Park, the lines traveled through residential areas (as seen in the top photo) and also through the city and to the Southern Pacific Depot.

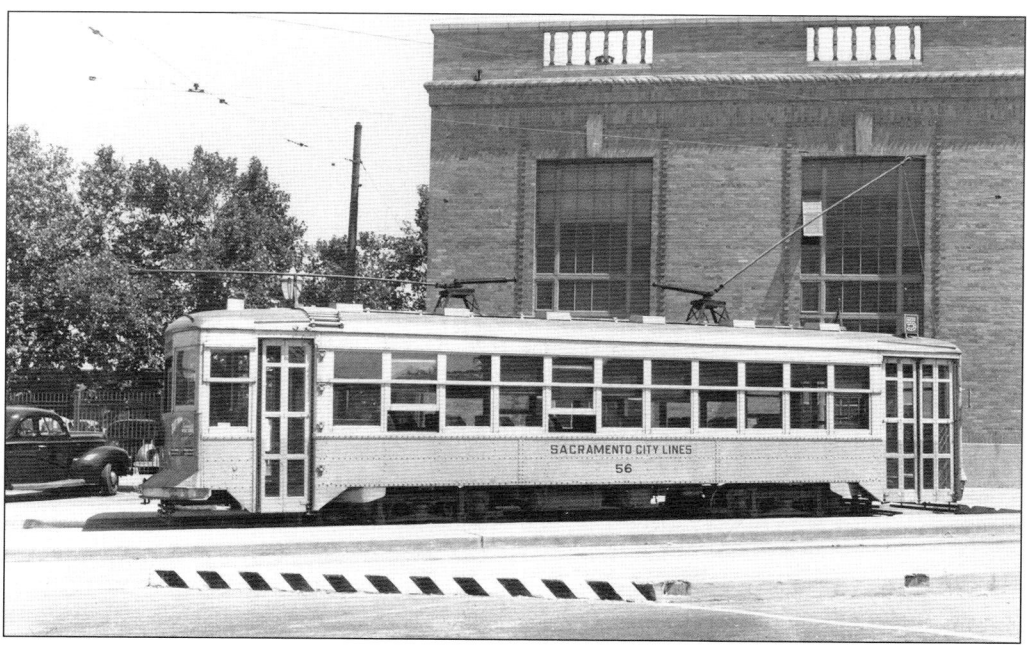

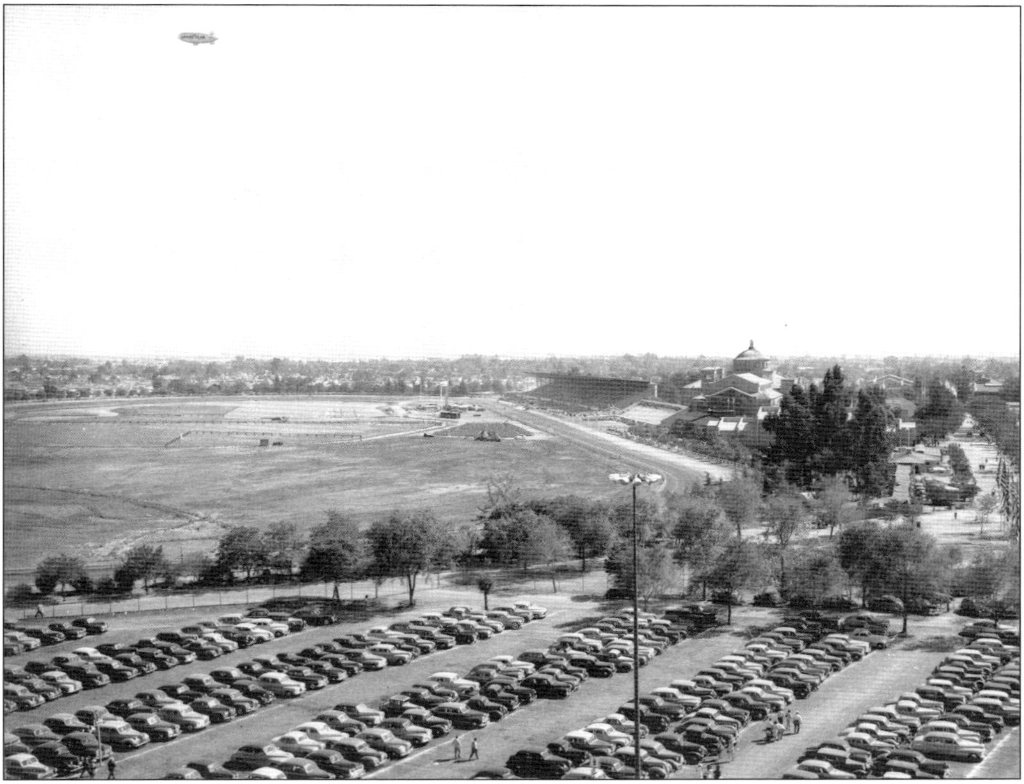

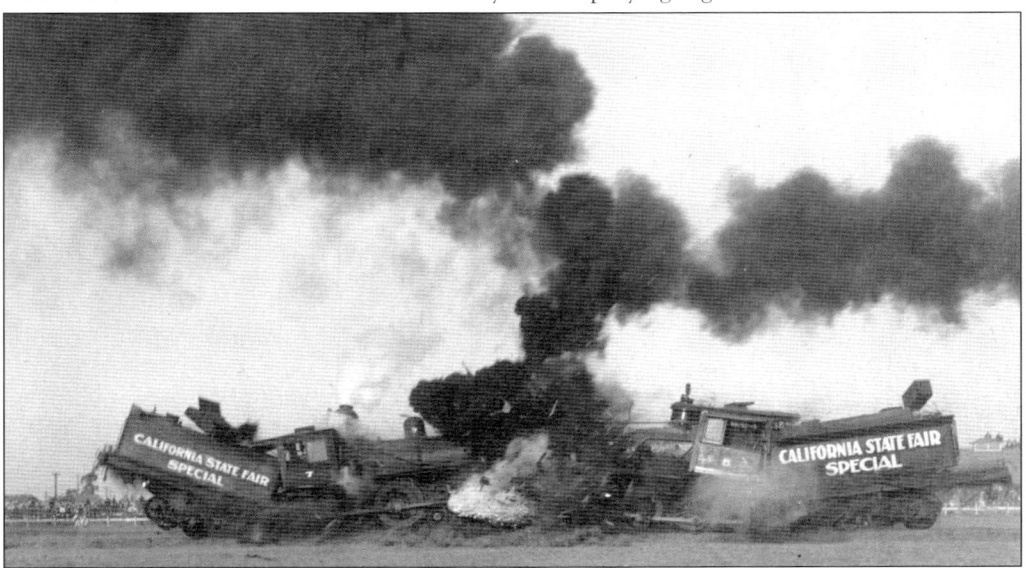

The parking lot at the state fairgrounds indicates that the day of the automobile had arrived. Notice the size of the lot as well as the Goodyear blimp flying high above the crowds.

This postcard, c. 1917, is from the California State Fair located at the fairgrounds in Oak Park. Train wrecks were a popular form of entertainment and the predecessor to the modern-day demolition derby.

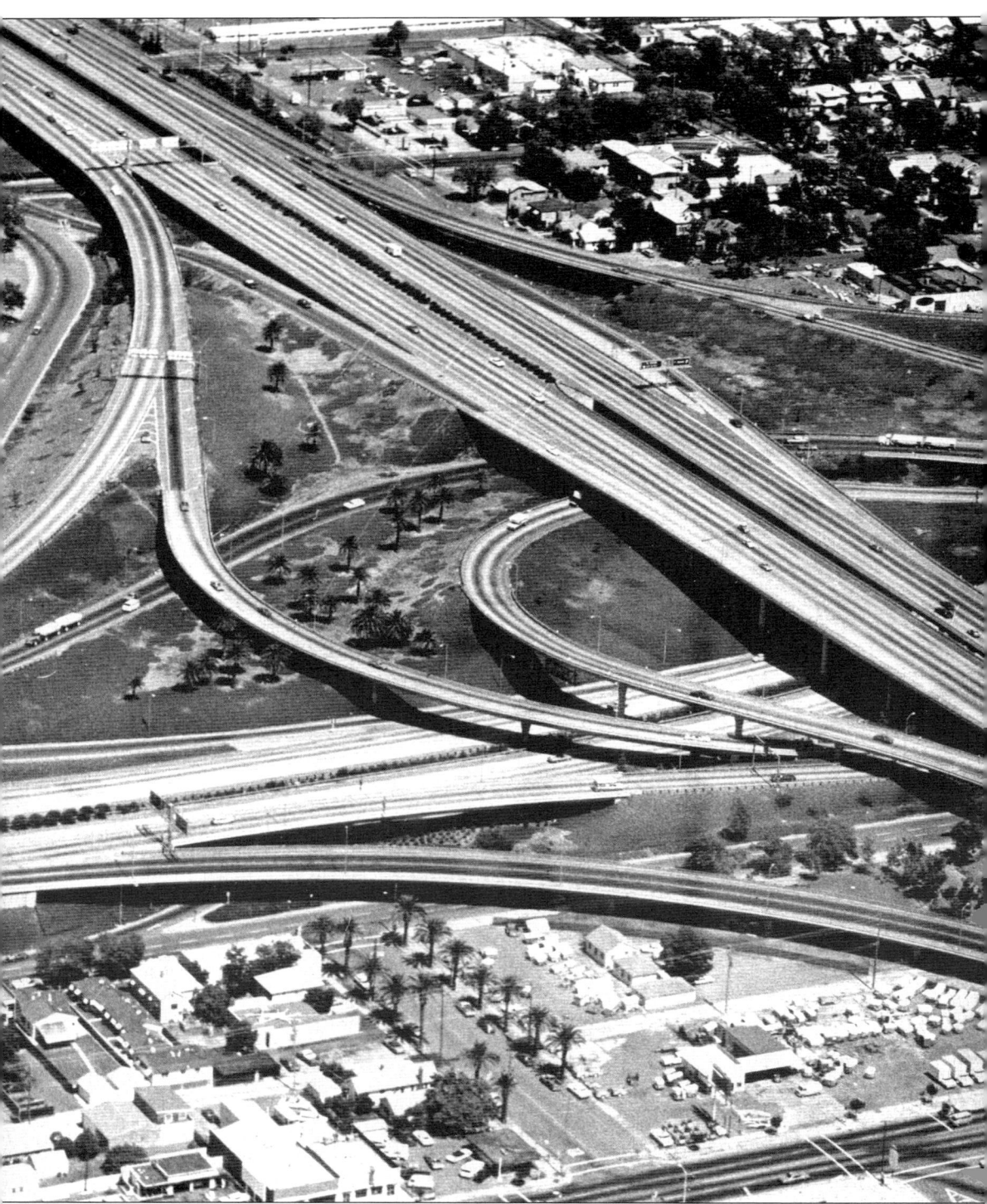

The construction of a freeway is a tremendous feat for the means of local transportation. This c. 1955 photograph of the Highway 99 interchange with Highway 50 shows the freeway

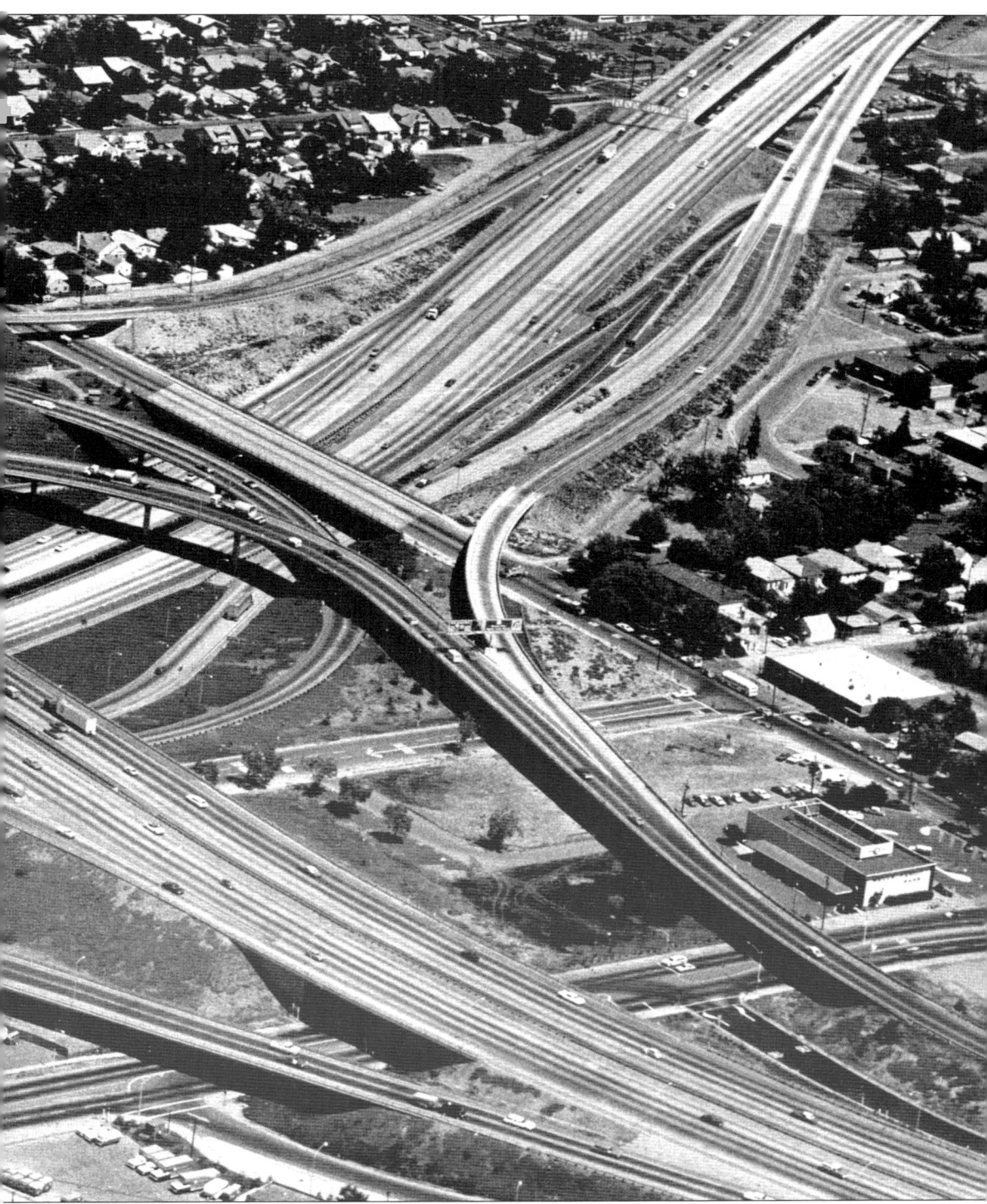
dividing Oak Park in half and destroying much of the local neighborhoods in its way.

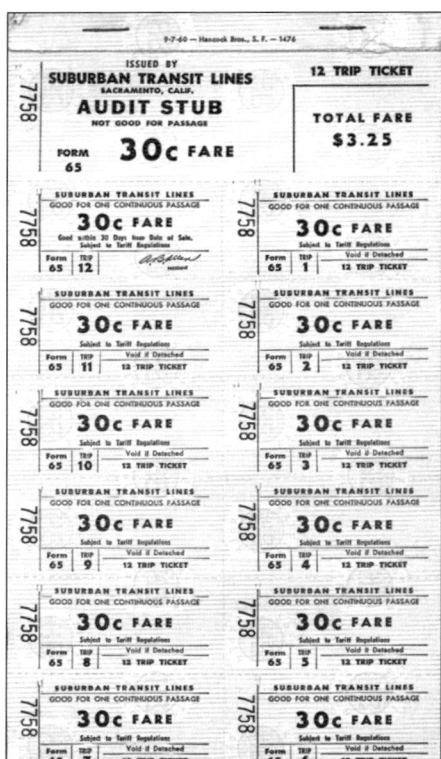

These tickets were used on the suburban bus lines in Sacramento. Similar tickets were used by Oak Park residents to travel about the city.

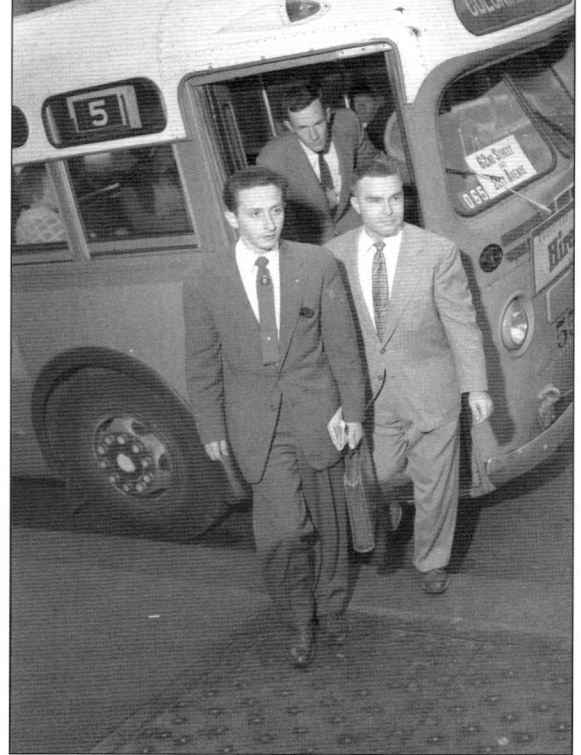

In addition to the trolley lines, the Sacramento bus lines became a major part of city transportation. This c. 1950 photo shows an Oak Park businessman stepping off the bus after a hard day's work.

Four

People of the Park
By Casey Wendt

In its earliest years, Oak Park was rural farmland just south of the city limits. There was no town or neighborhood. It was simply countryside made up of rich soil, where independent families could work the land for a humble living. Although Oak Park was yet to develop into the working-class suburb it became in later years, in many ways it was from this rural beginning that Oak Park earned its flavor as a working-class area. Throughout the years, as Oak Park shifted from farmland to suburb to slum to a neighborhood today looking to revitalize its image, Oak Park has remained working class.

The earliest Oak Park residents were primarily of Northern European descent and many were emigrants from New England. In the years following annexation into Sacramento, the suburb experienced a noticeable shift in the ethnic makeup of its residents. The largest ethnic group from the 1910s to the 1930s were Italians. They were joined by a smaller number of Portuguese and other Southern Europeans. This period also witnessed the movement of the first Mexican and African-American families into Oak Park. Japanese, Chinese, and other Asian residents were virtually non-existent in Oak Park, as they were purposely excluded from moving into the district. In many ways the shifting ethnic makeup of Oak Park provides a microcosm for the larger social and demographic changes of the time, affecting not only the rest of the Sacramento area, but ultimately cities all over the country.

It was not until World War II, as the nation was building up its wartime industry, that the African-American population in Sacramento—and subsequently Oak Park—began to increase noticeably. As was occurring all over the country, the great migration brought new families, new faces, and new diversity to almost all cities in the United States. Although Sacramento lacked a heavy war industry, it was home to several military bases, and, under the circumstances, increased opportunities began to open up for minorities. Nonetheless, it was not until the 1950s that African Americans began to move to Oak Park in substantial numbers. As urban renewal began to force African Americans out of Sacramento's West End, Oak Park's working-class neighborhood provided an affordable and attractive alternative.

The photographs that follow provide a glimpse into the diverse families that have made their home in Oak Park. In no way is this a complete portrayal of all of the families that have made Oak Park their home throughout the years. The photographs are drawn from a limited collection and thus provide only a sampling of images meant to convey the changing diversity of the area. In total, however, they accurately capture the deep working-class roots that lie at the heart of Oak Park.

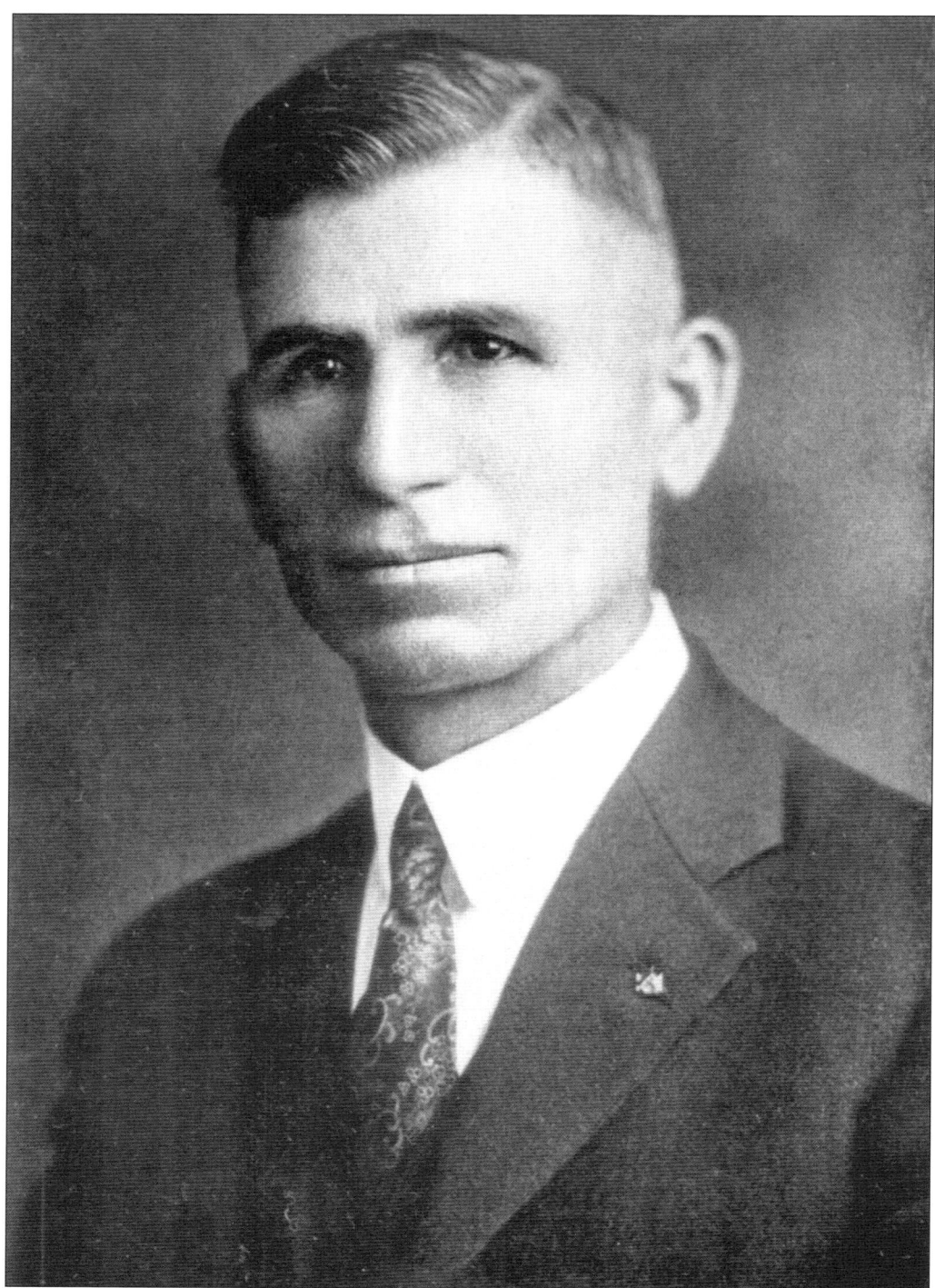

Owner of a vineyard on Fifth Avenue east of Stockton Road, Deo Cordano, shown in this c. 1920 photo, was one of the many Italian residents living in Oak Park from the 1910s to the 1930s. In fact, Italians made up the largest ethnic group living in Oak Park during this time.

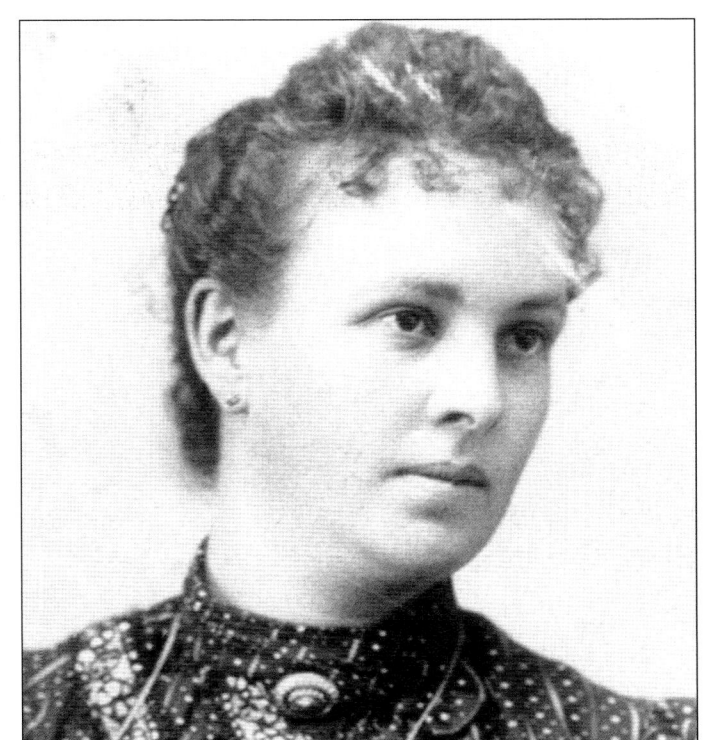

Anita Beckwith and her daughters, shown in these c. 1910 photos, represented Northern European immigrants to Oak Park.

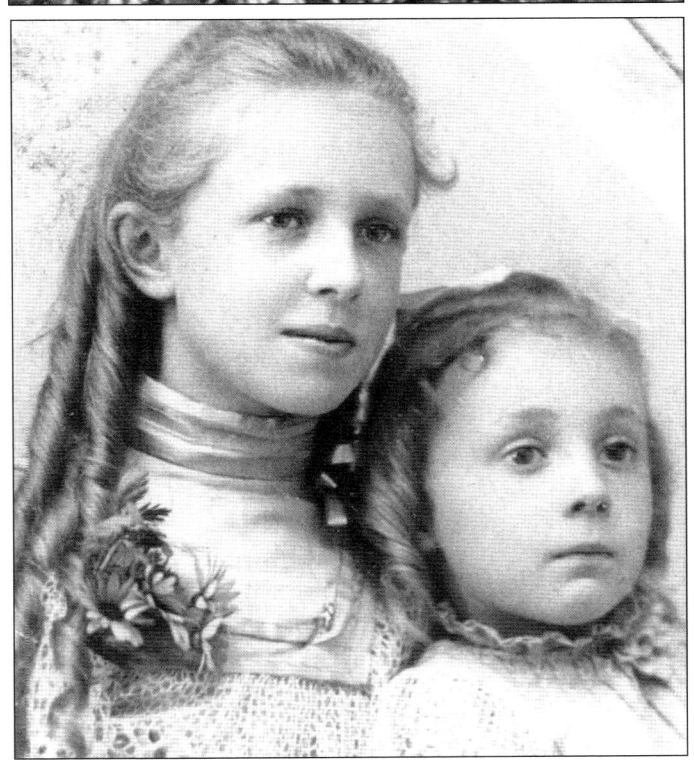

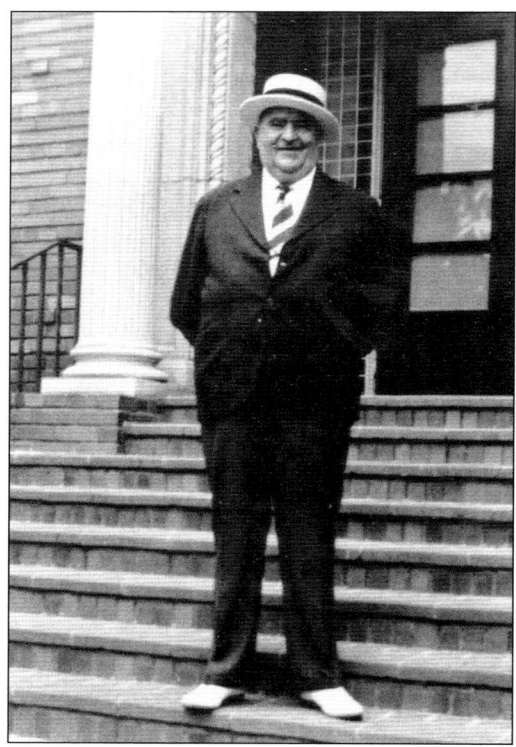

In this c. 1938 photo, James Ryle stands on the steps of the old Oak Park Library on Thirty-third Avenue. The library was replaced in 1982 by the Colonial Heights Library on Stockton Boulevard.

The Maleville children, Ralph, Jack, Elwood, and Eleanor, pose for a snapshot c. 1920. All of the Maleville children, including Edwin "Buddy" Robert (not pictured), were born at 3450 Second Avenue, the Maleville home in Oak Park. The children represent the third generation of Oak Park residents. Their grandparents were Judge John S. McMahon and Sara McMahon, some of Oak Park's first residents. Their parents were Lillian and Isidore Maleville.

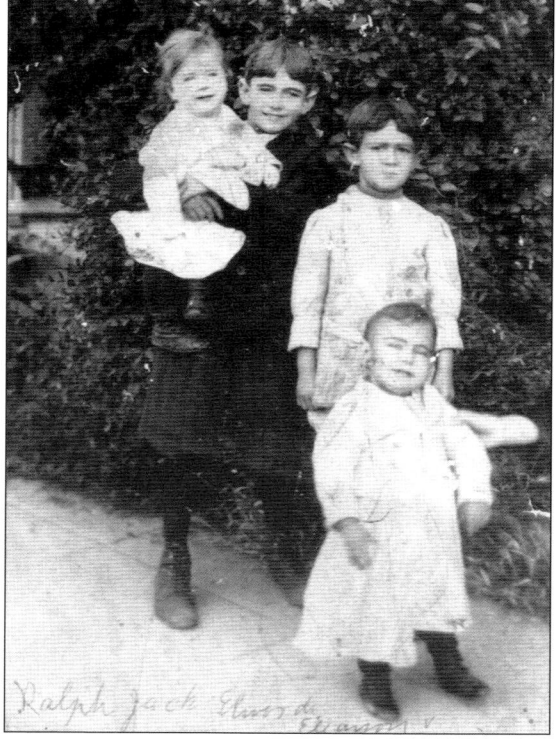

World War I called many young men out of their neighborhoods and into battle. Elwood Maleville, dressed in suit and tie in this c. 1918 photo, waits for his train as he leaves Oak Park to fight in World War I. Written on the family photo is the simple phrase, "Elwood going to war."

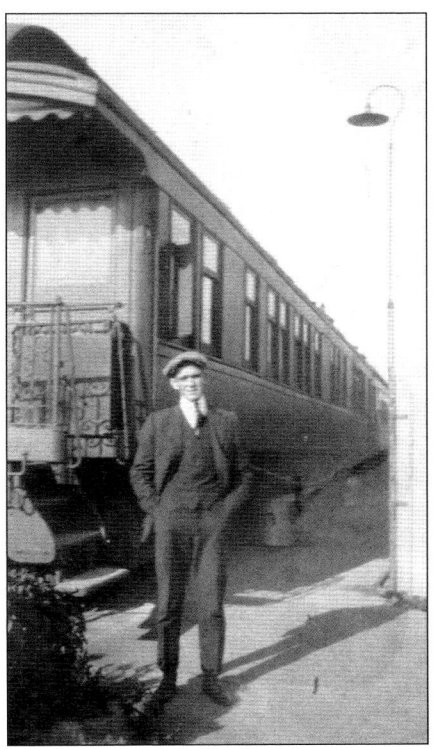

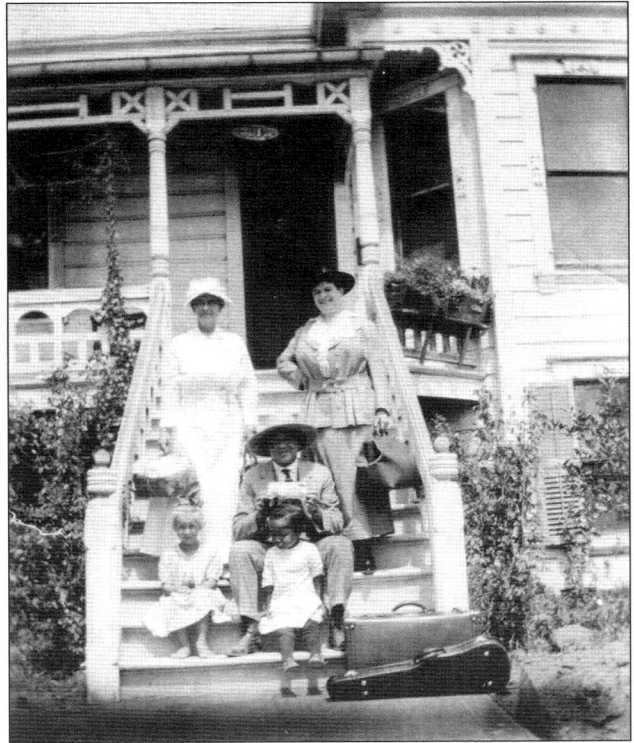

Perhaps a demonstration of pride in their homes, the front stoop appears to be a popular place to take photos of friends and family. Clarissa Hundley Wildy (front), Dorthea Martin (front left), and others pose in this c. 1917 photo with music cases in front of an Oak Park residence.

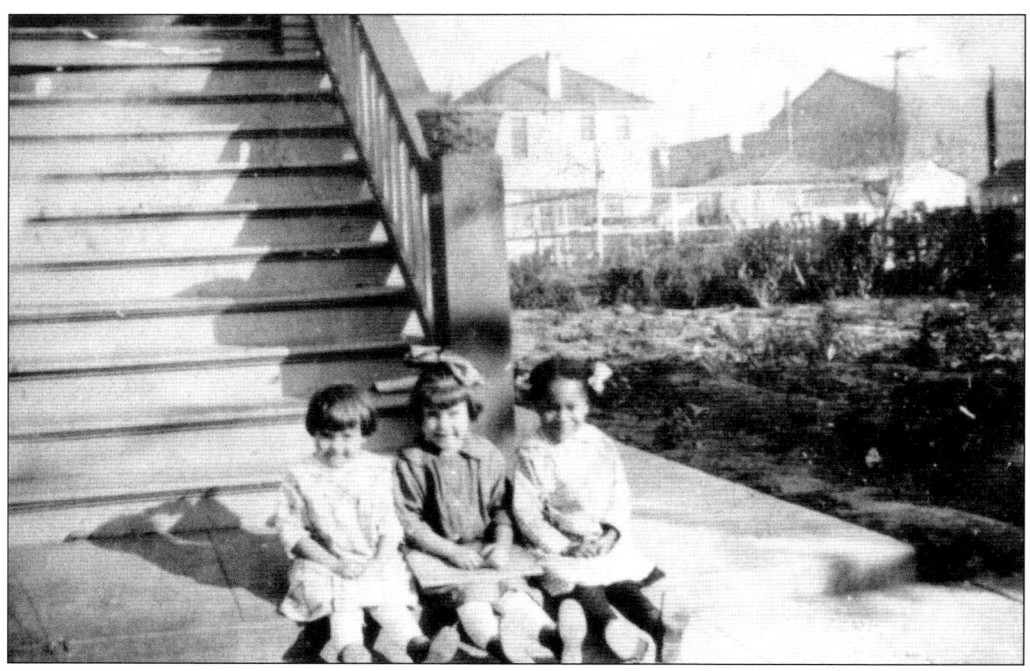

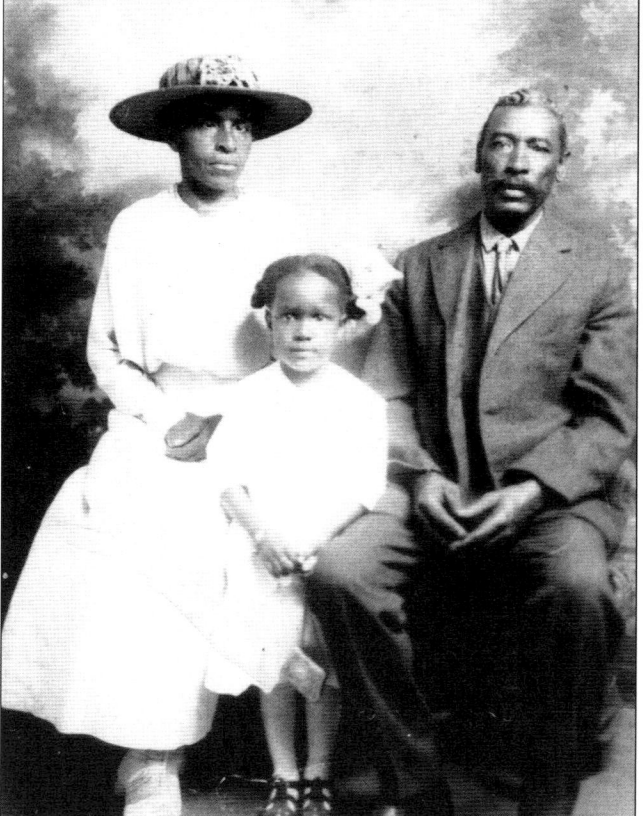

An important characteristic of Oak Park has always been the diversity of its residents, as demonstrated in this 1918 photo by these three young playmates, Hariette and Margaret Throckmorton and Clarissa Hundley Wildy (right) on the stoop of the Throckmorton home, 3419 Fourth Avenue.

The Hundley family—from left to right, Lucy Jane Ray, Clarissa, and David—pose for a family portrait in 1919. Clarissa's maternal grandfather, Francis Marion Ray, was a slave from Missouri who, at age five, was separated from his family when he was sold to a Texas plantation owner. It was not until 1877 that Francis Marion Ray was able to reunite with his family who had made their way to Sacramento. Several of Francis's children, including Lucy Jane, became early residents of Oak Park.

Pictured here, most likely in their Oak Park yard, are a smiling Clarissa Hundley Wildy (age 8) and her mother Lucy Jane (age 40).

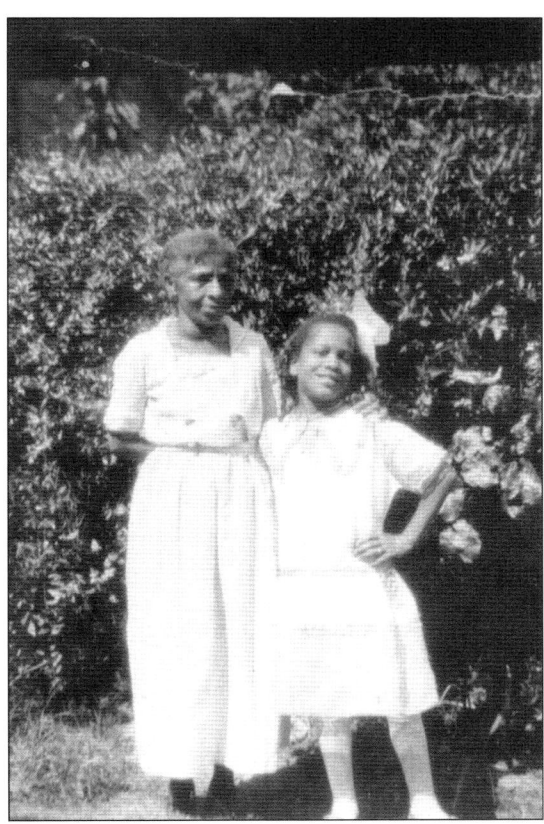

"Aloha Party for Clarissa—En Route to Honolulu" is penciled on the back of this group photograph, c. 1943. This farewell party was hosted by Jane Dunlap (standing). Clarissa, a clerk-typist, moved to Hawaii, where she worked at Pearl Harbor and later at Barber's Point. Pictured here are, from left to right, (front row) Doris Dunlap, Clarissa Hundley, and Marie Evans; (back row) Barbara Morgan, Audrey Dunlap, Marjorie Towns, Maude Brown, Julia ?, Madeline ?, and Irma ?.

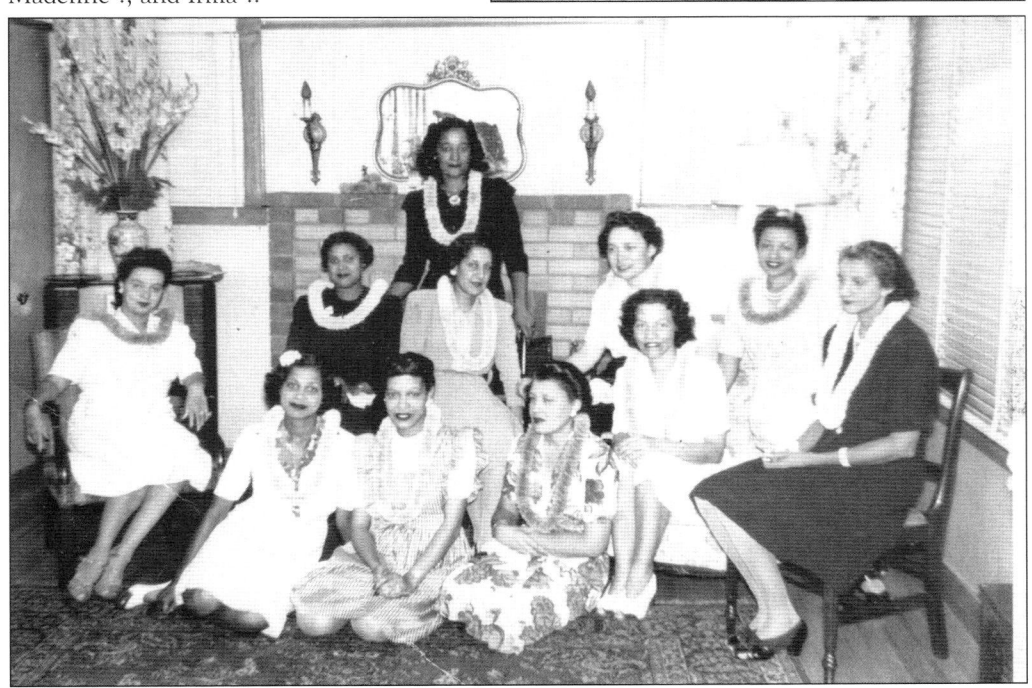

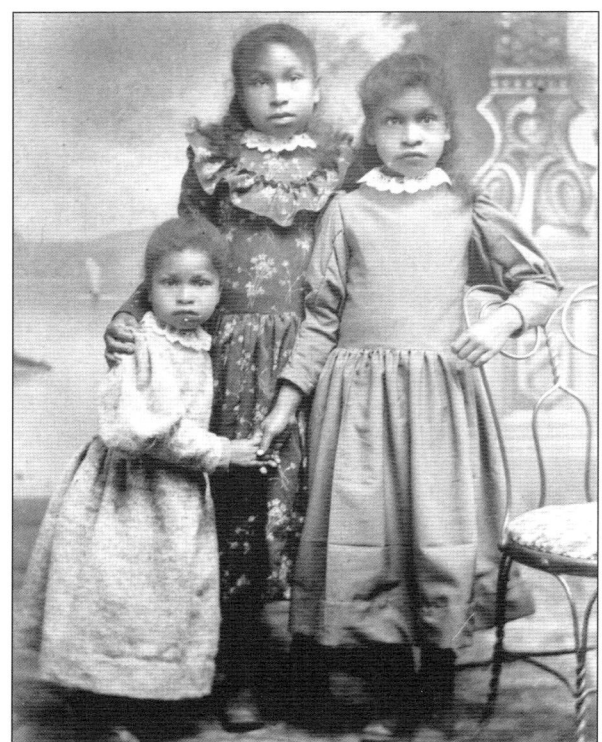

The Grubbs daughters—from left to right, Alma, Isabelle Clarissa, and Grace Evelyn—pose for a portrait. The Grubbs family photographs indicate the family lived a comfortable working-class lifestyle. Eugene Grubbs, husband of Fannie Ray and father of the girls, was a janitor for W.F. & Company. Around 1917 the family moved out of their Rose Street home to midtown Sacramento.

Despite racism and segregation, African Americans have served in the U.S. Navy since the Civil War. George Washington Ray, shown in this c. 1895 photo, brother of Lucy Jane and Fannie Elizabeth, served in the navy before making his home in Oak Park, where he worked for Castle Bros.

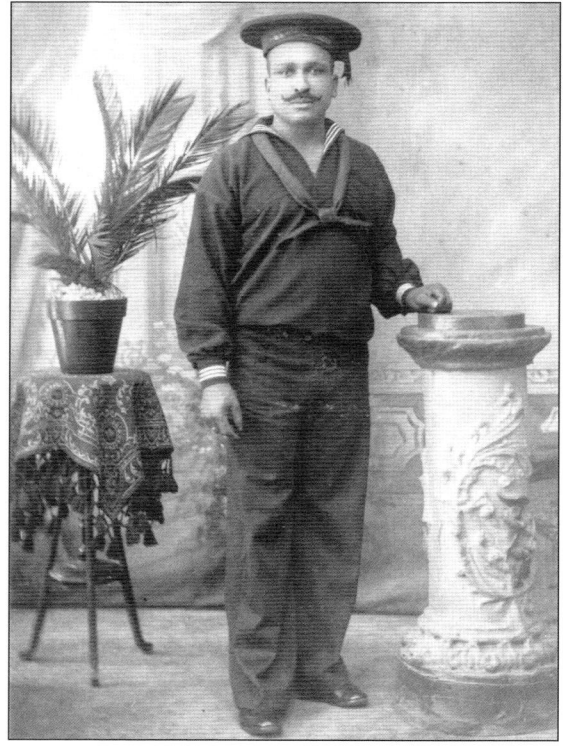

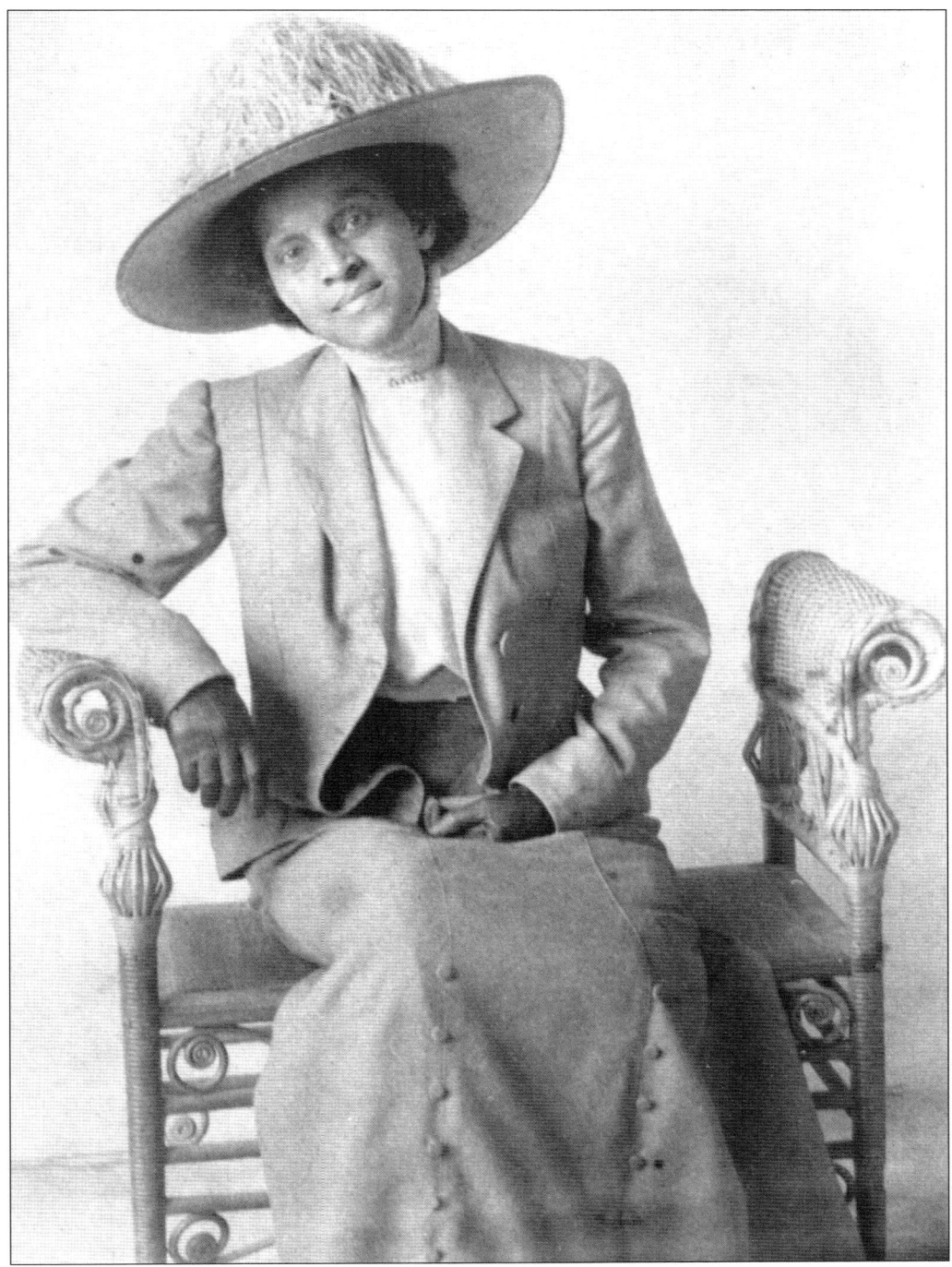

Maude Ray Simons poses for an elegant portrait. Maude was the sister of Lucy, Fanny, and George Ray and lived in Oak Park through the early 1900s.

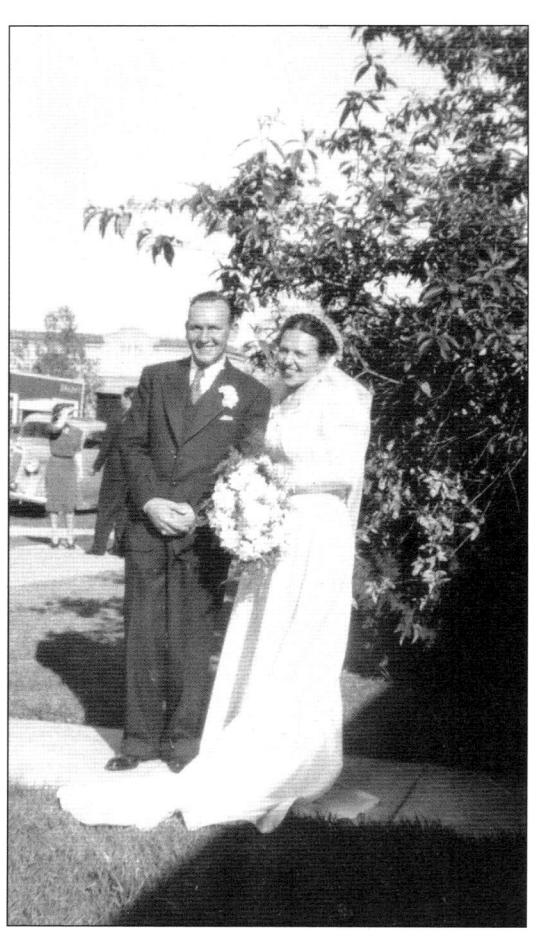

Married in 1942, Lloyd Hennesey and Mary Ansen Hennessey lived in Oak Park at 3764 Miller Way from the year they were married until the 1990s. Mary was the daughter of Russian immigrants. She graduated from Chico State Teacher's College in 1934 and taught for many years at Elder Creek School. W. Lloyd Hennessey was a janitor at Sacramento Junior College.

Perhaps after returning one afternoon from a hunting trip c. 1945, Lloyd Hennessey poses in his Oak Park backyard with his game.

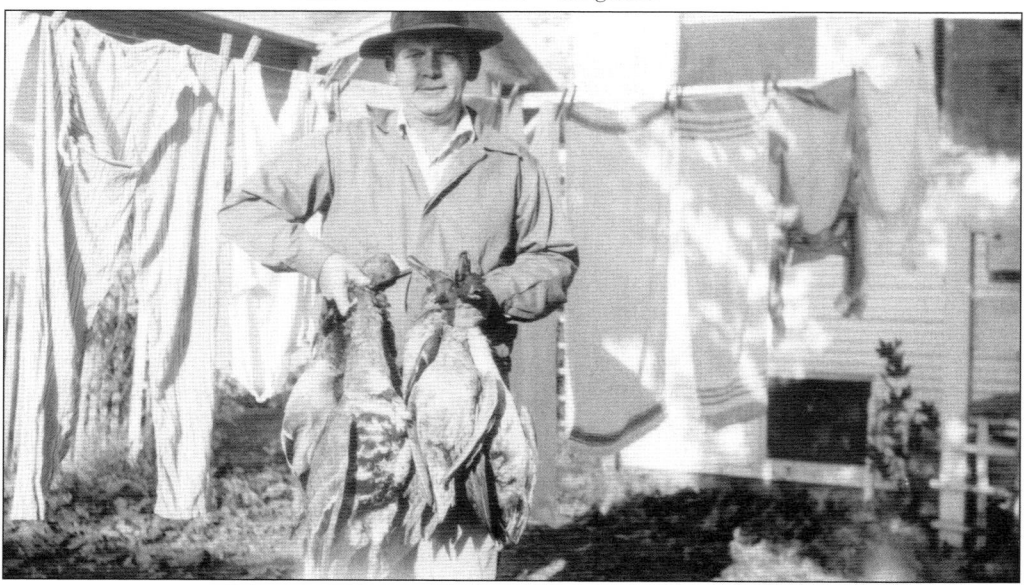

Steven Bellew spent his early childhood in Oak Park. He is pictured here with his mother (at right) and in his wagon (below) in front of the family home c. 1950.

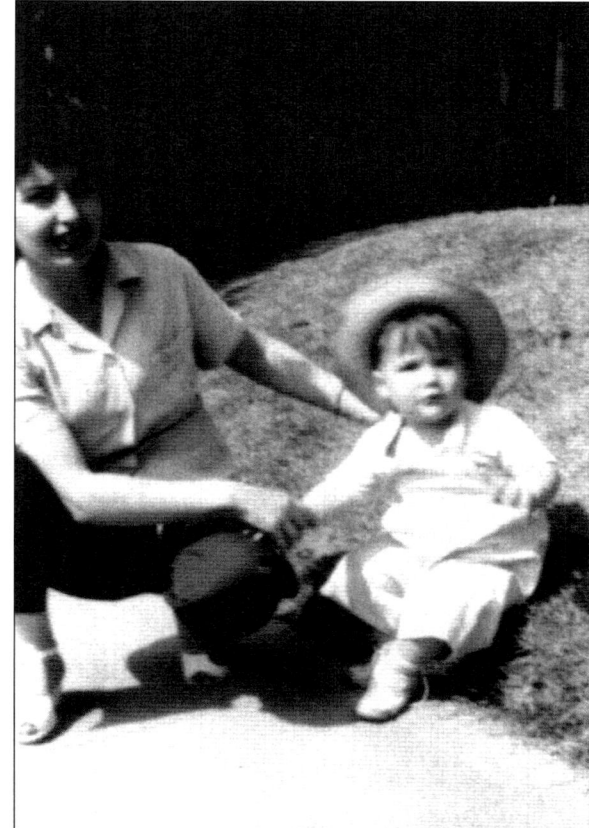

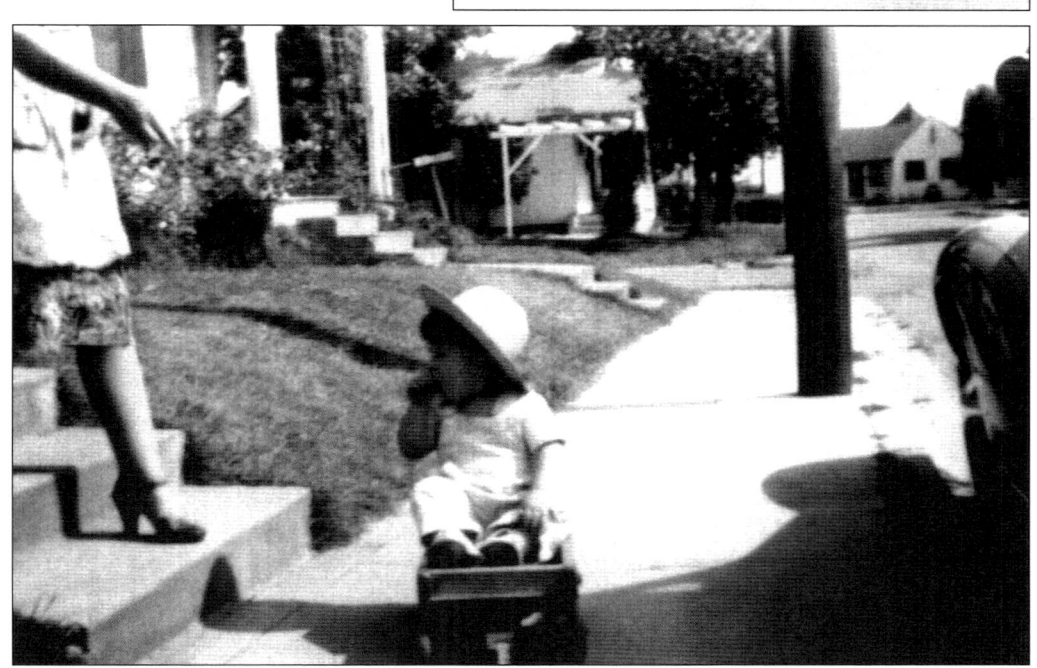

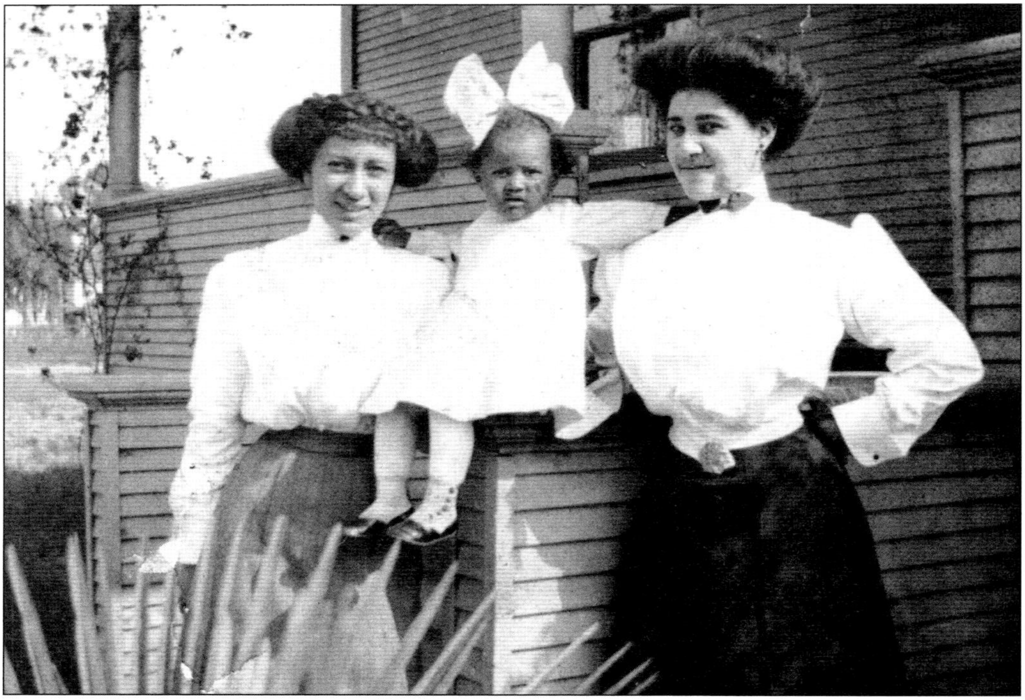

Louise Dunlap, Audrey Dunlap, and Adel Smith pose c. 1910 in front of the Dunlap's Fourth Avenue home. The home later became Dunlap's Dining Room.

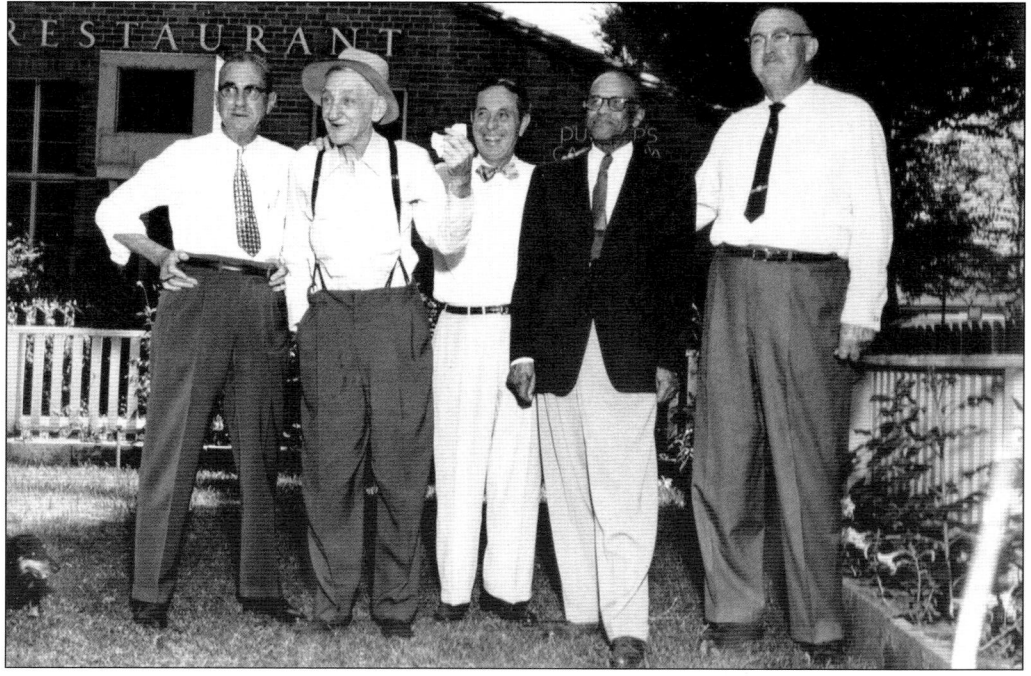

Standing in front of the famous Oak Park restaurant, Dunlap's Dining Room, is George Dunlap, second from right.

Five

MAKING ENDS MEET
By Gabe Aeschliman

Prior to the introduction of the streetcar in 1891, most Oak Park residents relied on farming for work. A variety of crops and animals provided subsistence, but income came primarily from vineyards and dairy farms. The rise of industrial and entrepreneurial activities after the turn of the 20th century finally caused a decline in agricultural dependence.

The extension of the streetcar line permitted Oak Park residents to seek work further away from home. At 5¢ a ride, even laborers could afford to commute. From 1891 through the first part of the 20th century, more and more Oak Park residents worked for the Southern Pacific Railroad, just a short ride down the main line. For those residents who chose to labor closer to home, a small business district developed to supply needed services to the growing suburb. Early businesses such as Steen's Corner Saloon, Daly Bros. Grocery, and Clifton's Furniture Store laid the groundwork for sole proprietorships in Oak Park.

New Oak Park businesses, such as the Sacramento and Citizens Banks, began to add an independent character to the still blossoming area, and they set the tone for area businesses for the next century. Men such as Harry C. Muddox found new opportunities in Oak Park to expand beyond their original business interests. Muddox ran the sewer and pipe company that supplied materials for sewer construction following annexation in 1911. In 1910 he also established the Citizens Bank, which he managed until his death. Another enterprising businessman was Judge John S. McMahon. An emigrant in 1873, McMahon left a permanent mark on Oak Park both as justice of the peace and as builder of some of Oak Park's important public buildings. Most notably, he erected the Oak Park post office in 1915. In 1911, these pioneering proprietors established the Oak Park Business Men's Association, headed by local jeweler J.W. Babcock, to serve as a veritable chamber of commerce.

The stock market crash of 1929 brought Oak Park prosperity to a screeching halt. The community finally found economic salvation in a number of new military bases established in the Sacramento area. Oak Park became a prime settlement area for new working-class military men including a significant number of African Americans. This demographic shift also led to the rise of new black-owned businesses. Three months after the crash, George Dunlap, a resident since 1906, opened Dunlap's Dining Room for business. The restaurant became a symbol of the new Oak Park community.

Unfortunately, while most of America climbed out of the depression in the 1940s and 1950s, Oak Park businesses remained depressed. Businesses failed and others fled, opting for more prosperous suburbs. By the 1960s Oak Park was notorious for criminal activities, not the working-class ideal on which the community was founded. However, in 1973 the Oak Park Redevelopment Project Area was formed with the intention of reshaping the struggling community. Today the Oak Park business community is rebounding. The revitalization effort has revived the working-class ethic that existed in the early days of the community.

FACTS FOR FARMERS

Helpful Suggestions For the Agriculturist.

HINTS THAT ARE INTERESTING.

Some Good Advice for the Ruralists—A Budget of Knowledge That May Prove Beneficial.

"Facts for Farmers" ran as a regular section in the *Oak Park Ledger*. The column offered advice and farming tips for local farmers. The section ran on the front page until 1904, when increasing industrialization became more important in the growing suburb.

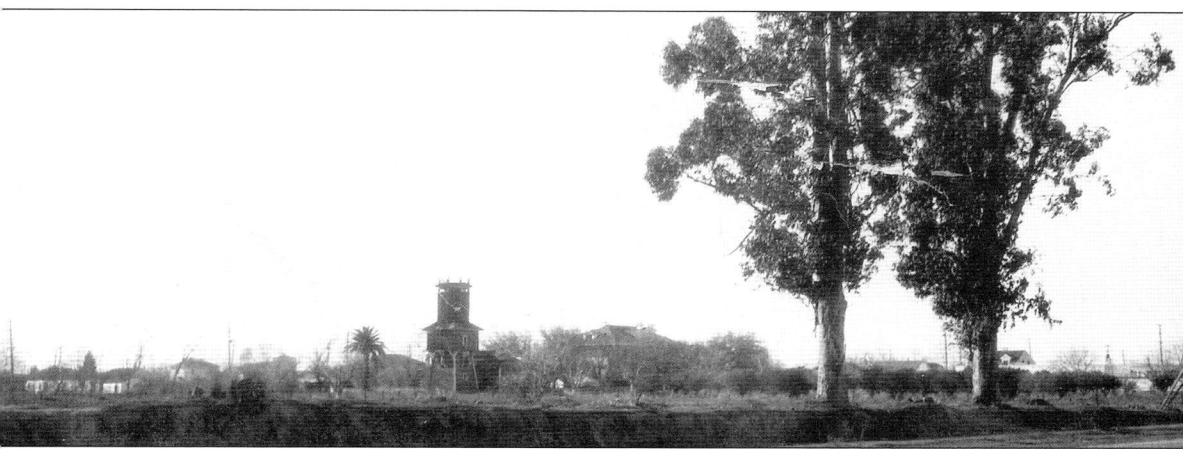

Although this picture was taken in 1938, it offers a glimpse into Oak Park's past. The location at Stockton Boulevard and Miller Way has an orange grove in the near distance. Oak Park was littered with such groves prior to development. Today, the Coca-Cola bottling plant stands at this location.

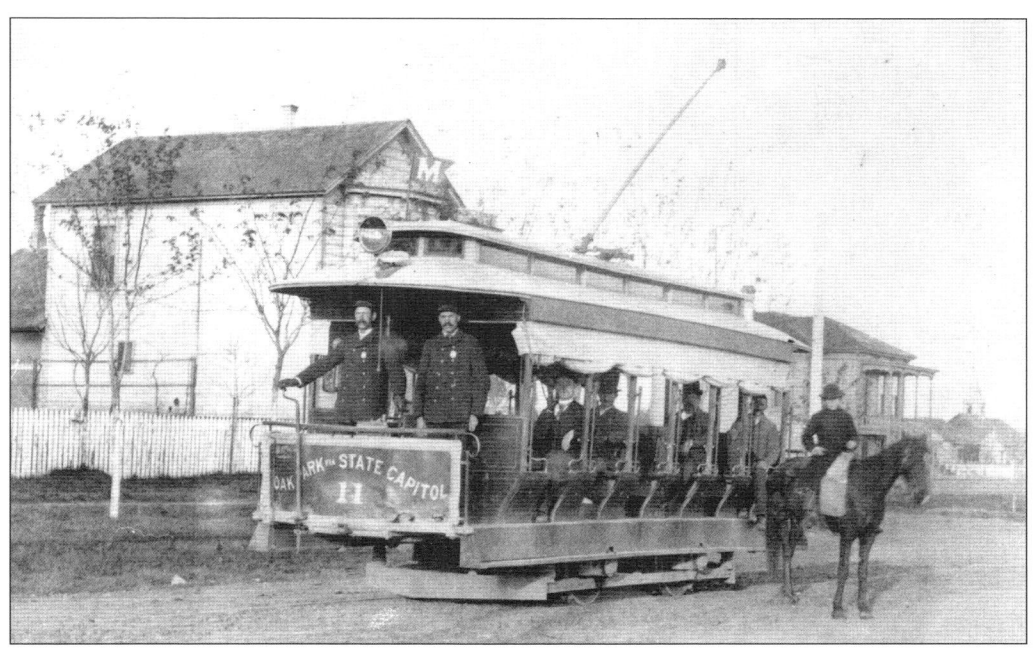

The Sacramento streetcar line extended to Oak Park in 1891. This line gave laborers the opportunity and ability to reside outside of the downtown business area. This picture, taken c. 1900, depicts German and Irish workers, possibly shop foremen, riding the line that stopped at the Southern Pacific Depot.

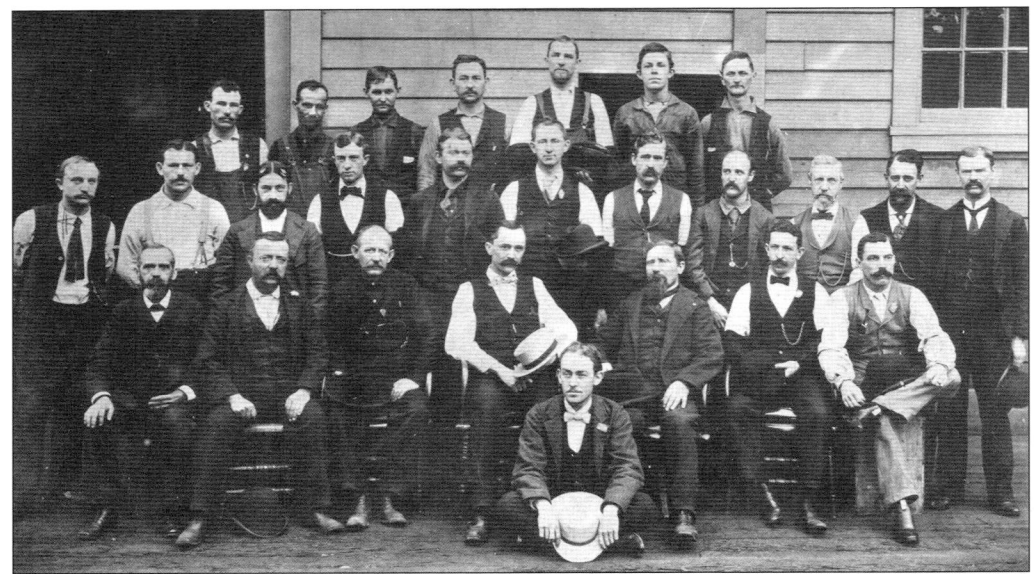

This picture depicts the store department employees of the Southern Pacific Railroad Company in 1898. The railroad was a large employer of Oak Park laborers.

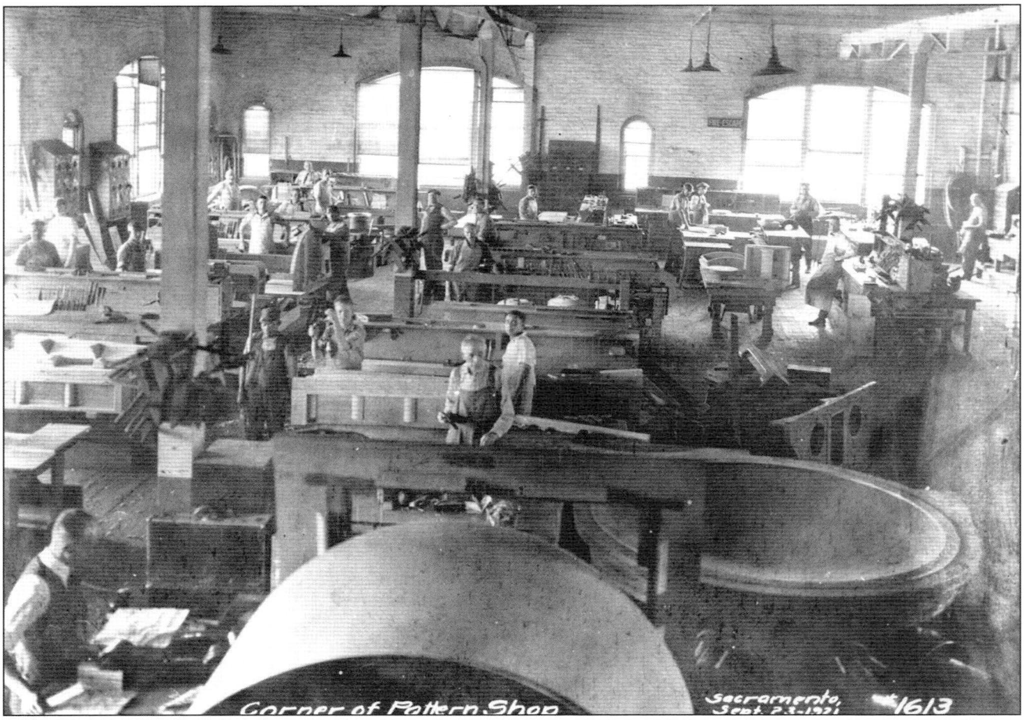

Although no information confirms the identity of these Southern Pacific Railroad shop workers, a large number of Oak Park residents were employed by the railroad giant. This picture was taken on September 23, 1921, and shows the general operations of the pattern shop.

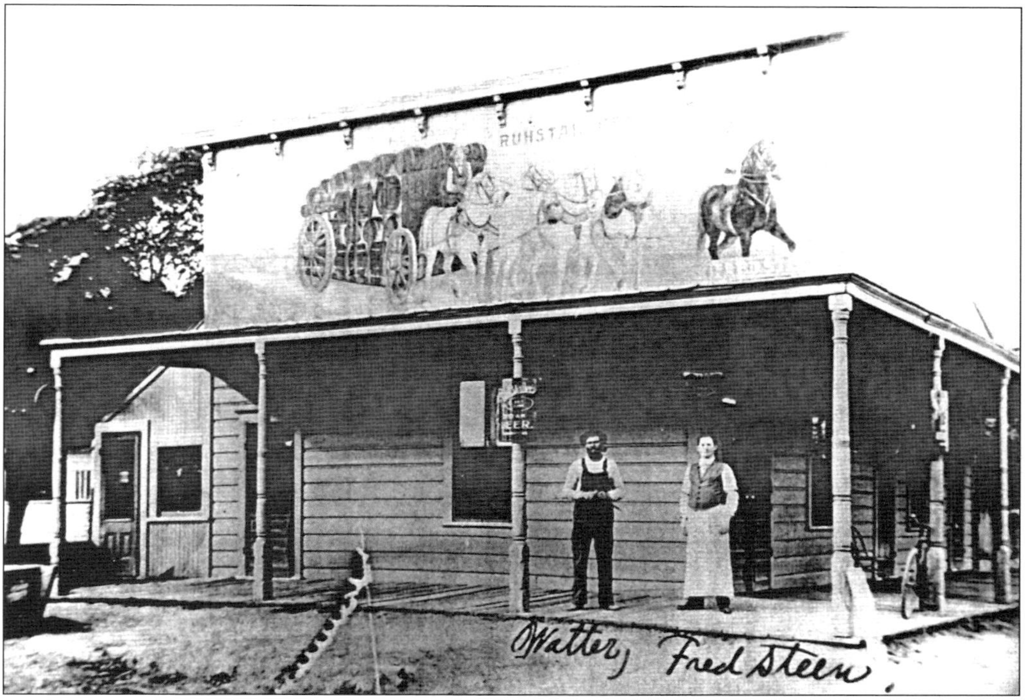

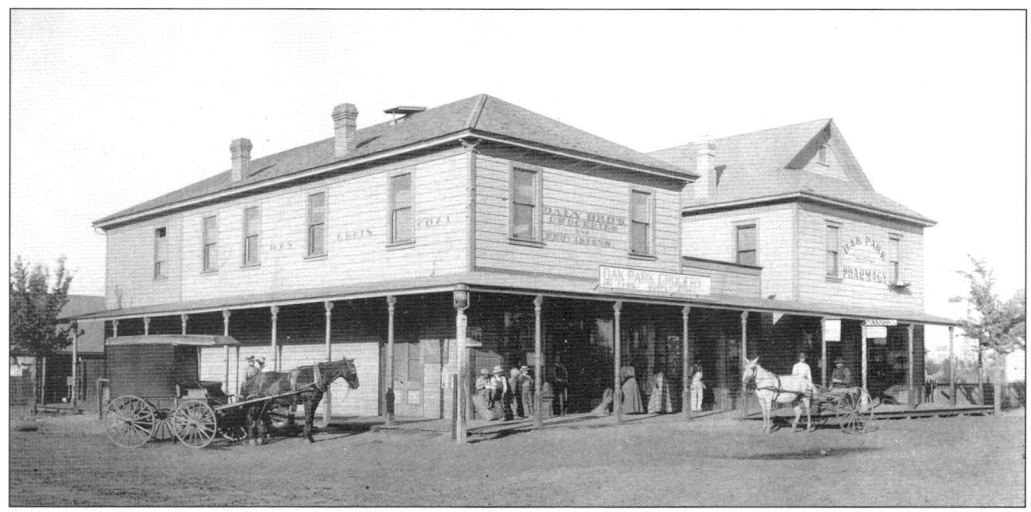

Steen's Corner Saloon was erected in 1893. Established by a German immigrant, John Steen, this saloon was the first Oak Park business. Steen's Corner became a popular watering hole for residents. During Prohibition, the saloon survived by pouring soft drinks instead of beer.

The Daly Bros. Grocery Store was an early addition to Oak Park, catering to the working-class population of the area and in the early part of the twentieth century to the small farmers who populated the area. This photo was taken c. 1890, before the introduction of power to Oak Park.

Politics played an important role in working-class life in the early 20th century. This advertisement, taken from the November 3, 1910 edition of the *Oak Park Ledger*, demonstrates labor's concern with Prohibition.

EVERYBODY IS INVITED TO JOIN

LABOR'S PROTEST AGAINST PROHIBITION

Saturday Evening, November 4th

BIG STREET PARADE BY WORKINGMEN AND WOMEN WHOSE LIVELIHOOD WOULD BE DESTROYED BY THE ADOPTION OF EITHER OR BOTH OF THE PROHIBITION AMENDMENTS.

BIG MASS MEETING AT THE GRAND THEATER

IMMEDIATELY AFTER THE PARADE

Miss Mary Field, the well-known woman worker; Supervisor Andrew Gallaghar, of San Francisco; President John A. O'Connell, of the California Trade Union Liberty League, and J. B. Osborne, the well-known California blind orator, will be the speakers.

Music and Entertainment

Under auspices of Sacramento Branch, California Trades Union Liberty League.

Archie W. Clifton's Oak Park furniture store is the second oldest business in Oak Park. In 1902 Clifton emigrated to Sacramento to work at John Breuner's furniture store. By 1910, Clifton became confident in the potential of Oak Park and opened his own store there. Upon retirement Clifton deeded the store to his two sons, M.C. and H.C. Clifton.

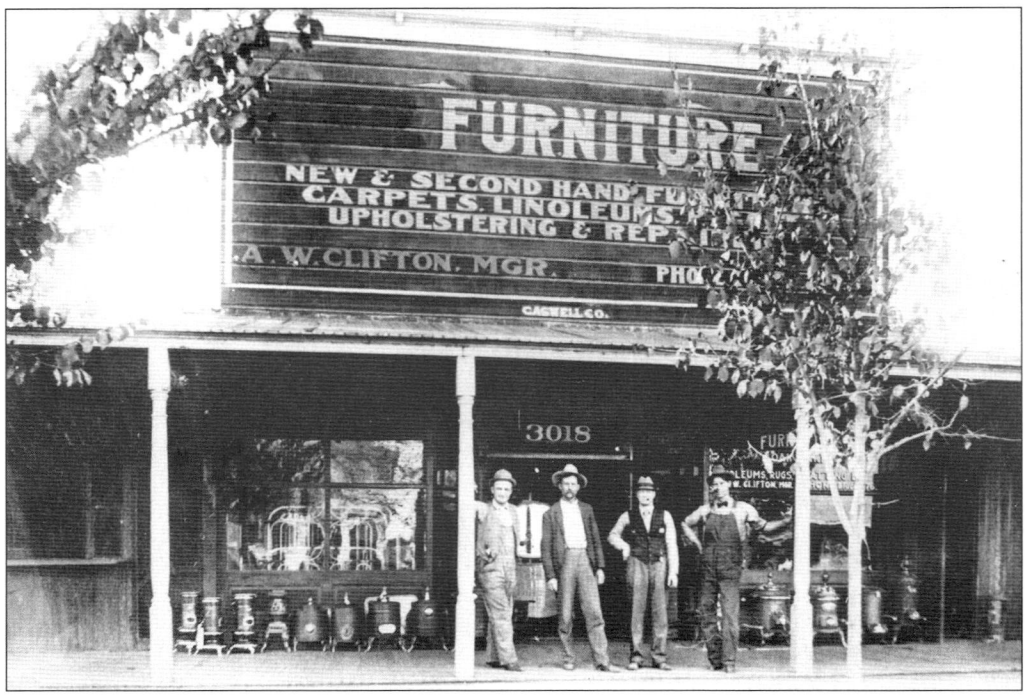

This advertisement for Clifton's Furniture Store ran in the *Oak Park Ledger* on September 29, 1911.

AT HOME

After September 20th Mr. Clifton Will Show You His New Line of

Heaters, Cook Stoves and Ranges

of all Descriptions. Something That Will Fit Everybody's Pocket Book.

CALL AND SEE US

OAK PARK FURNITURE STORE

A. W. CLIFTON
3018 35th St.   Phone Black 1871

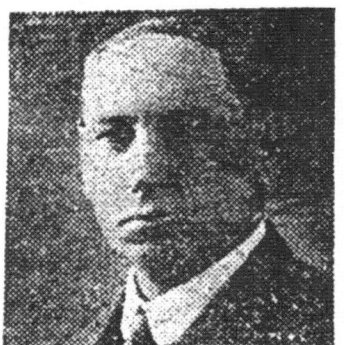

VOTE FOR
J. W. Babcock
JEWELER
CITY COMMISSIONER
SHORT TERM
First Name On The Ballot

The Oak Park Business Men's Association was created in 1911 to bring a non-partisan interest into the economic affairs of Oak Park. The group, comprised of local businessmen, lobbied to obtain city benefits for the newly annexed area, including sewers. J.W. Babcock, a local jeweler, served as the first president of the association. He later ran for city commissioner in 1915.

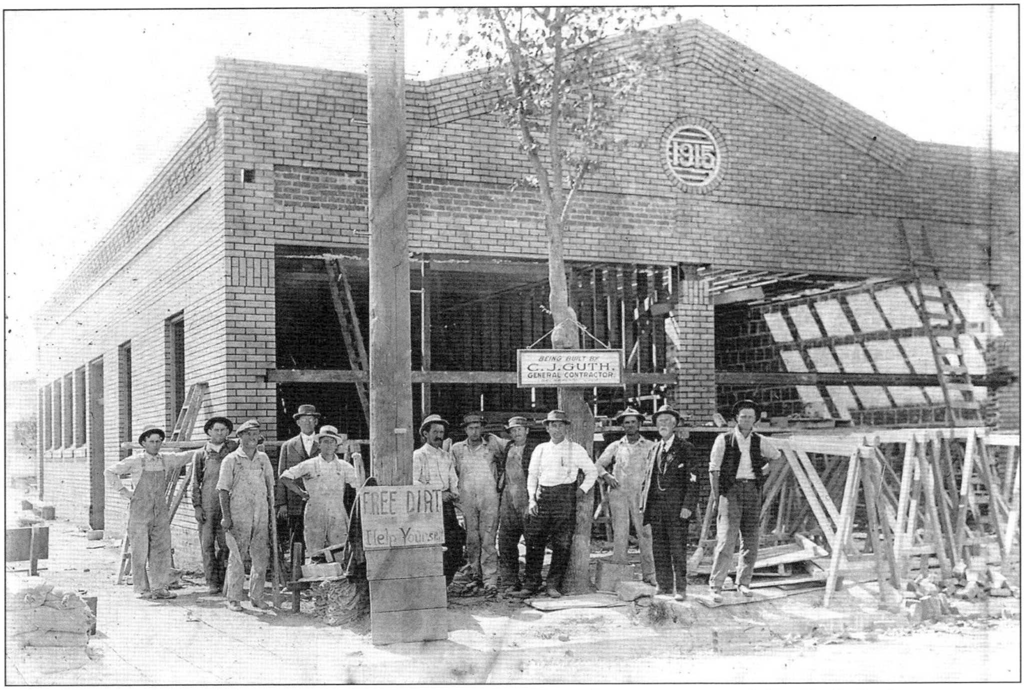

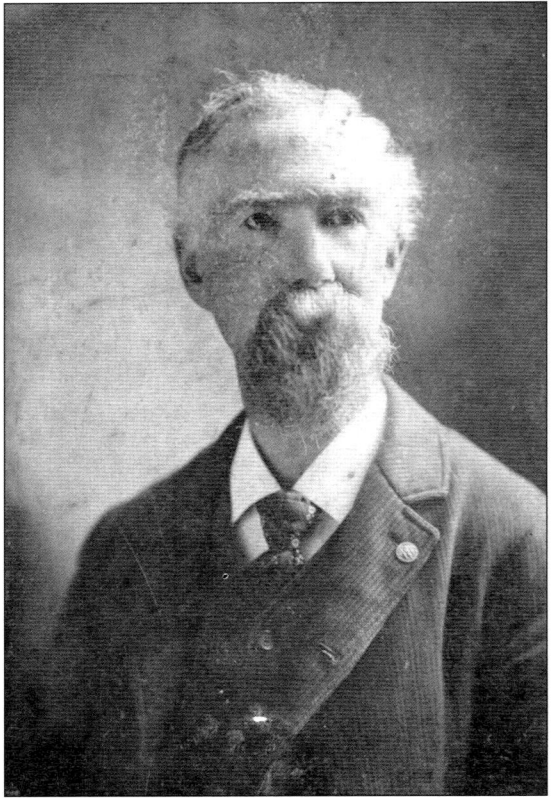

Construction of the Oak Park post office, funded by Judge John S. McMahon, began in late August 1915. According to the *Oak Park Ledger*, this building was the "first in Sacramento to be faced with ferred brick." This picture depicts the building in mid-construction. The man in the dark suit near the right side of the group is believed to be Judge McMahon.

Judge McMahon was considered a friend to labor. He joined the Printer's Union in 1864, one of the earliest union groups in California. McMahon once described his reasons for residing in Oak Park: "There was a street car. . . . That was one of the reasons, together with the cheapness of the lots, that caused my wife and me to buy here. It was attractive to a workingman. All this was then outside the city."

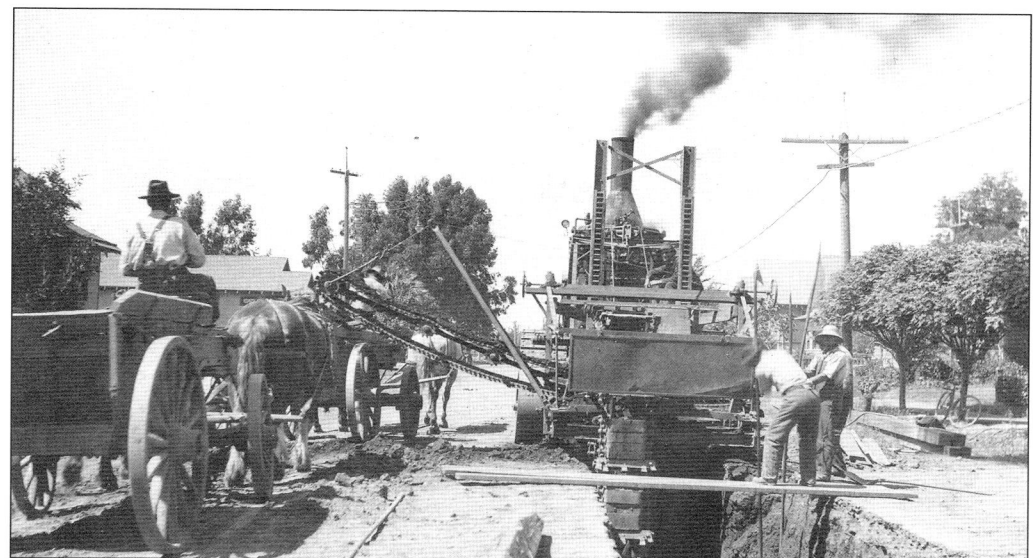

The need for city-funded sewer lines was a major factor in favor of annexation into Sacramento. This was also one of the first activities performed after annexation. Harry C. Muddox, an Oak Park resident and community leader, provided the pipe that went into the Oak Park sewers. This 1915 photograph shows actual digging of a Sacramento sewer.

The Thomas Scollan Company, located on T Street in Sacramento, plastered many buildings in the Oak Park area, including the exquisite Sacramento Bank located at Thirty-fifth Street and Broadway. This picture depicts a plastering crew in 1910. During a period when segregation ruled much of the country, this company integrated the workforce.

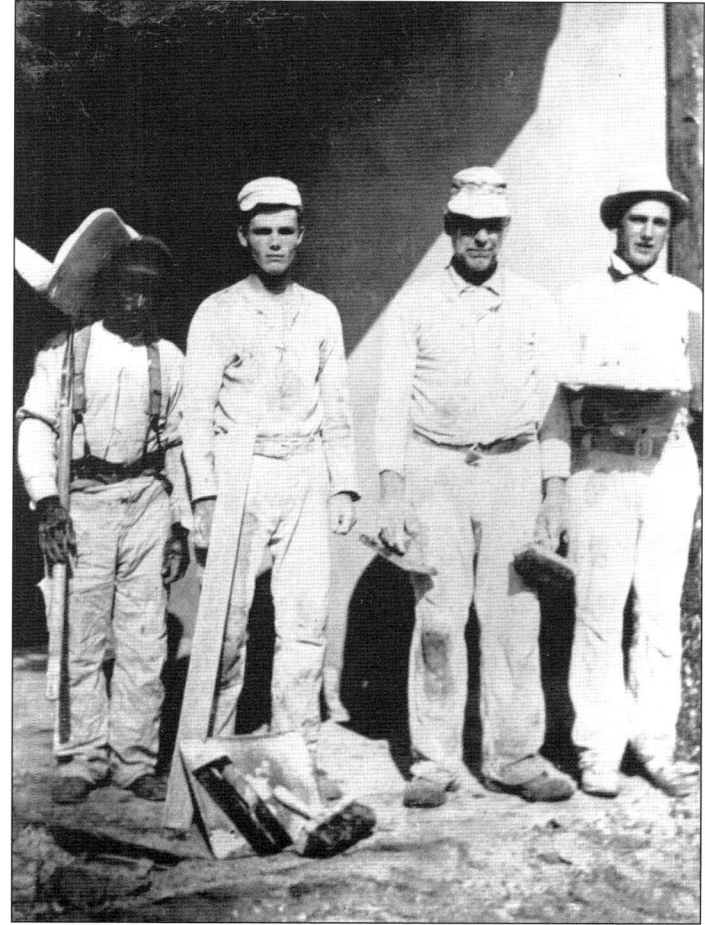

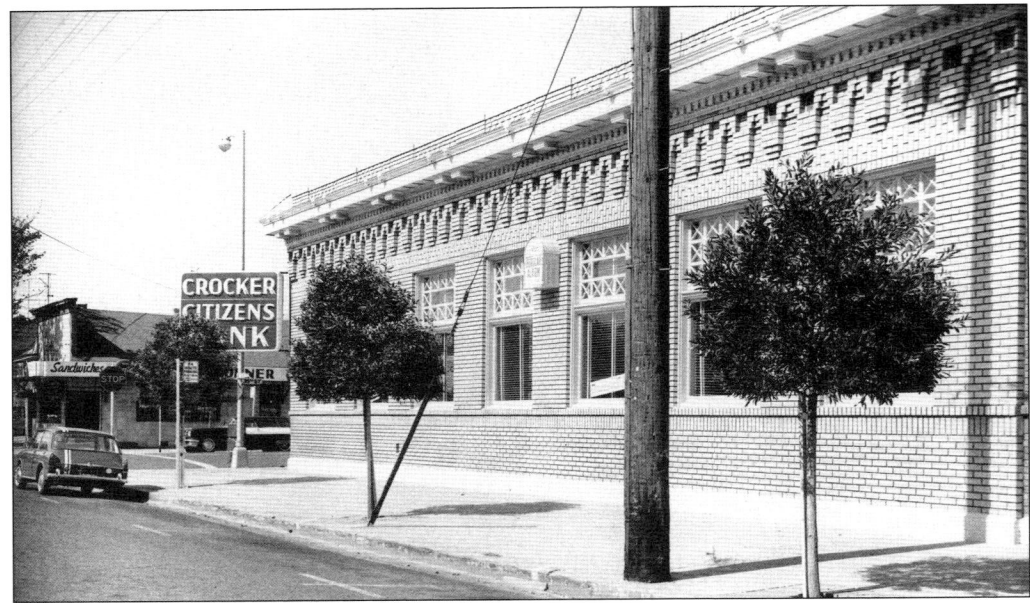

With money from the installation of Oak Park sewer lines, Harry C. Muddox opened the Citizens Bank in 1912, the first bank opened in Oak Park. This is the second location of the bank, which moved in 1917 to compete with the opening of the Sacramento Bank.

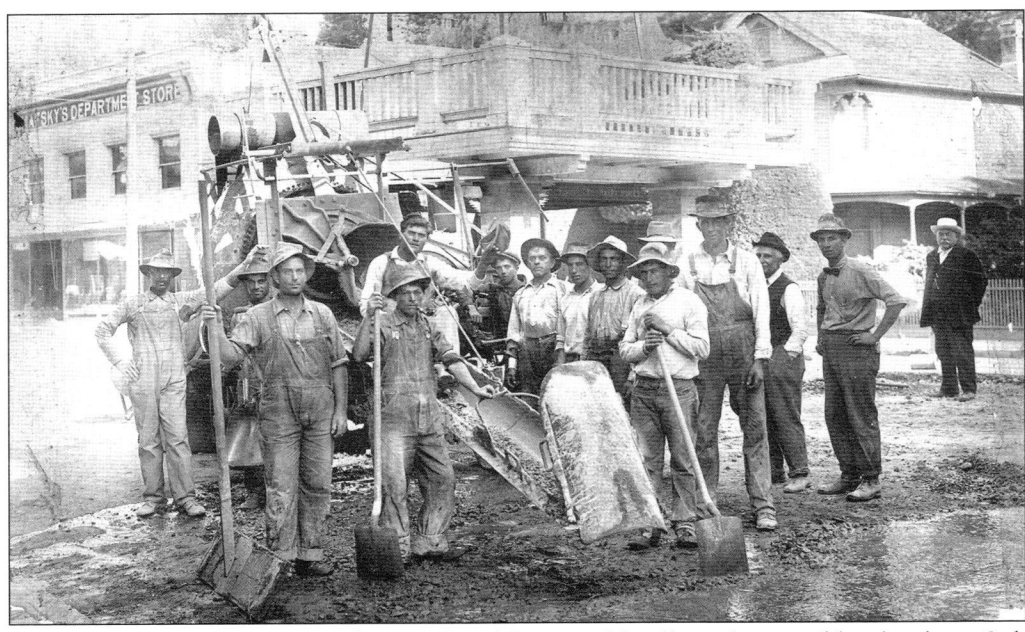

On the far left in this c. 1910 photo is David Bennett Hundley, who raised his family in Oak Park where he labored as a cement worker. His daughter Clarissa Wildy was educated by Oak Park schools and eventually attended college in Hawaii.

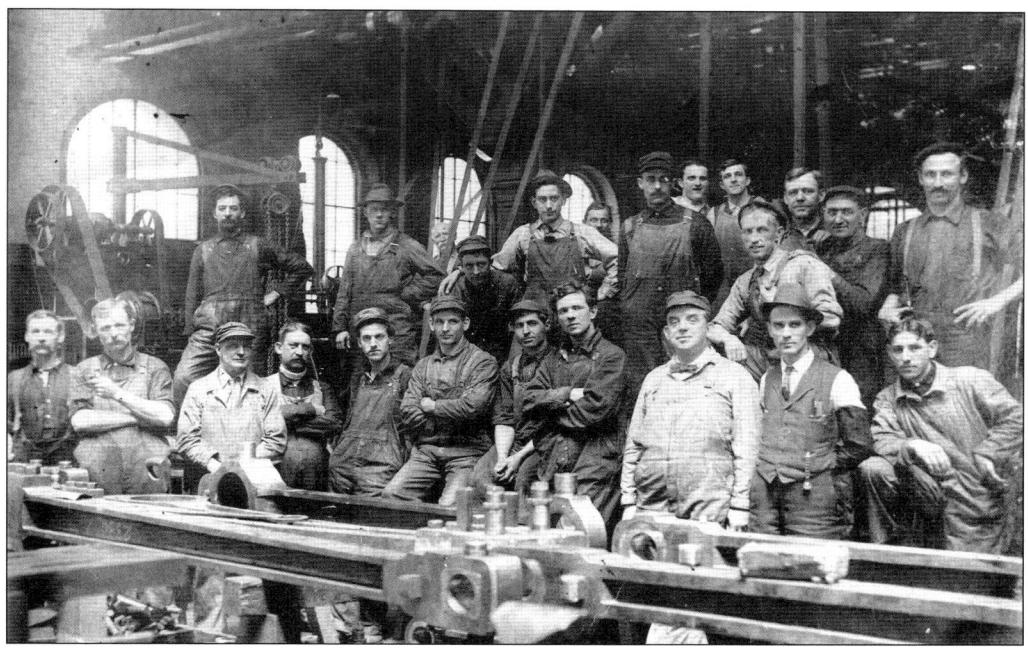

By the 1920s, Oak Park saw an influx of Italian immigrants who assumed the same positions as other Oak Park workers. This c. 1920 photo depicts a group of unidentified Italian shop workers of the Southern Pacific Railroad.

Announcement

✢

MRS. GEORGE DUNLAP

announces the opening of an exclusive

DINING ROOM

at her residence

Saturday, March 29th, 1930

where Southern Cooked Dinners will be served, specializing in Fried Chicken and Baked Ham

Price $1.00

Residence, 4322 Fourth avenue

Phone Capital 335-W   Hours 4:30 to 8:30 p. m.

No service on Monday except on holidays

Reservations Preferred

This card announced the opening of Dunlap's Dining Room, Saturday March 29, 1930. The restaurant specialized in Southern cooking.

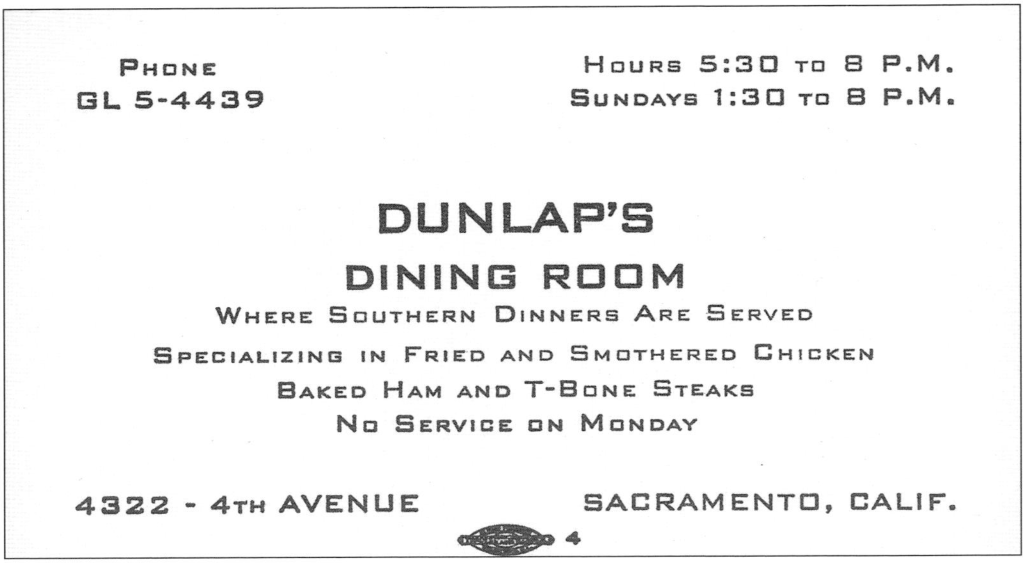

PHONE
GL 5-4439

HOURS 5:30 TO 8 P.M.
SUNDAYS 1:30 TO 8 P.M.

DUNLAP'S

DINING ROOM

WHERE SOUTHERN DINNERS ARE SERVED
SPECIALIZING IN FRIED AND SMOTHERED CHICKEN
BAKED HAM AND T-BONE STEAKS
NO SERVICE ON MONDAY

4322 - 4TH AVENUE   SACRAMENTO, CALIF.

George Dunlap's business card advertised the delights of Southern cooking to be found in his Oak Park restaurant.

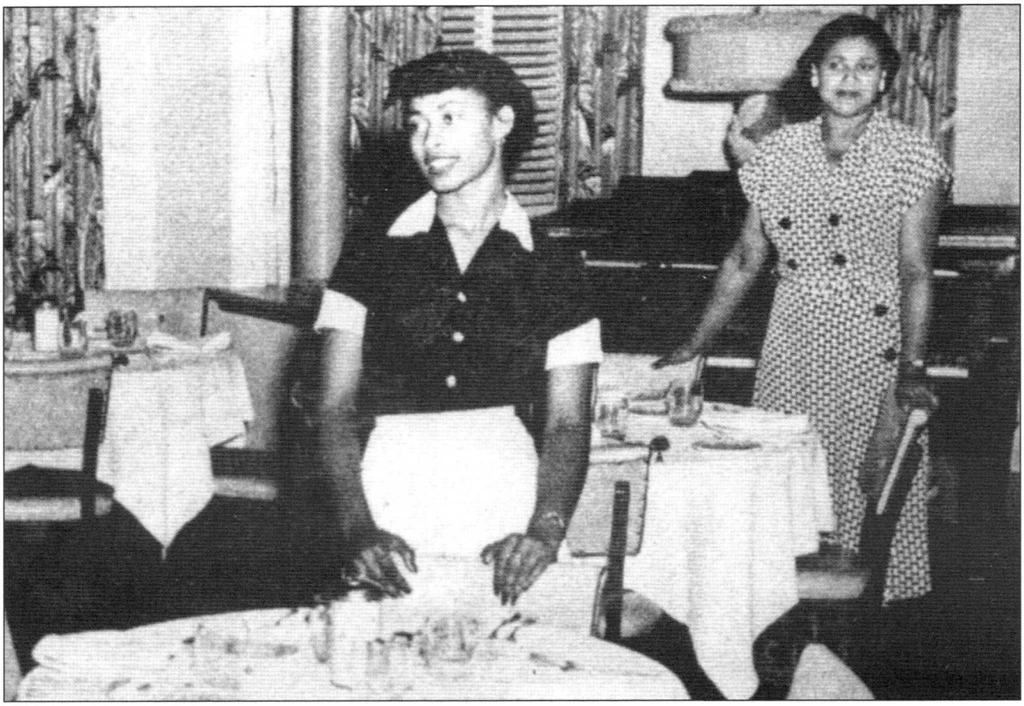

Prior to the liberation movements of the 1960s, women had little opportunity to acquire work in a male-dominated world. This c. 1930 photo, taken inside Dunlap's Dining Room, shows a waitress and a hostess, both relatives of George Dunlap.

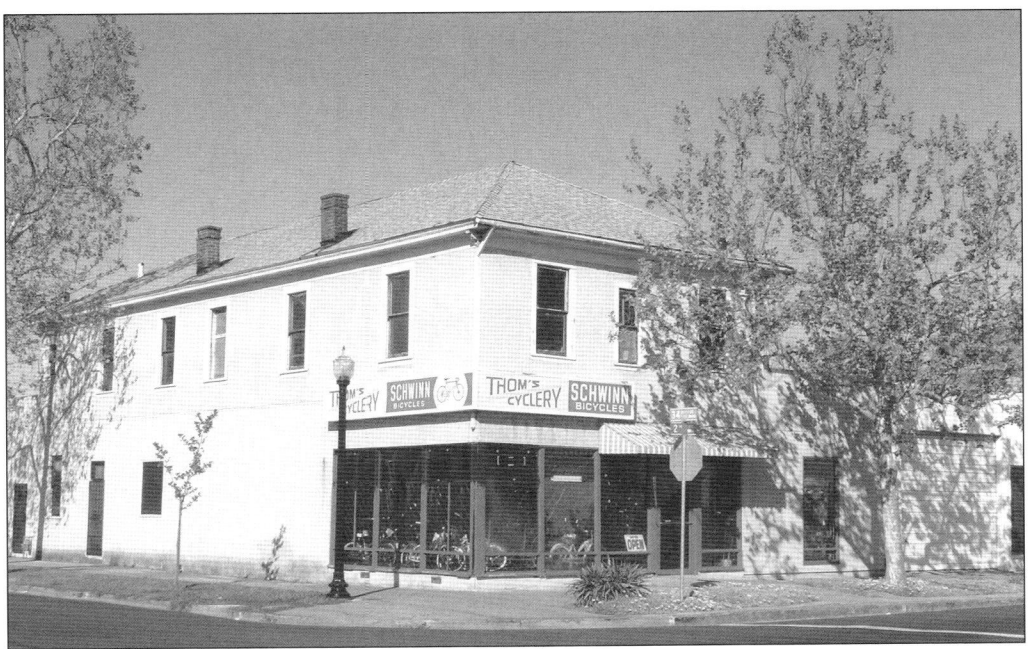

Some businesses were able to stay afloat in the Depression. Thom's Cyclery, located in the old Daly Bros. grocery store, was started by Thom in 1937 and remains open today. (Photo by Gabe Aeschliman, 2004.)

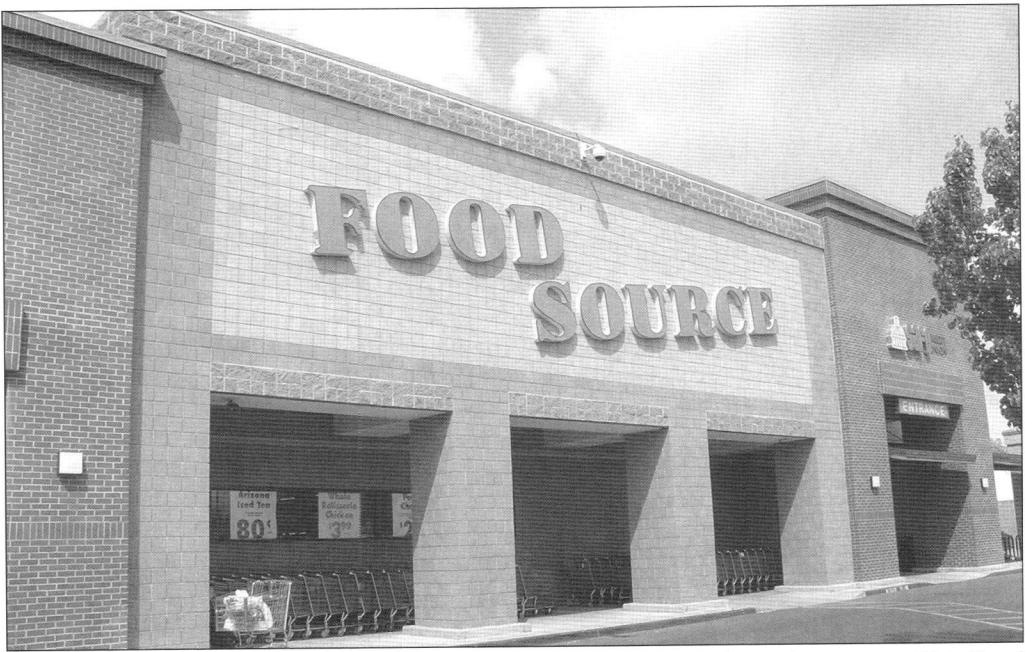

The recent revitalization of Oak Park includes the recruitment of new businesses. This Food Source Shopping Center, coupled with a Rite Aid and Hollywood Video, was erected in the late 1990s. Early Oak Park could boast numerous grocery stores; prior to the opening of this business, Oak Park had none. (Photo by Gabe Aeschliman, 2004.)

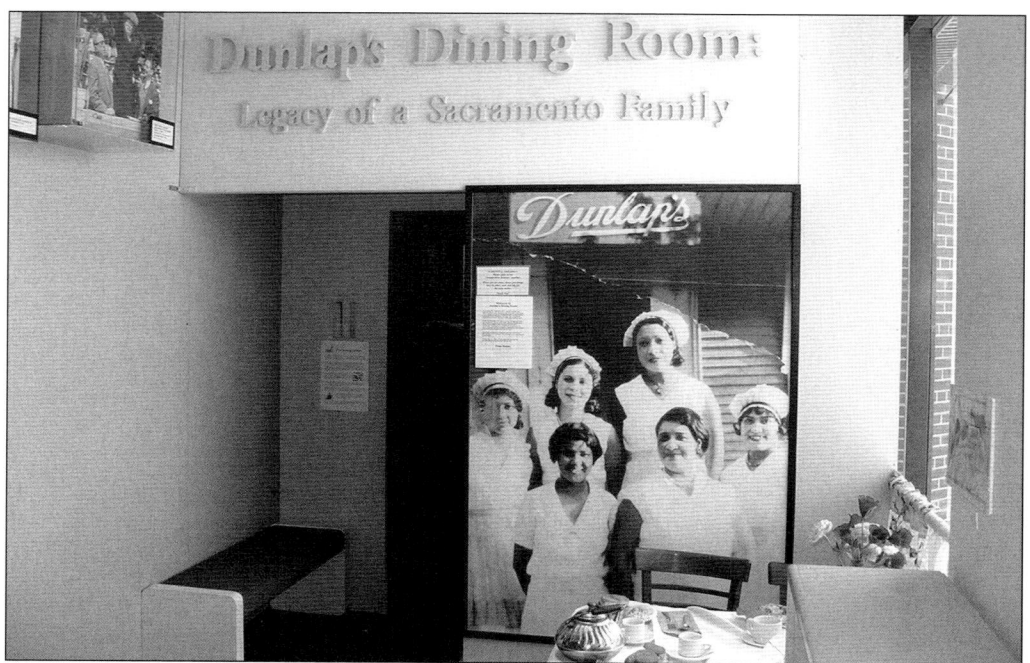

The achievements and impact of past Oak Park businesses have not gone unnoticed by the larger Sacramento population. The Sacramento Discovery Museum History Center, located in Old Sacramento, has dedicated an entire display to the Dunlap's Dining Room Restaurant. The display, shown in this 2004 photo, offers a recreated model of this important African-American business. (Photos by Gabe Aeschliman.)

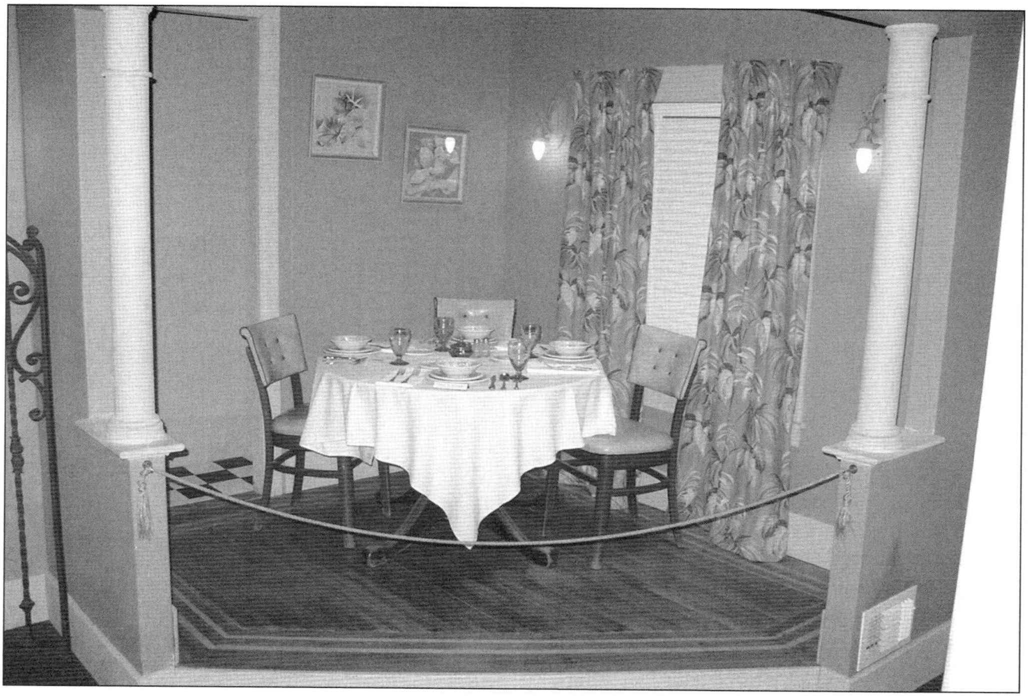

Six

A Walk in the Park
By Michael Farda

From its founding, Oak Park was a great retreat for leisure activities. One of the community's first attractions was the amusement park named Joyland, which opened in 1889 on Thirty-fifth Street and Fifth Avenue. Joyland was the brainchild of the Sacramento Gas, Electric, and Street Railroad Company, which was looking for a way to entice more riders on weekends. Joyland started out slowly over the years; however, people started to become more intrigued in 1913 when it came under different ownership. On June 13 of that year, more than 10,000 eager people swarmed into the park to experience the park's reopening and enjoy all its offerings, including a roller coaster, skating rink, pool, zoo, and numerous concession stands where an ice cream, soda, or lemonade could be purchased for 10¢ each.

However, in 1920 the roller coaster came to a screeching halt. A huge fire at Joyland destroyed most of the rides and buildings. The amusement park lay dormant for two years during renovation. After the renovation, Joyland reopened to a much smaller crowd; it could no longer compete with William Land Park south of downtown. This new park along with middle-class migration to suburban areas led to the park's demise. It finally closed in 1927 when Mr. and Mrs. Valentine McClatchy bought the amusement park from PG&E and gave away the park as a gift to Sacramento. The park was renamed James McClatchy Park for Valentine's father. McClatchy Park was still a place of great interest for the community, but it had nowhere near the draw that Joyland had once cherished.

Another big draw for Oak Park was the California State Fair, located on Stockton Boulevard where the U.C. Davis Medical Center now stands. The fair opened in Oak Park the summer of 1909 and stayed on its 80-acre lot for the next 58 years. In 1968 the fair left Oak Park for a larger venue in North Sacramento, the Cal Expo at Arden Fair. Sacramento was a growing city and the fair needed to be well represented. If the fair were to stay in Oak Park, horse racing, parking, and increased attendance, which were high income producers, would have had to be abandoned or sharply curtailed. After years of research and debate, the California State Fair Commission chose a 356-acre site next to the American River as the new home of the fair.

In addition to Joyland/McClatchy Park and the California State Fair, there were still many activities in Oak Park. The community held numerous parades downtown to celebrate holidays. These parades attracted huge crowds. Oak Park also had a swimming pool called the "free plunge," where anyone could take a swim on a beautiful day. Little league baseball was also a popular activity on nice spring days. Many little league teams formed in Oak Park to celebrate the nation's pastime.

The closures of Joyland and the California State Fair led to a steady decline in the economy of Oak Park. However, today St. HOPE Academy provides new activities for residents. St. HOPE is a youth organization that is committed to providing people with educational and cultural programs, including the popular artist-in-resident program. Even in Oak Park's renovation, it still has activities to enjoy.

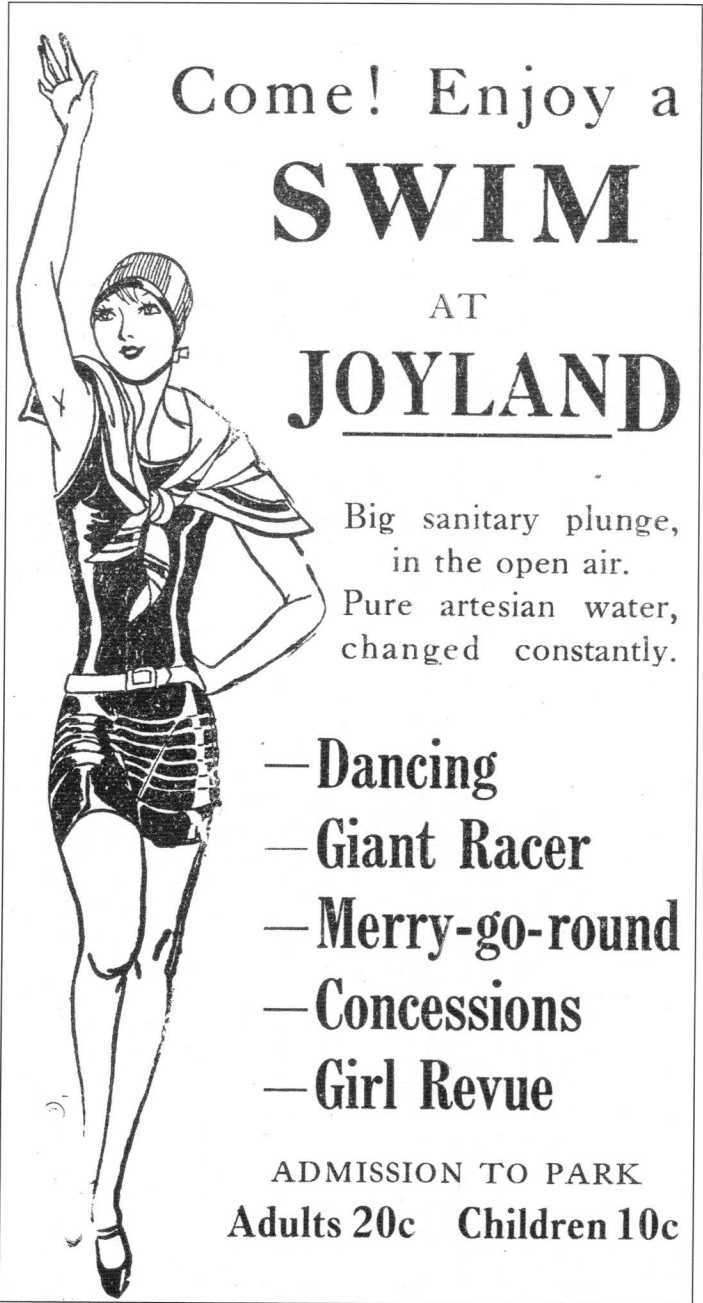

An Advertisement in *Lee's Sacramento Guide*, July 1926, for Joyland Amusement Park, describes all the fun at the amusement park, especially the big sanitary plunge.

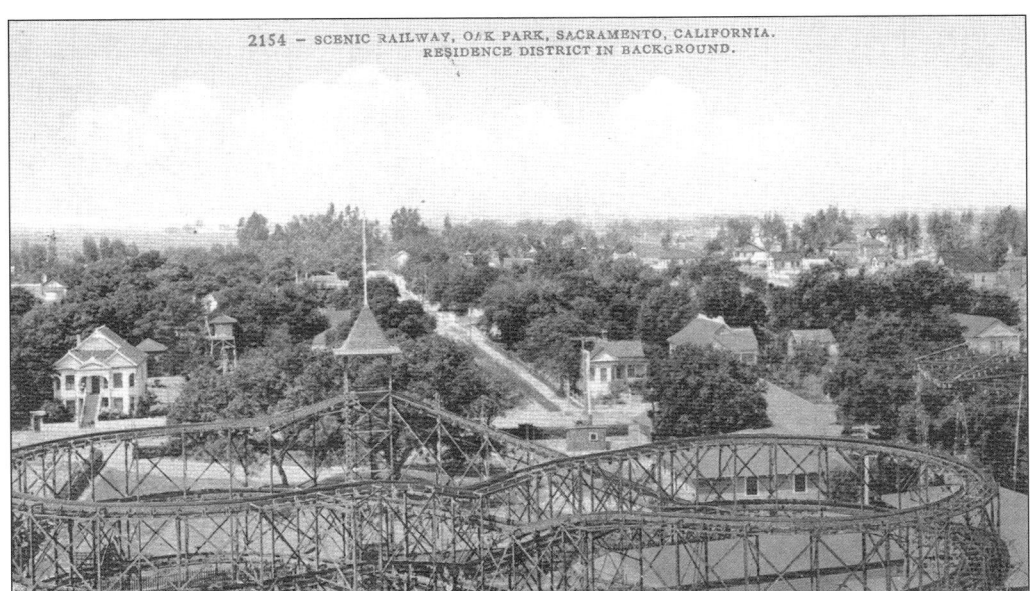

This postcard is a scenic picture in the early 1900s of the roller coaster at Joyland amusement park. This massive structure attracted many patrons on weekends. Pictured in the background is the Oak Park residential district.

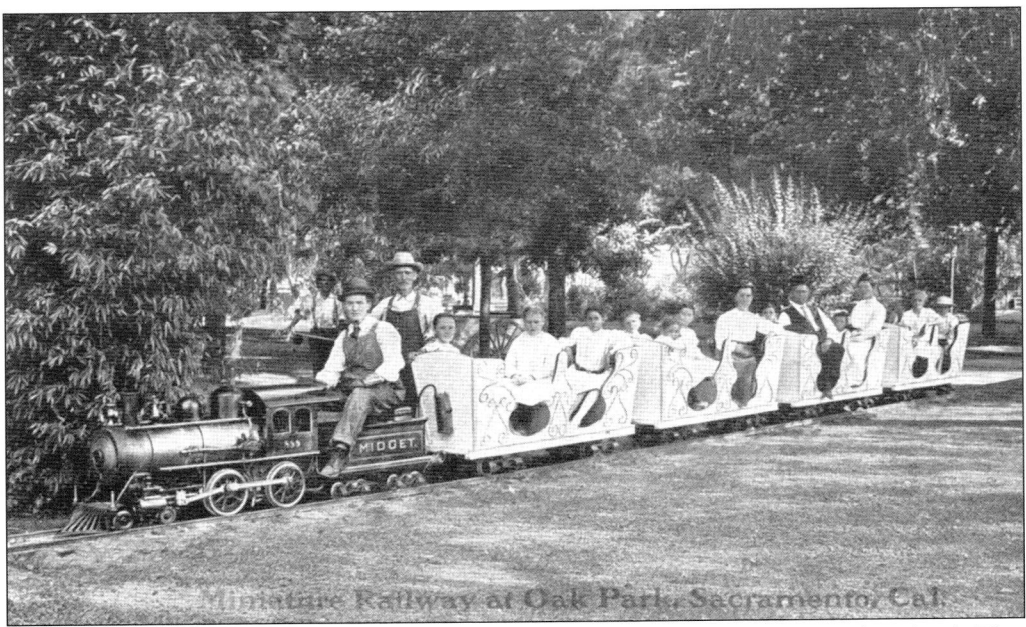

In this 1910 postcard, the miniature railway in Oak Park is en route around Joyland. This miniature railway was a way for children to enjoy a nice relaxing train ride while taking a break from other activities at the park.

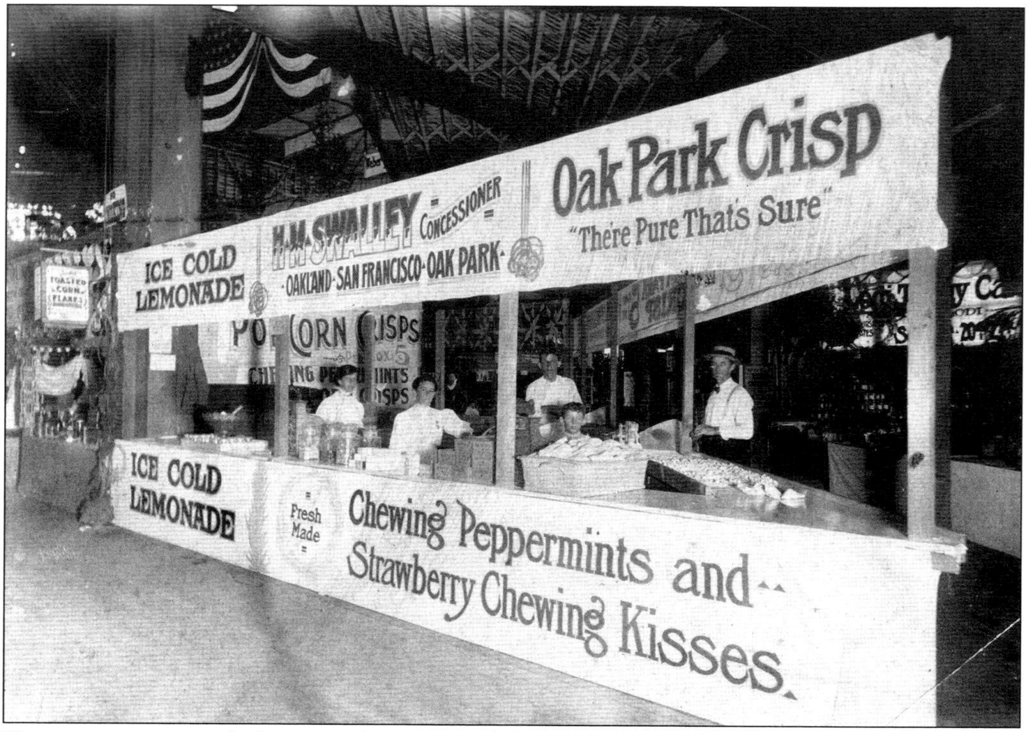

The concession stands shown in these 1900 photos were located in the rollerskating rink inside Joyland. Visitors could find a nice sweet or cold treat for a good price.

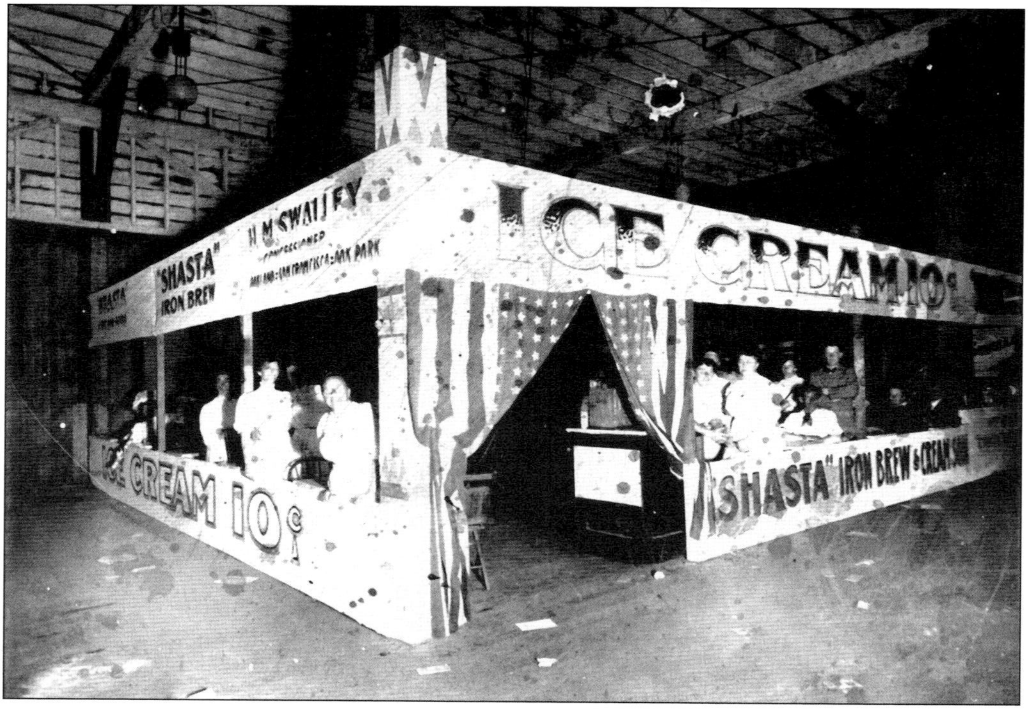

This flagpole and plaque commemorate the dedication of McClatchy Park.

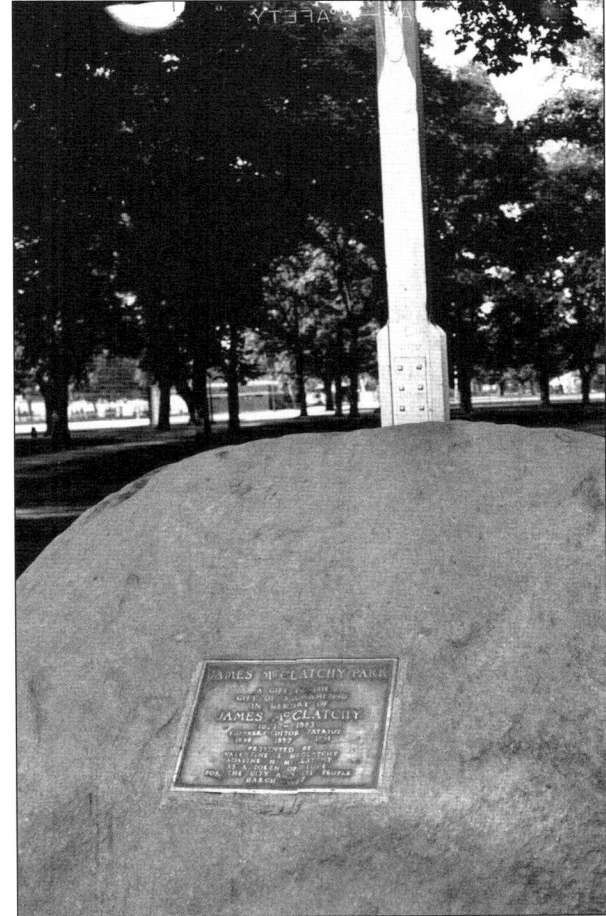

Shown in this 1952 photo, McClatchy Park, with its beautiful tree-laden grounds, was the location of the once exuberant Joyland amusement park. Although Joyland is no longer in existence, McClatchy Park is still a popular destination for rest and relaxation.

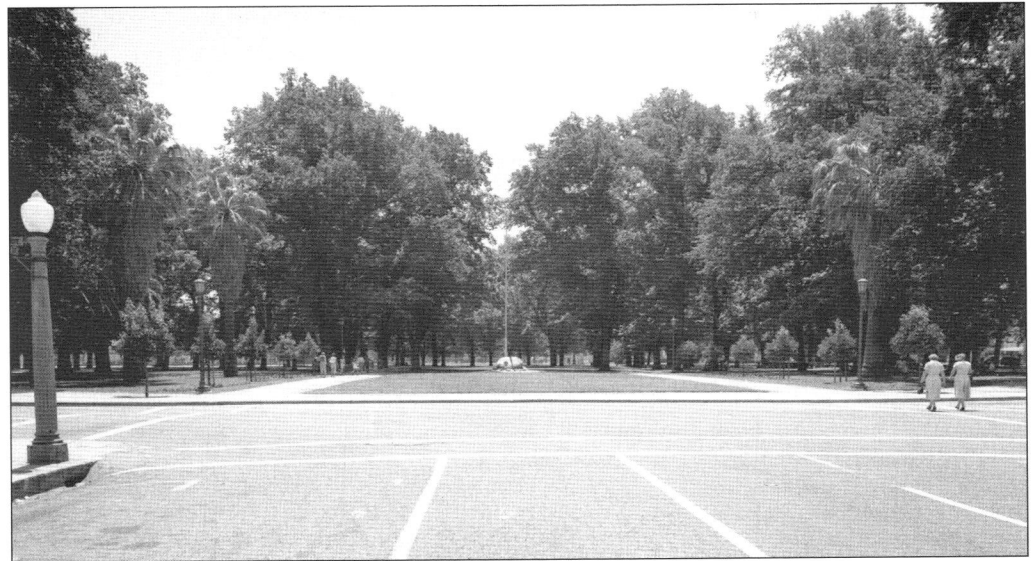

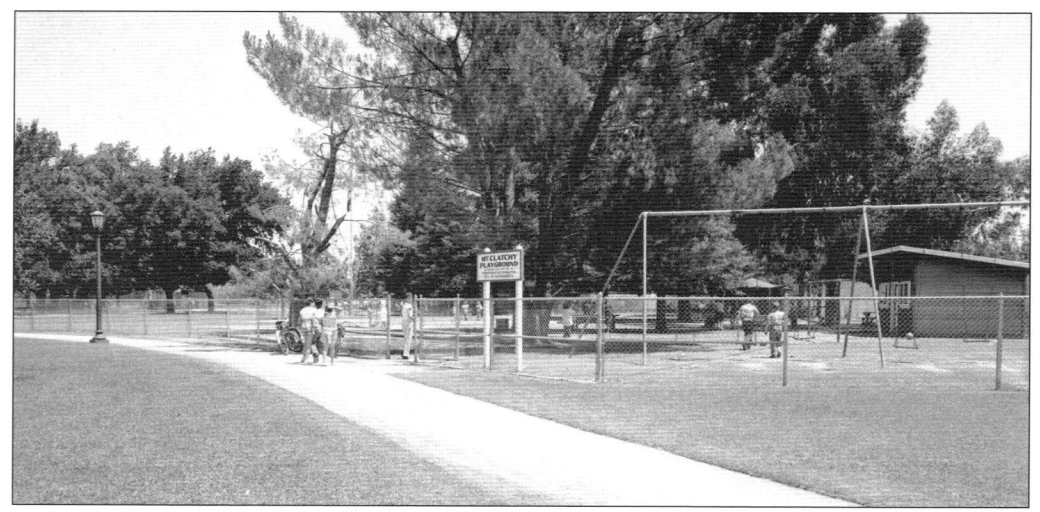
In this 1952 photo, children play on and around the swing set at McClatchy playground.

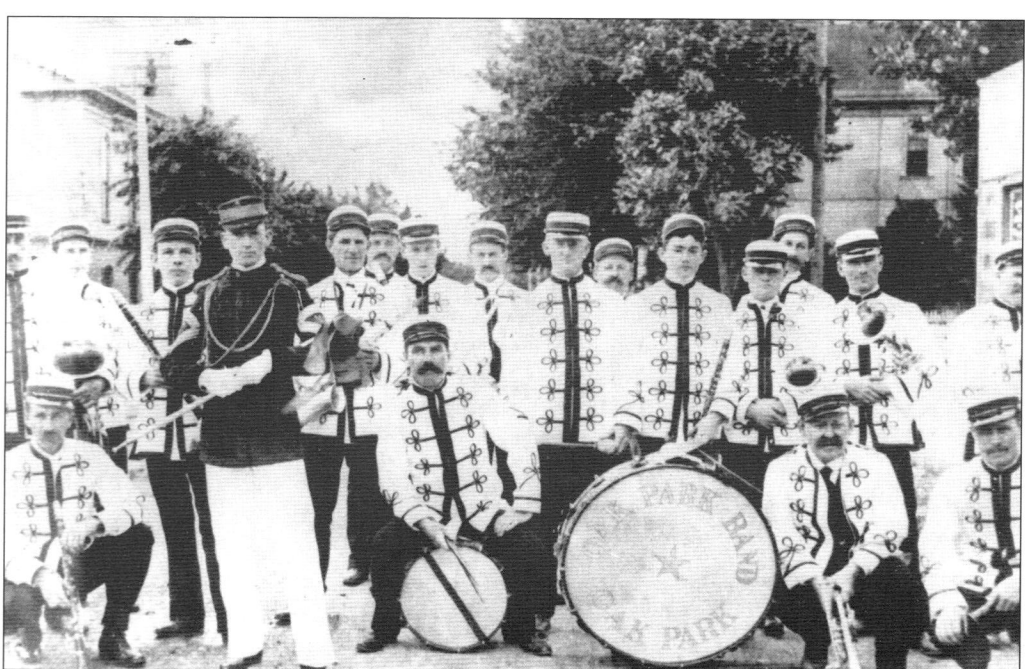
The Oak Park band represented the community spirit of the neighborhood. Ready to play for any and all parades, the band is shown here c. 1900.

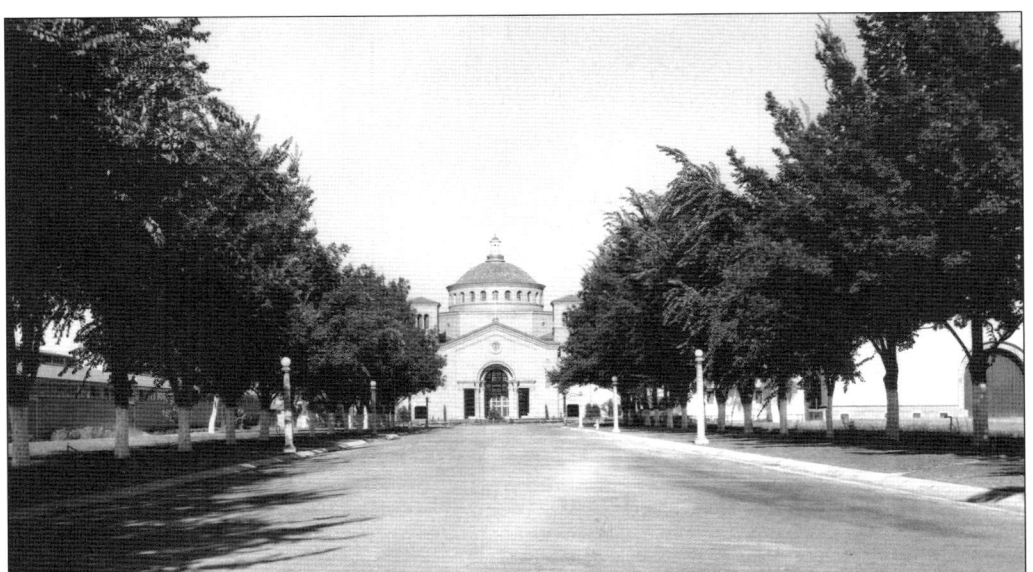

Trees line the front entrance of the California State Fair in the 1940s. Until 1968, the fair made its home on Stockton Boulevard in Oak Park. Today this property is now home to the U.C. Davis Medical Center.

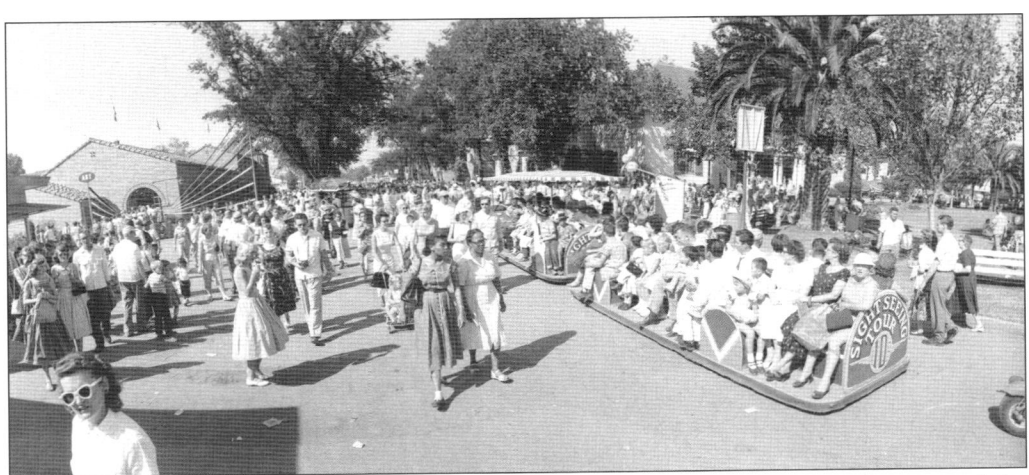

A diverse audience is evident in this photo from the 1952 State Fair. Note the view of the crowds and the tour trains that provided transportation around the 80-acre site.

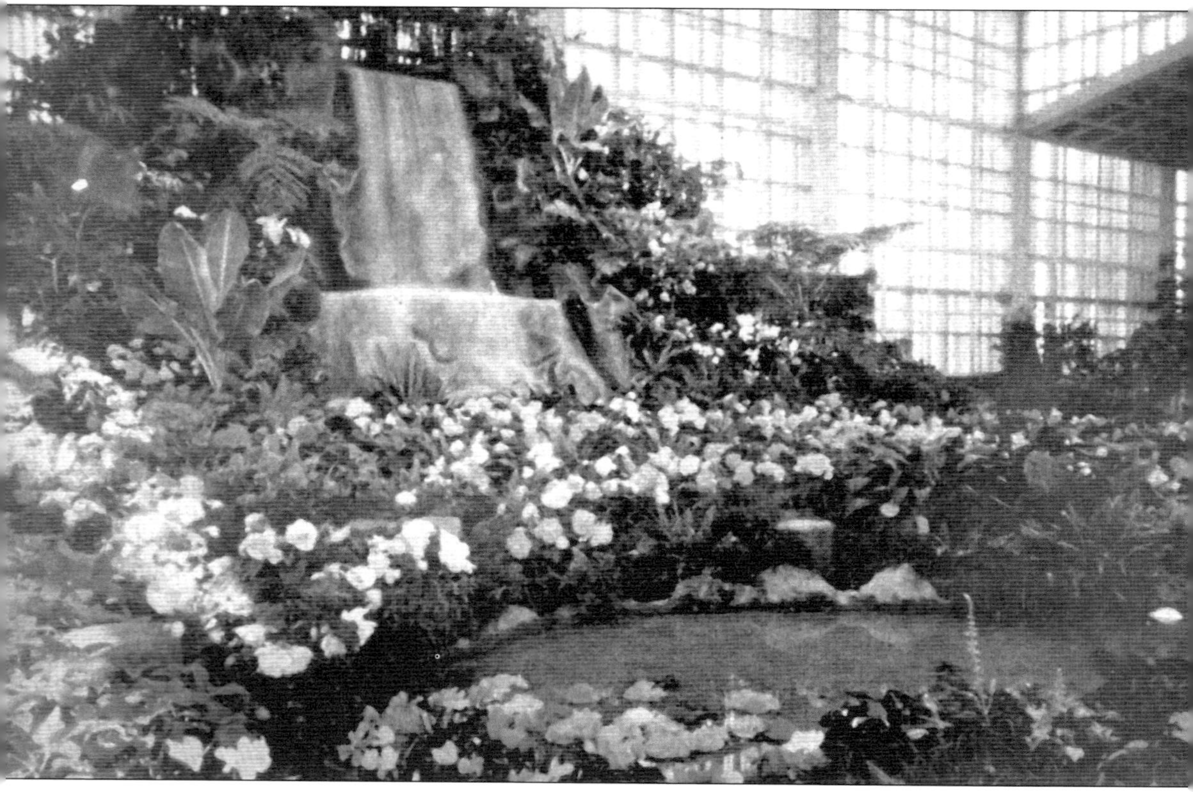

The state fair provided an opportunity to celebrate the agricultural economy of California. The agricultural building held the popular county agricultural exhibits in which volunteers created displays that best depicted their counties. The building is shown here in the 1940s (above) and in 1956 (below).

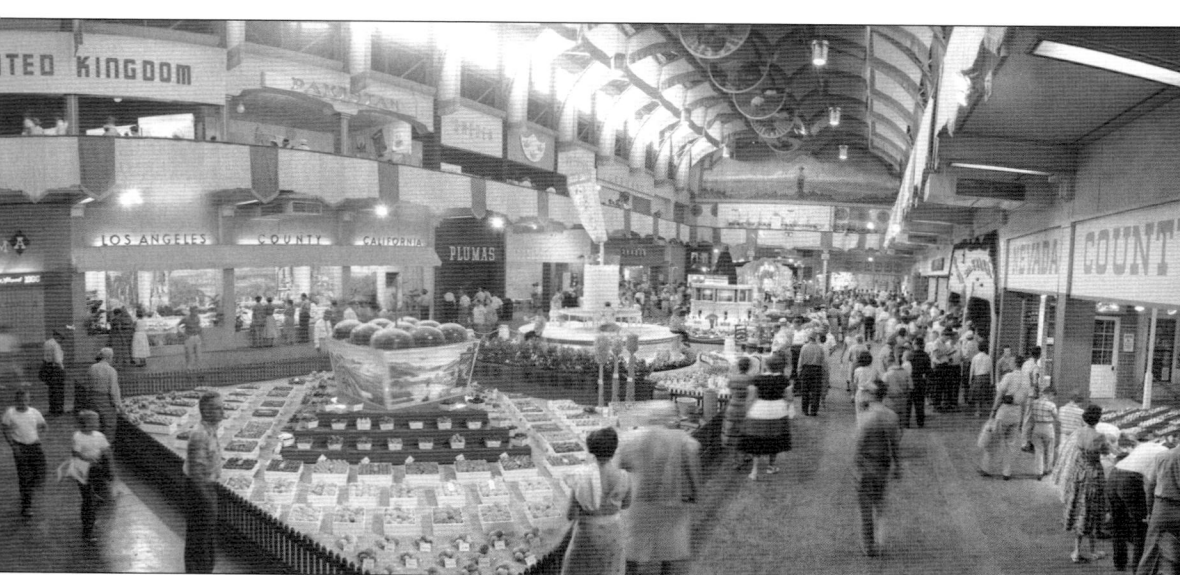

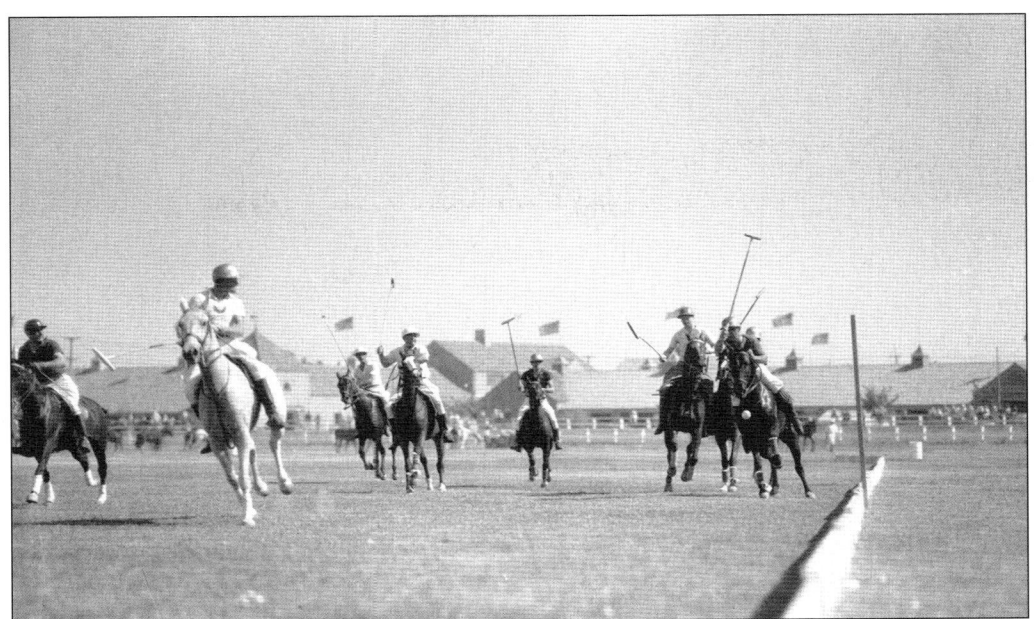

The sport of kings, polo, was played at the California State Fair in 1932.

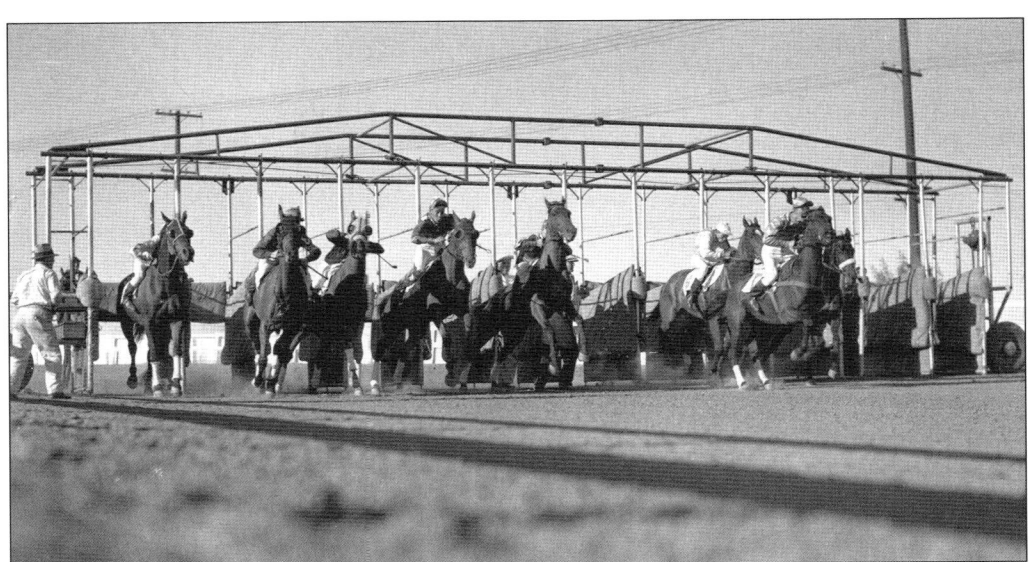

Crowds gather in this 1932 photo to watch horse racing at the California State Fair. Increased demand on the horse track and other facilities provided the impetus to create a state-of-the-art track at Cal Expo in the 1960s.

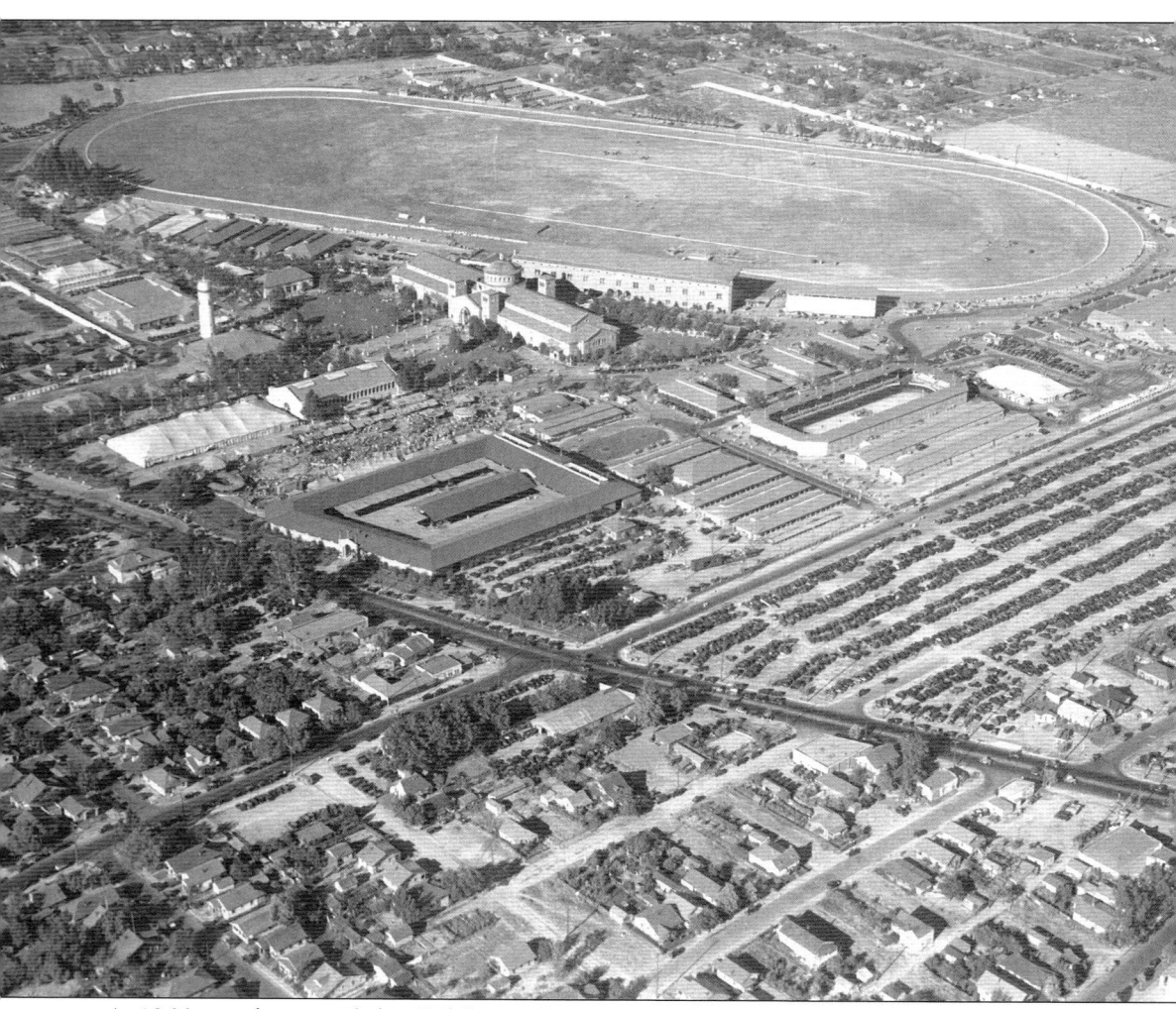

A 1966 aerial view of the California State Fair parking lots, race track, and surrounding neighborhoods provides evidence of the need to relocate the fair grounds. By the late 1960s, the Oak Park site no longer provided adequate space for fair crowds.

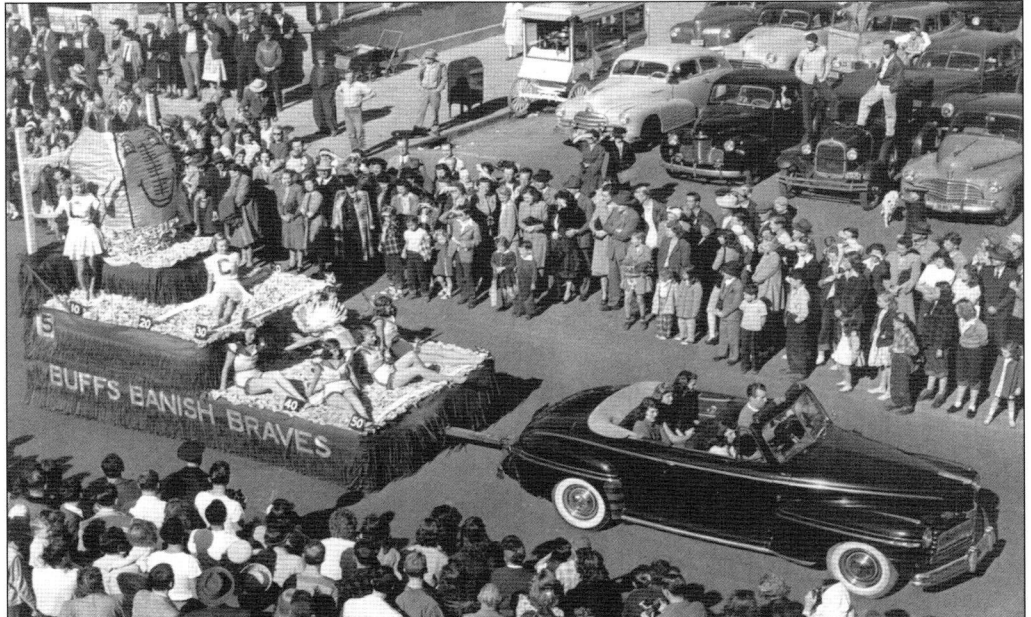

Like most Americans, Oak Park residents enjoy a good parade. Crowds gather to watch the meticulously crafted floats drive by in this July 4th parade from the late 1940s. (Photo courtesy of Steven Ballew.)

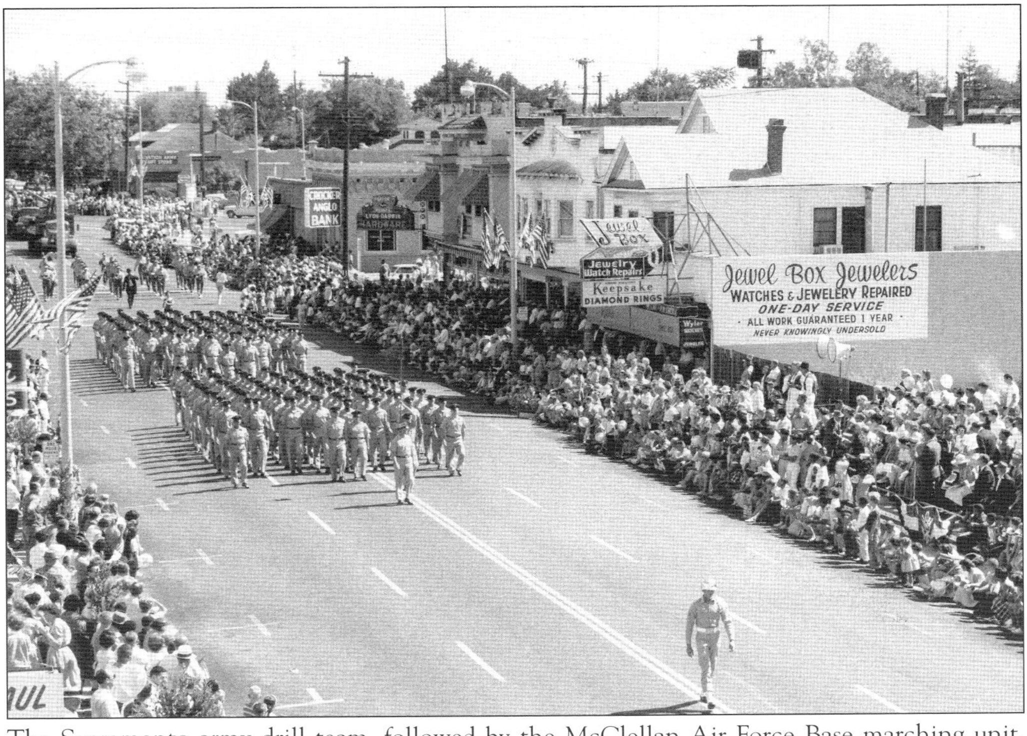

The Sacramento army drill team, followed by the McClellan Air Force Base marching unit, marched in Oak Park during this Fourth of July parade in 1963.

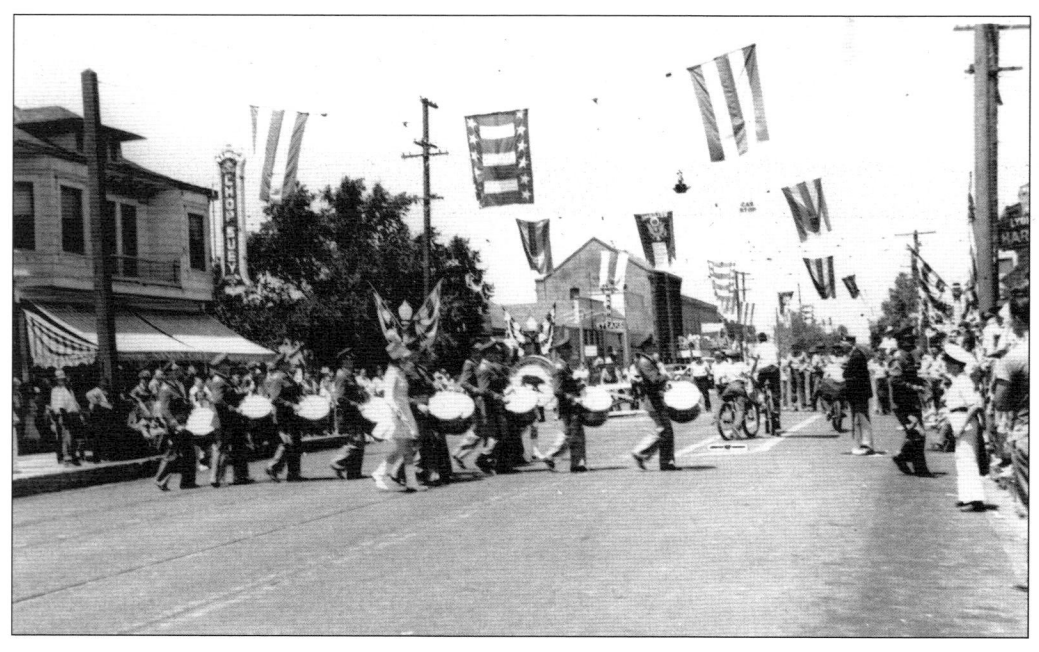

The Native Sons of the Golden West, Drum Corps. No. 3, marched in the Fourth of July parade of 1942.

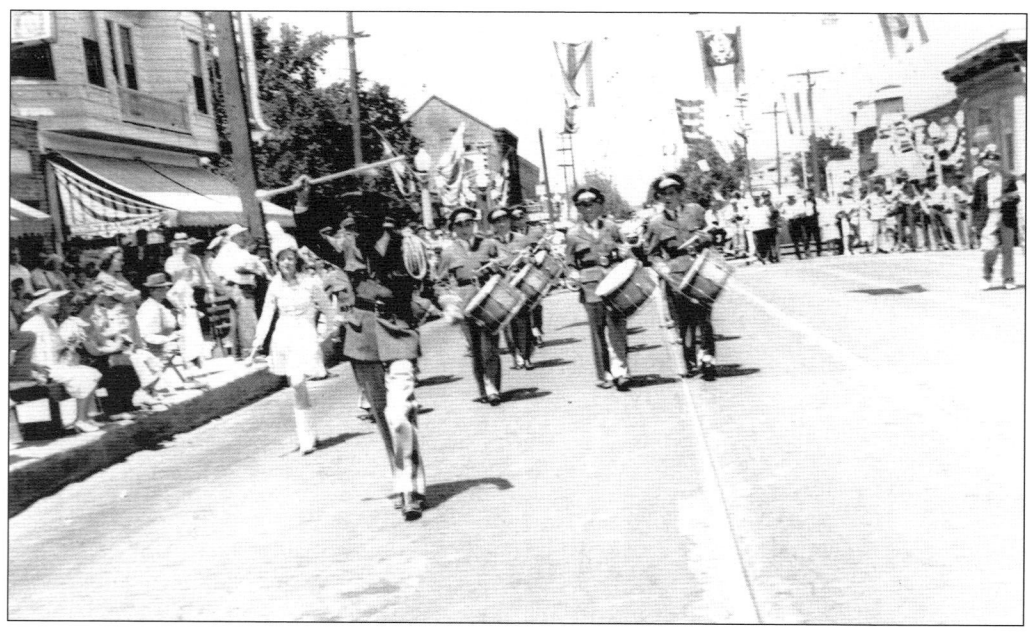

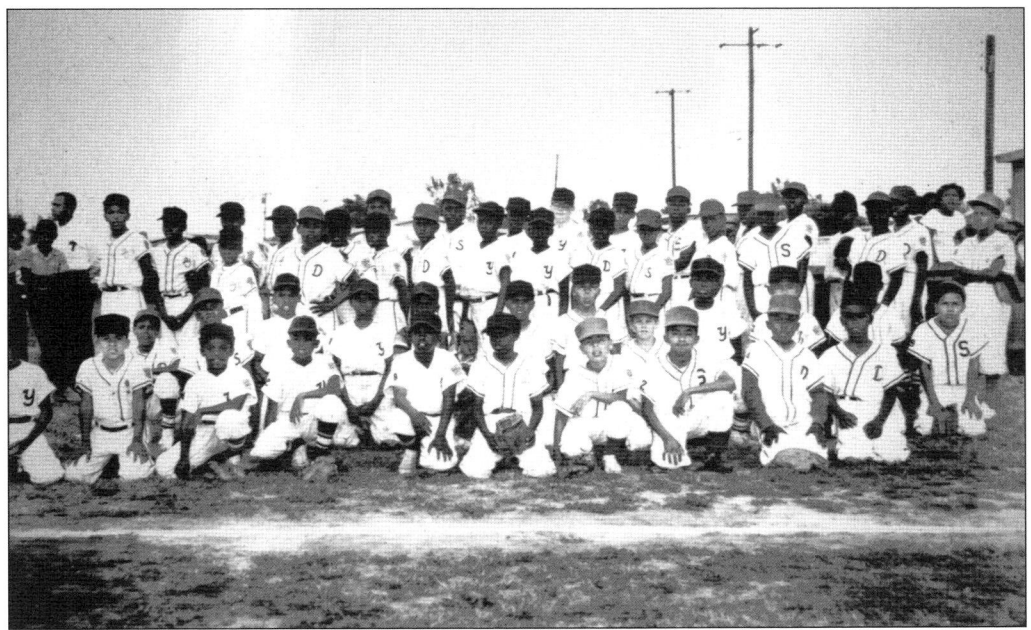

Oak Park children participated in the great American pastime. This is a group photo, c. 1967, of members of the Glen Elder Little League team located in Oak Park.

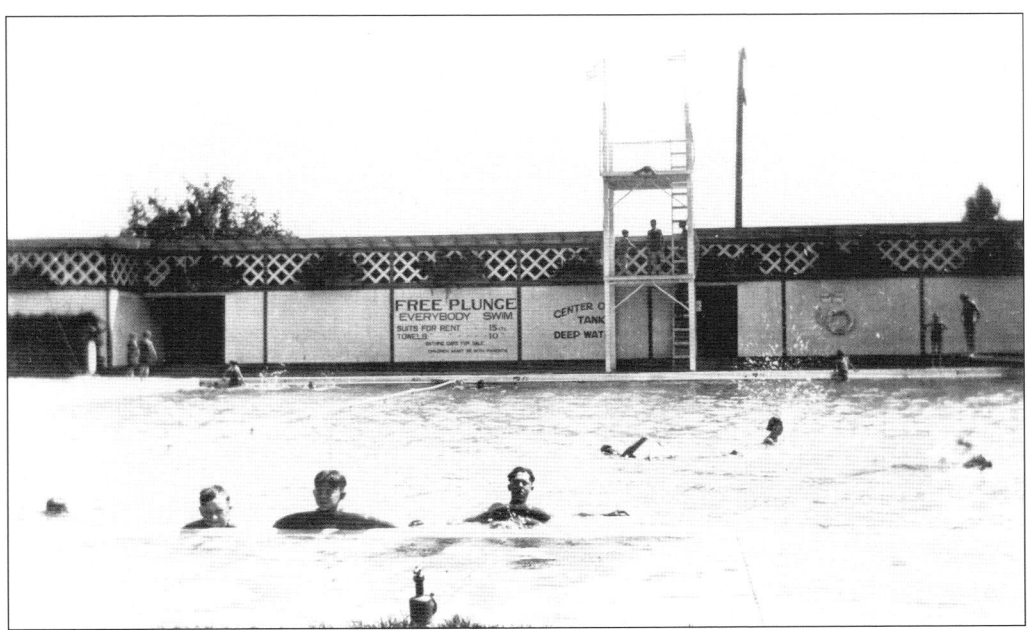

The free-plunge swimming pool, shown in this 1950 photo, was a great place to go on a hot summer day. Anyone could swim in the pool, and swim suits and towels were available for rent.

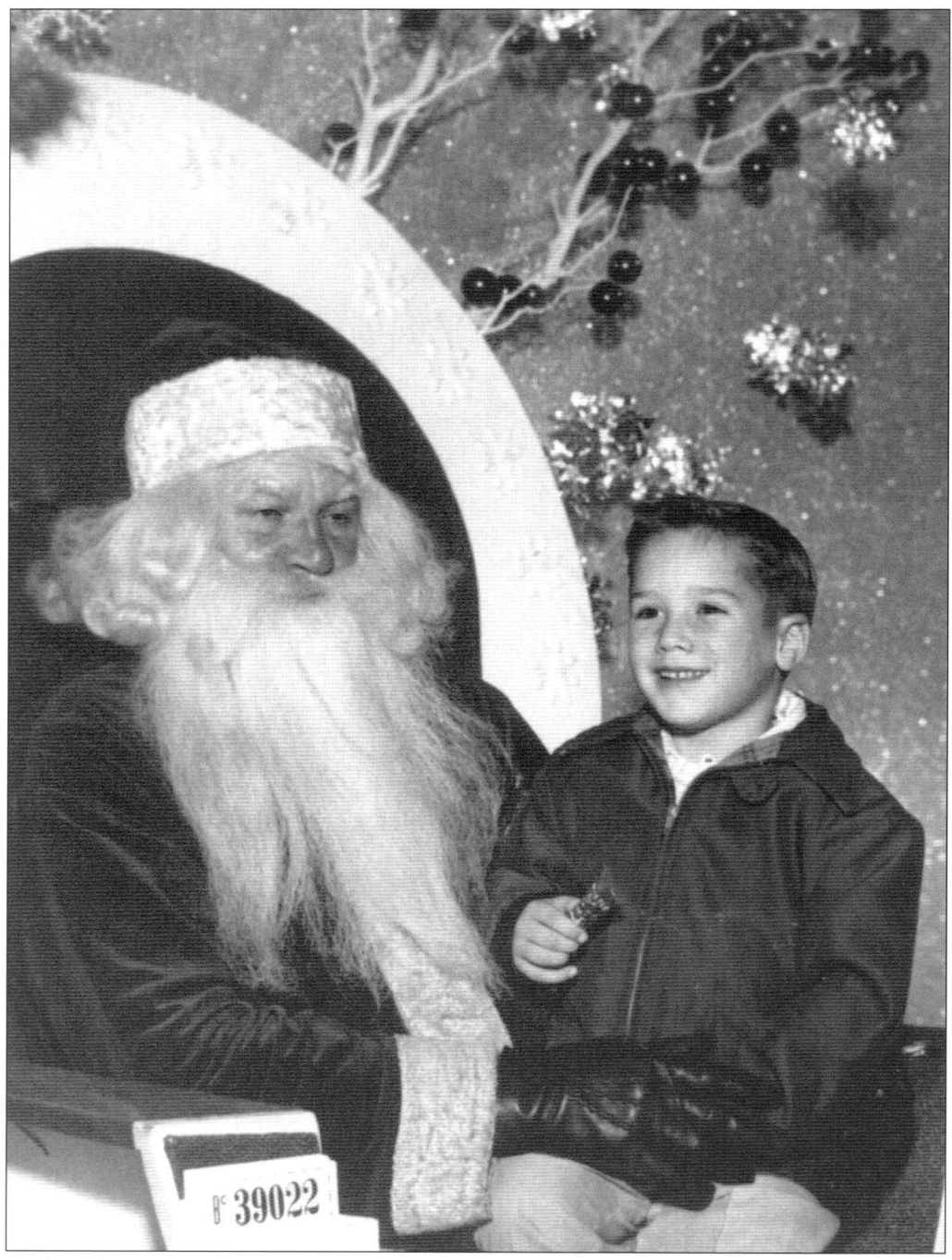
Mark Ballew sits on Santa's lap at the Weinstocks on K Street in this *c.* 1954 photo. This was an annual tradition for many Oak Park children. (Photo courtesy of Steven Ballew.)

Seven

EDUCATION IS GOLDEN
BY PATTIE BASTIAN

The history of the public school system in Oak Park mirrors the history of public education in both the state and in the nation—and reflects the economic realities of this working-class community. Just as the city is in need of revitalization, so too is the educational system. On a positive note, however, what began as a segregated system for white children evolved into a system open to all regardless of race and ethnicity.

The Oak Park public school system, like other systems throughout California, is the direct result of language in the California constitution. In 1849 California held its first constitutional convention and addressed the need for public education and school funding. The California legislature approved school funds and decided to appoint a superintendent of public instruction to oversee the direction of public education statewide. Within a few years, the legislature passed additional laws that assured public education for white children only throughout California. No mention of education for minorities appeared in the legislation until 1855, when a teacher from a school for children of color sought aid from the board of education. By 1863 black children were allowed to attend public schools, but Chinese and Mongolians were excluded. Thus during the first 50 years of statehood, only minimal efforts were implemented to provide minority children with education.

Oak Park established its public school system with the opening of Oak Park Elementary. In 1912 overcrowding led the Sacramento Board of Education to propose building an auxiliary primary school on Thirty-fifth Street. After a heated and protracted debate over the location and its proximity to saloons, Bret Harte School was opened and replaced Oak Park Elementary School. As the population of Oak Park expanded, so did its school system. Donner School, located on Stockton Boulevard, offered elementary education and provided overflow classroom space for the larger Sacramento School District. The district also chose Oak Park as the location for a new high school to replace the city's original high school built in 1856. Sacramento High continues to operate at its location on Thirty-fourth and Y Streets.

Today, Oak Park houses Oak Park Pre-School, a year-round school; Oakridge Elementary School; the American Legion Continuation School; and two new charter schools, Sacramento High School and PS7 elementary school. The current Sacramento High School charter is the outgrowth of a school in jeopardy of closing its doors permanently due to low test scores. Thanks to the efforts of members of local organizations such as St. HOPE Academy, whose overall mission is to provide and assist Oak Park's educational system, Sacramento High School is experiencing a dramatic turnaround. St HOPE Academy stresses academic excellence and seeks to motivate students to succeed to higher levels of education. Oak Park schools are returning to the concept that education is golden.

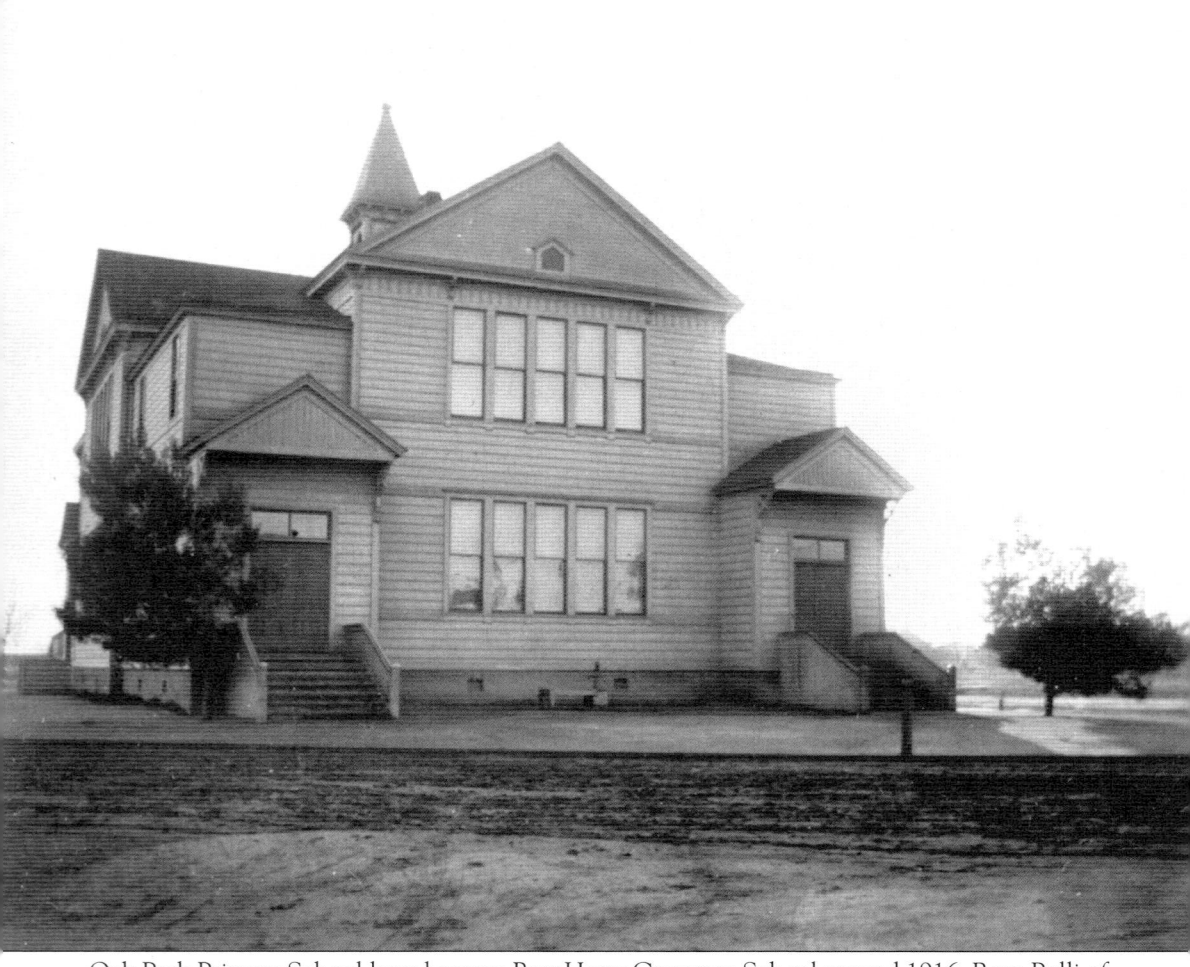

Oak Park Primary School later became Bret Harte Grammar School around 1916. Rose Polli of San Francisco taught at Bret Harte briefly under the direction of Principal Louise Gavigan Bartlett. Today the old grammar school is occupied by a Methodist Church.

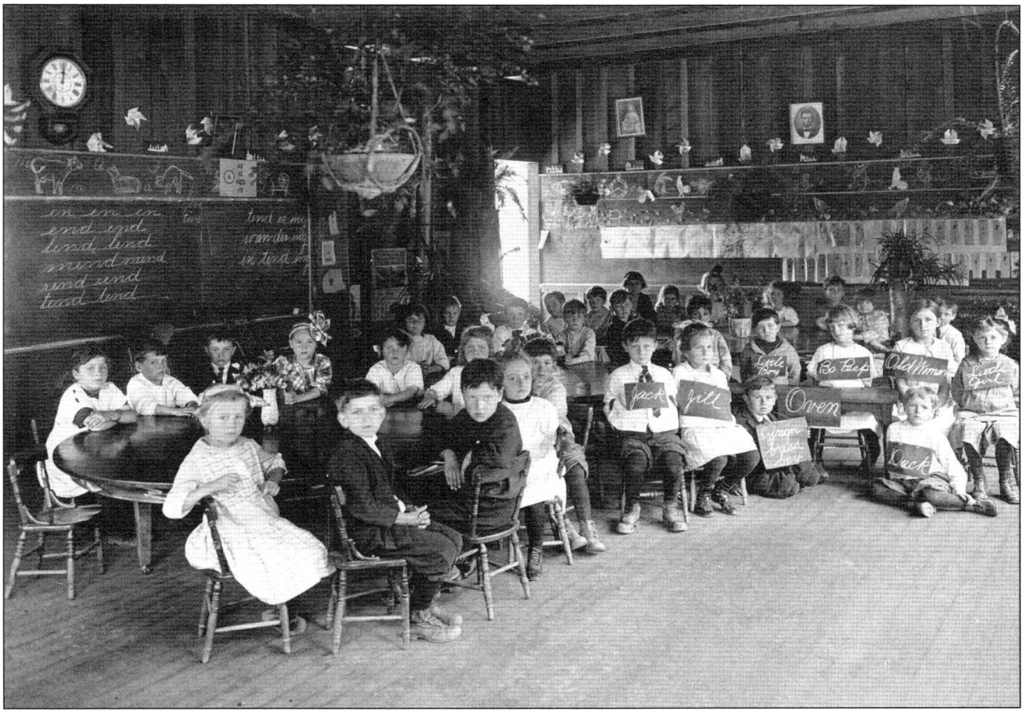

In these 1914 pictures, primary school students at Oak Park School take a break from their studies of nursery rhymes (top) while older students practice their sewing skills (bottom).

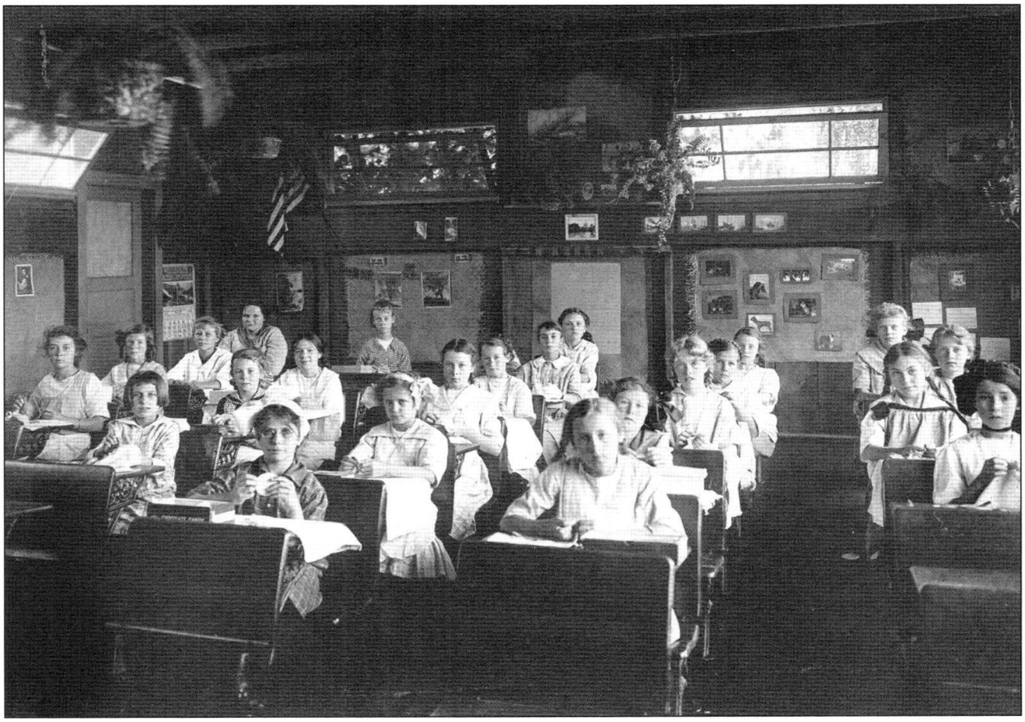

83

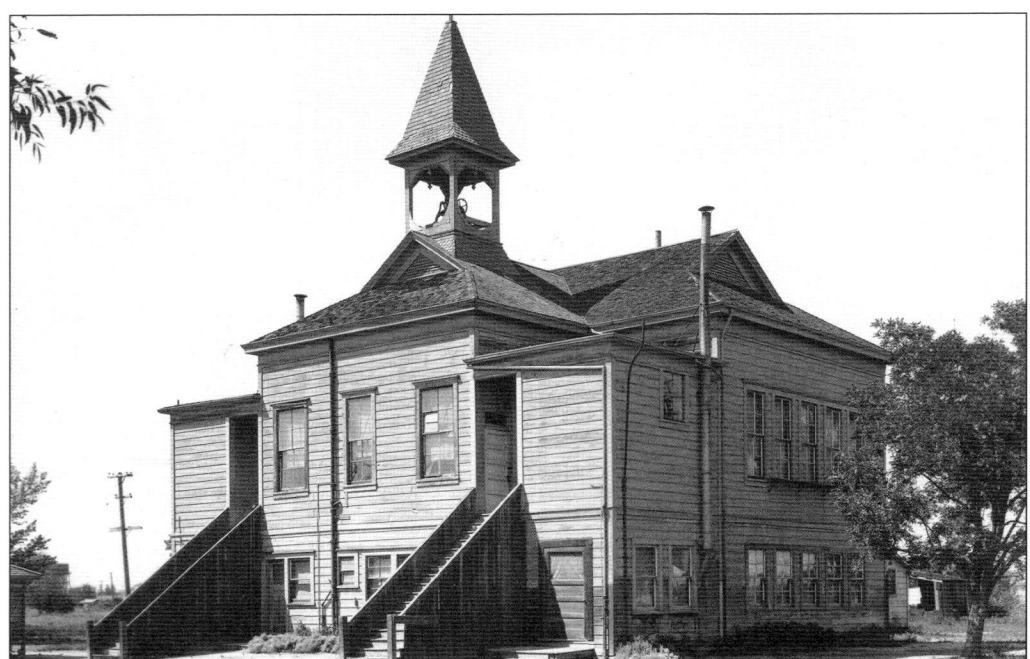

This 1910 two-story schoolhouse, Franklin Grammar School, was located on Forty-fourth Street and Fourteenth Avenue. Some high school students were schooled here due to overflow until the new high school was built on Thirty-fourth and Y Streets.

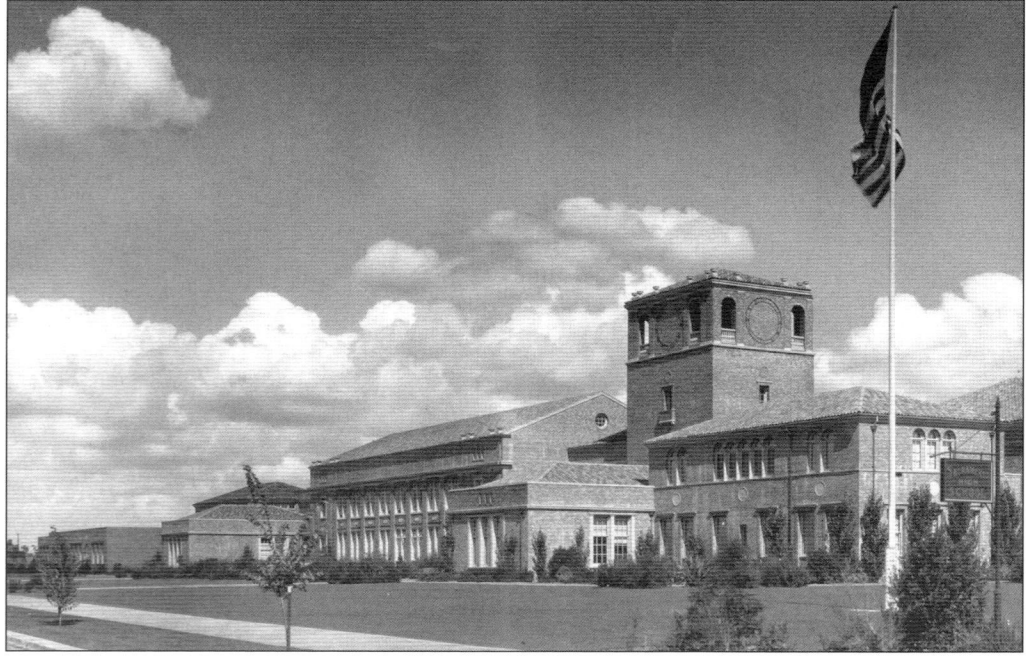

Sacramento High School is currently located at Thirty-fourth and Y Streets. The 1856 high school building on Ninth and M Streets was torn down due to Sacramento's growing population and the need for a larger facility.

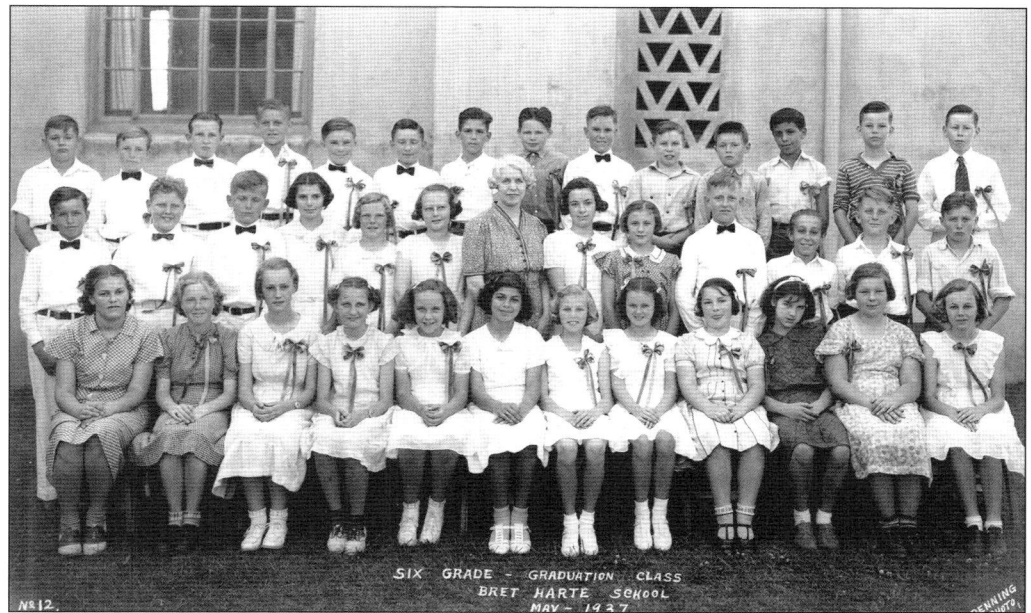

Dressed in their best for picture day in this 1937 photo, the members of the sixth-grade graduating class of Bret Harte School pose for one of their last school pictures together.

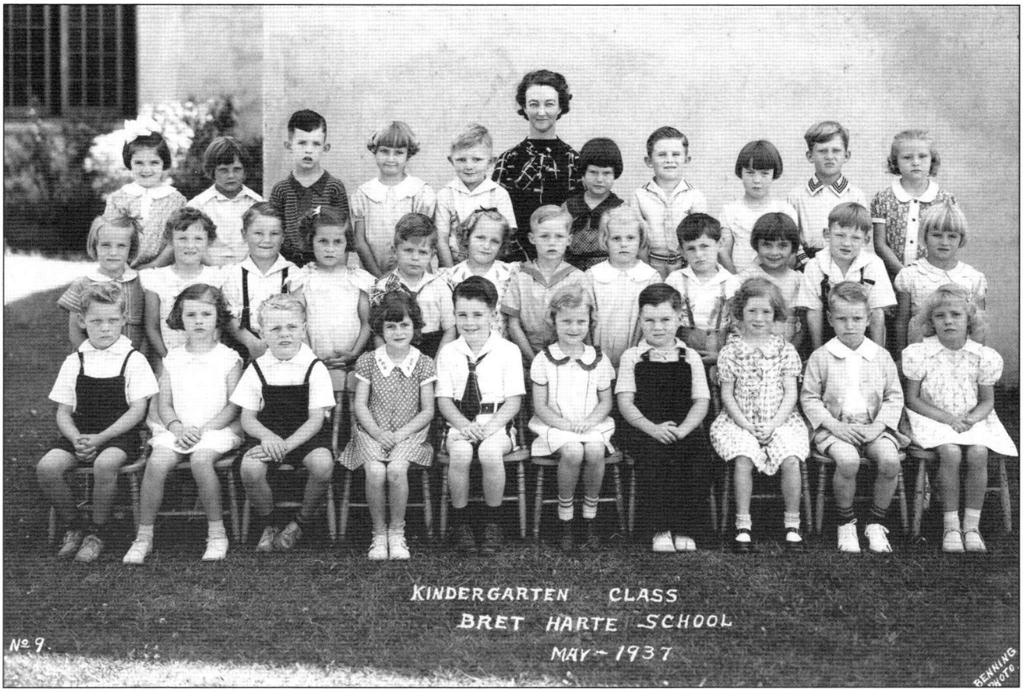

Just beginning their education at Bret Harte School in 1937, these eager kindergartners sit just long enough for their photo to be taken before they run off to play.

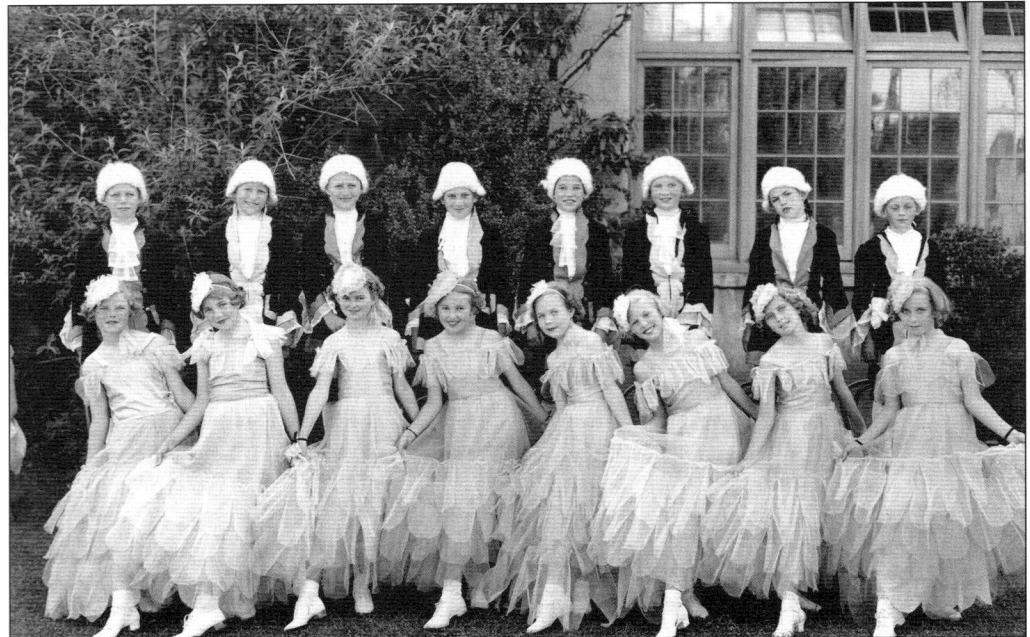

The May Day celebration of 1937 included participation by the entire Bret Harte School. Pictured here are young girls and boys in beautifully detailed costumes. Notice the wigs on the boys.

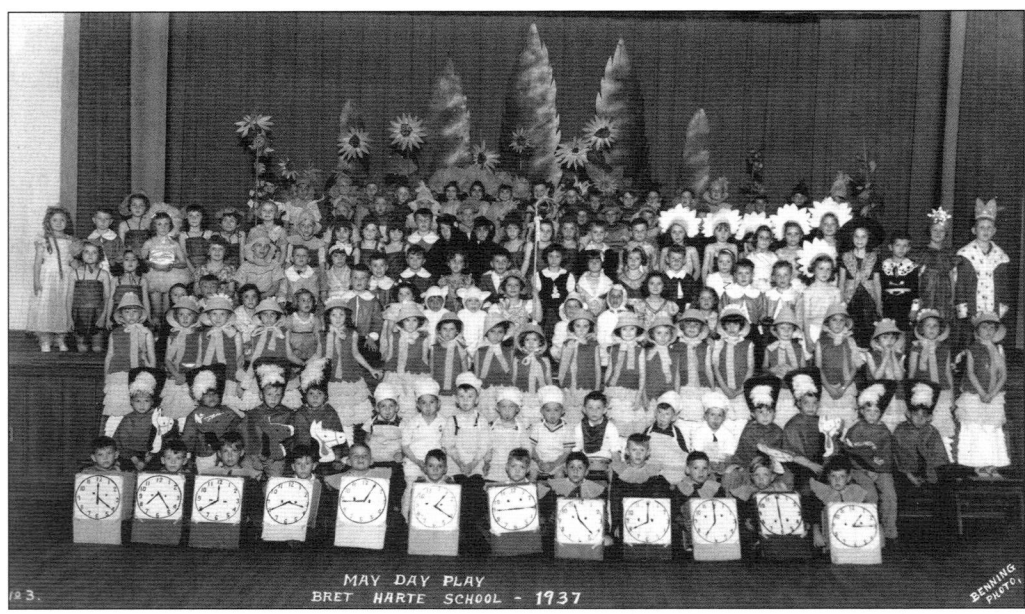

The May Day celebration of 1937 included a celebration of cultural diversity. This all-school picture includes children in different international costumes perhaps meant to depict children from around the world. Notice the clocks in the front row illustrating the different time zones.

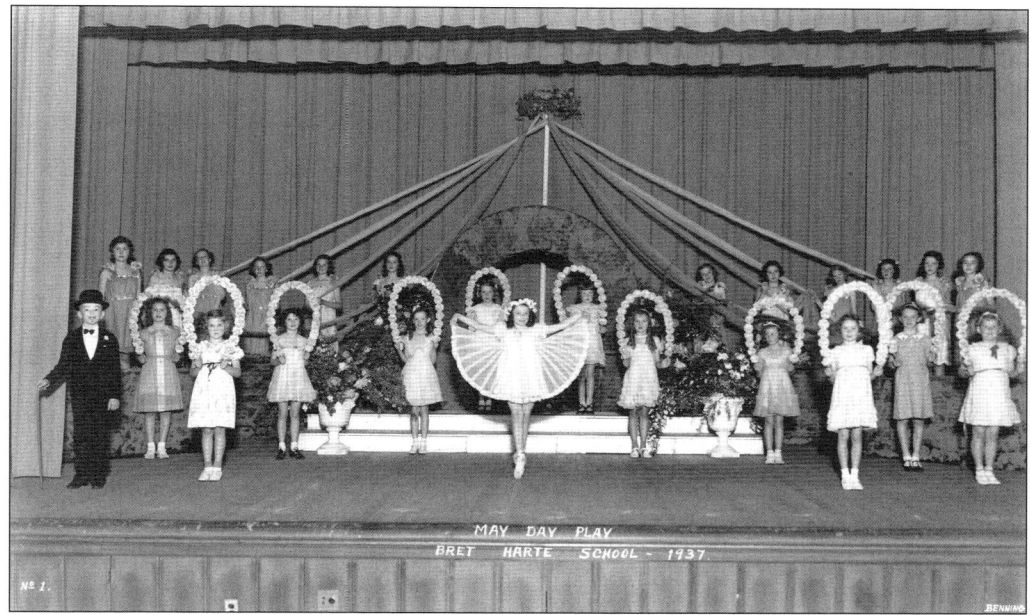

Proud parents snap a photo while the boys and girls of Bret Harte School sing and dance on stage in 1937.

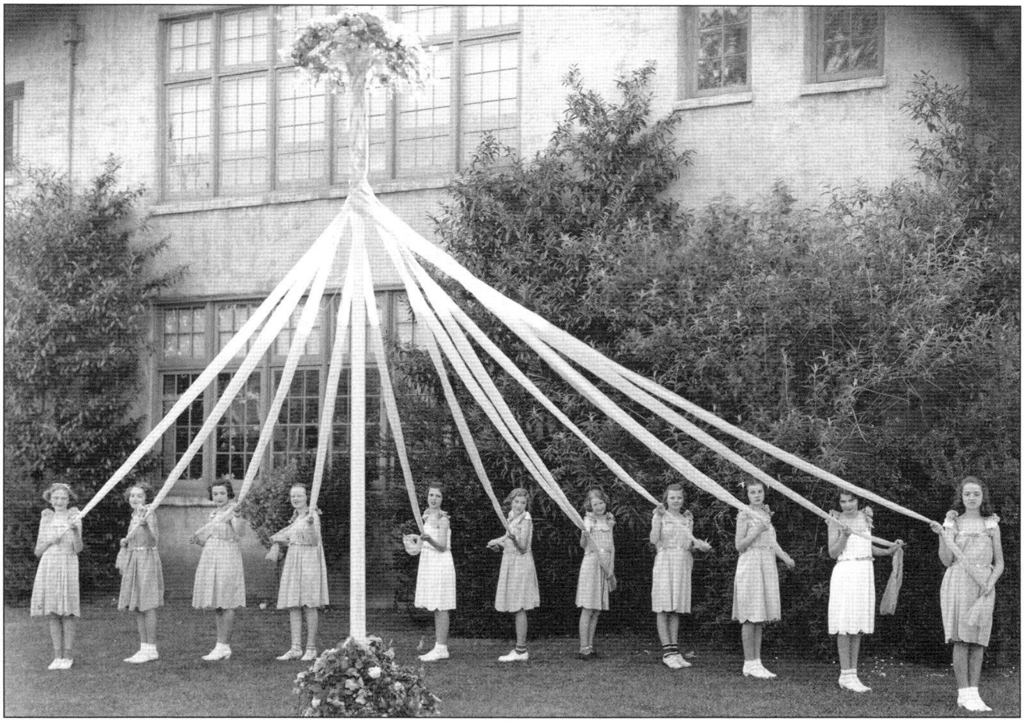

Sixth-grade dance around the maypole for the 1937 May Day celebration.

87

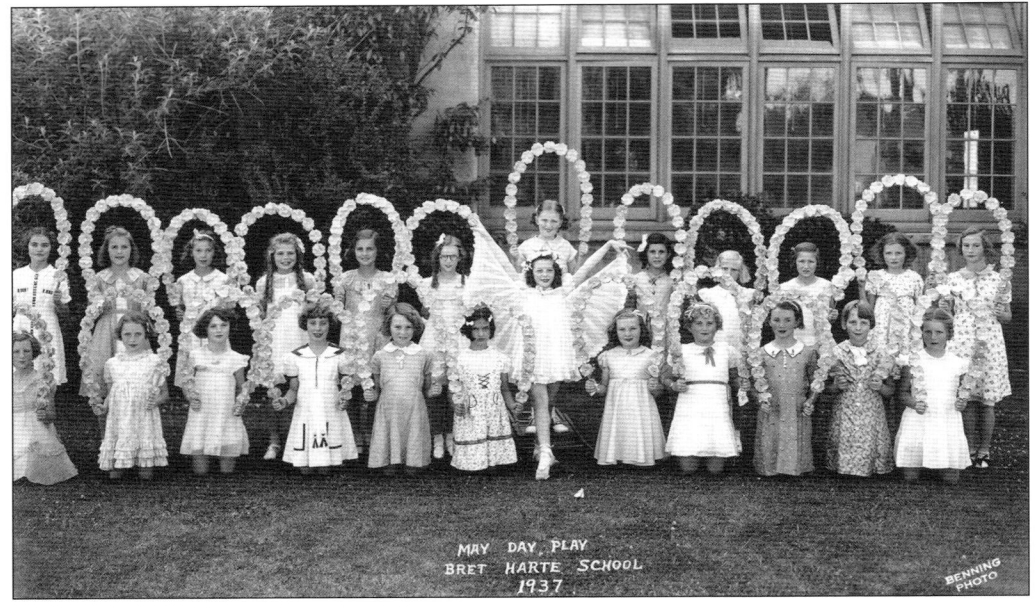

Flower wreaths make angels out of these May Day dancers.

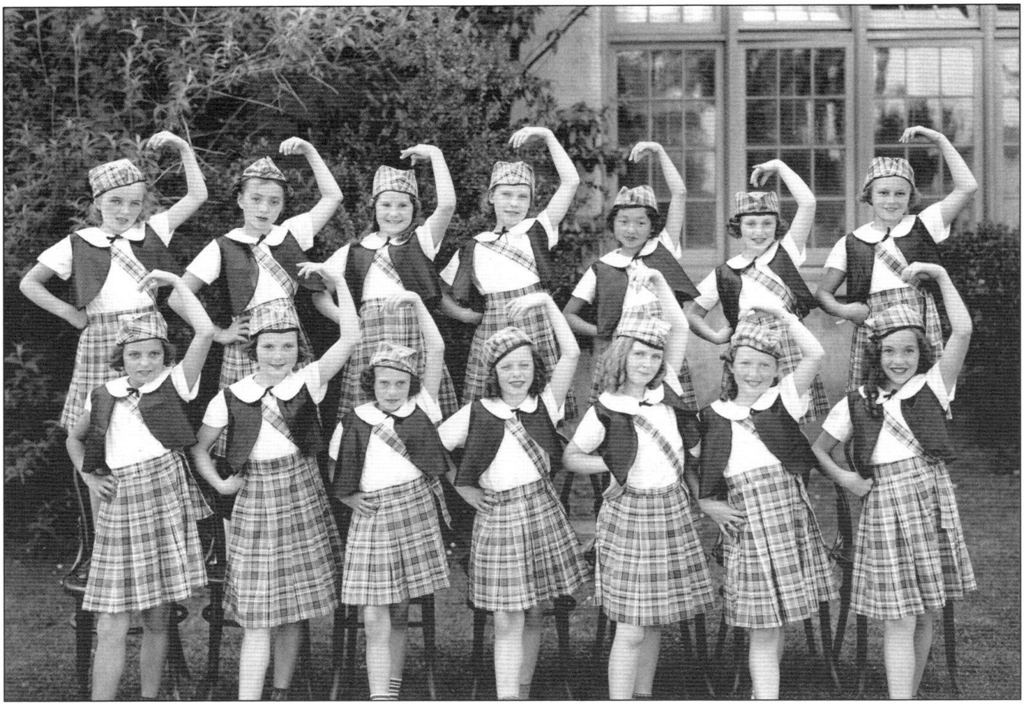

Fifth and sixth graders line up in their Scottish costumes posing as dancers in 1937.

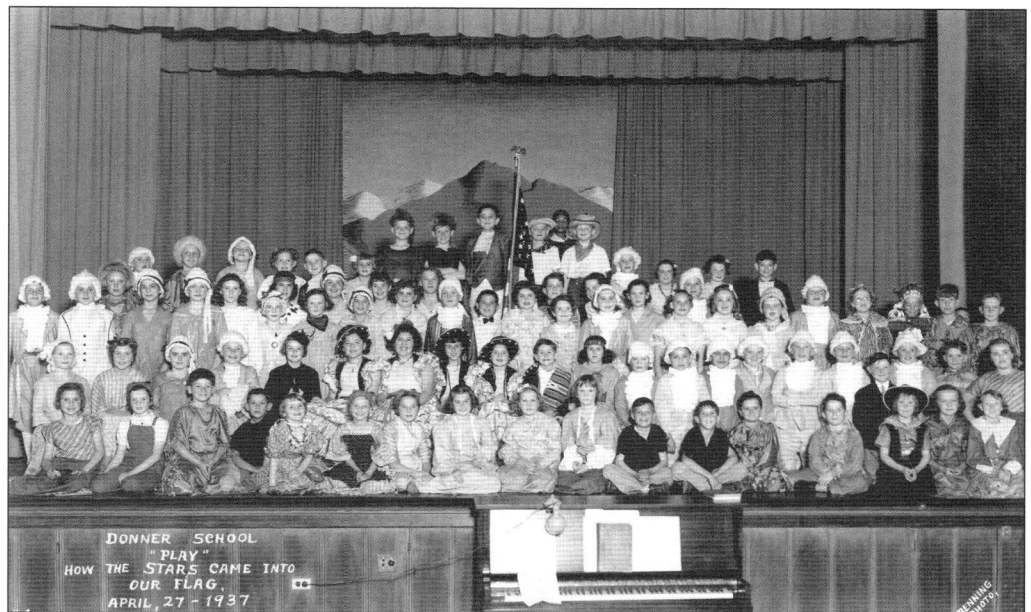

Not to be outdone by Bret Harte School, the children of Donner School staged a patriotic spring play of their own in 1937 entitled "How the Stars Came into Our Flag."

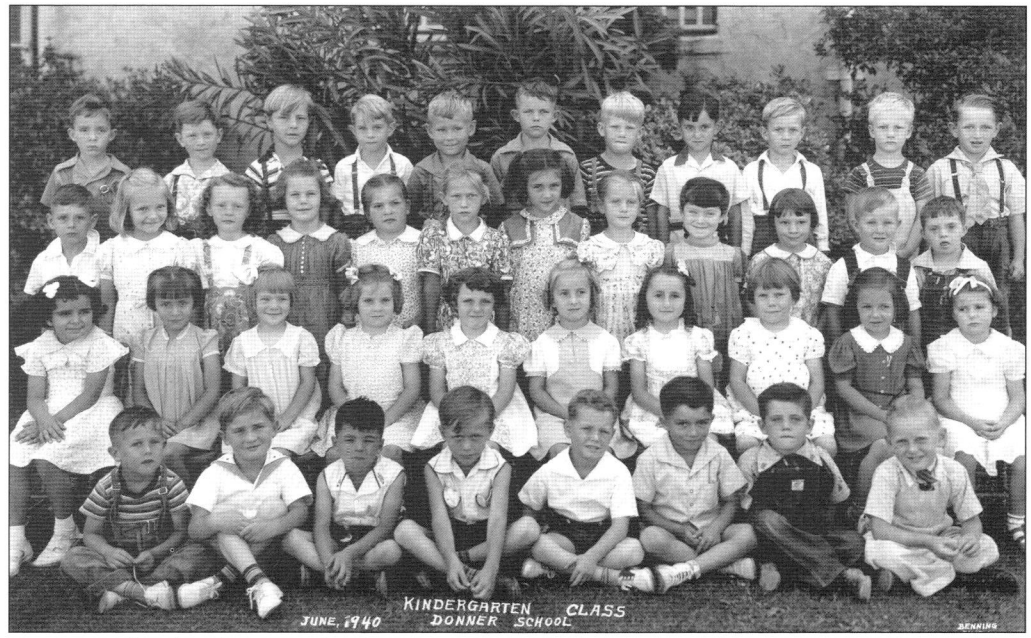

Donner School's afternoon kindergarten class of 1940 reflected a predominantly Western-European Oak Park.

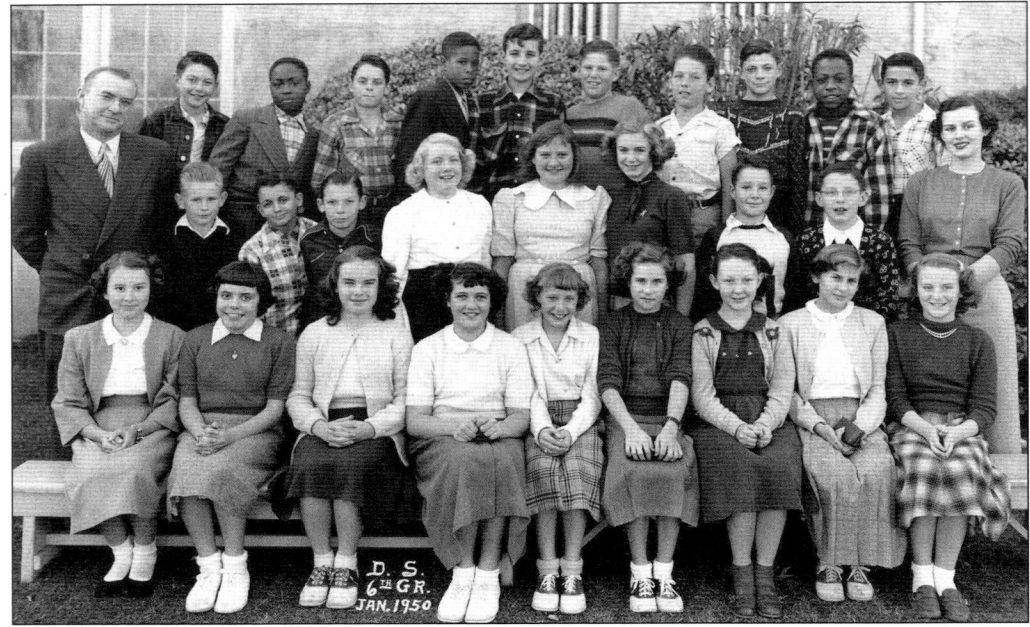

The Donner School sixth-grade class of 1950 poses with the teacher as well as the school principal. Notice the different nationalities among the children, indicating the ethnic diversity of Oak Park.

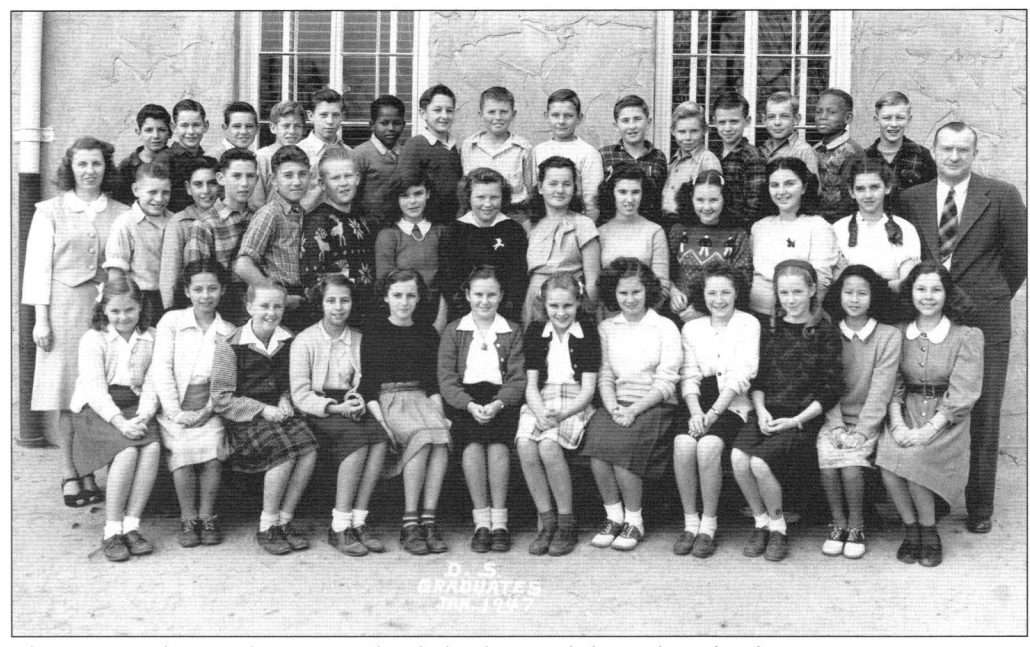

The 1947 graduates of Donner School clearly reveal the Oak Park's diversity.

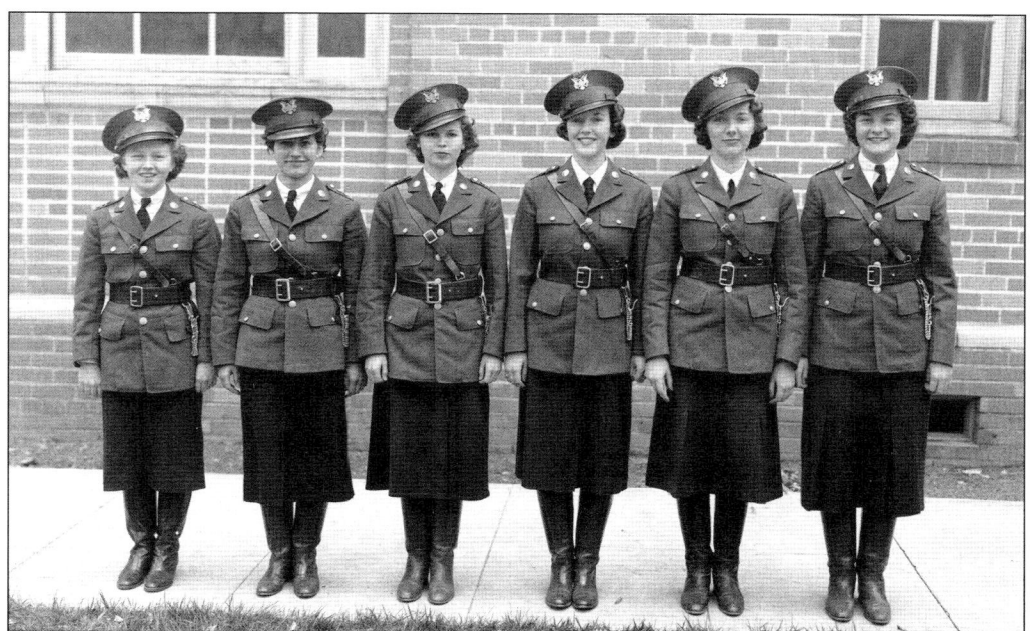
The 1938 Sacramento High School ROTC Girls represented the first female ROTC organization offered at a local high school.

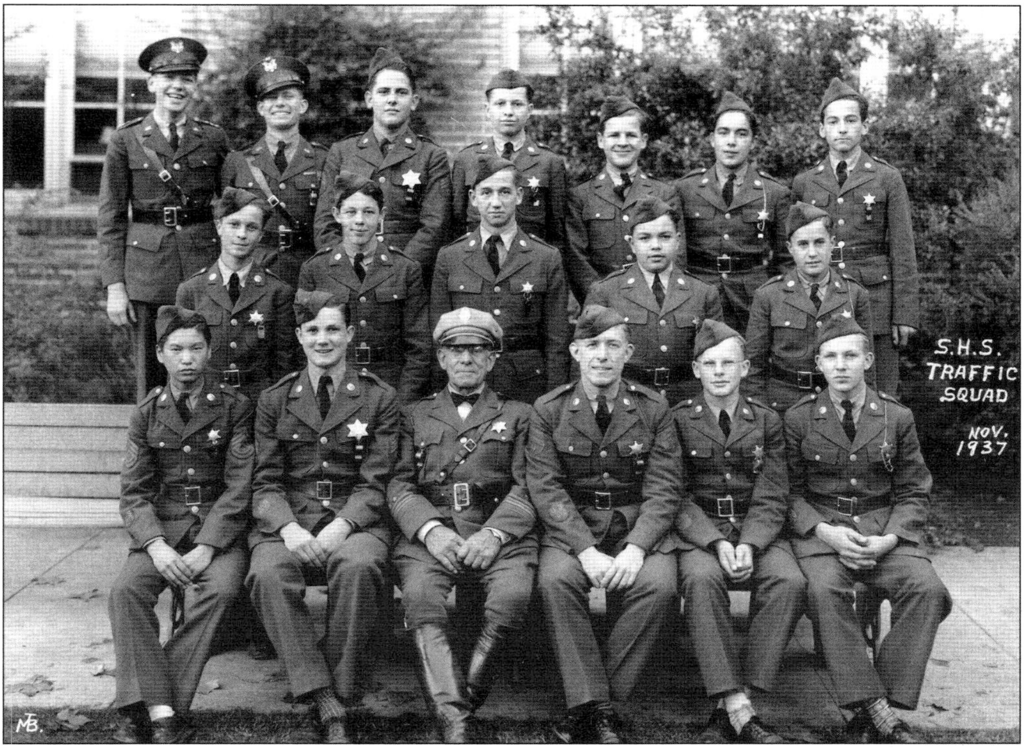

The Sacramento High School Traffic Squad team of 1937 pose before marching off to duty.

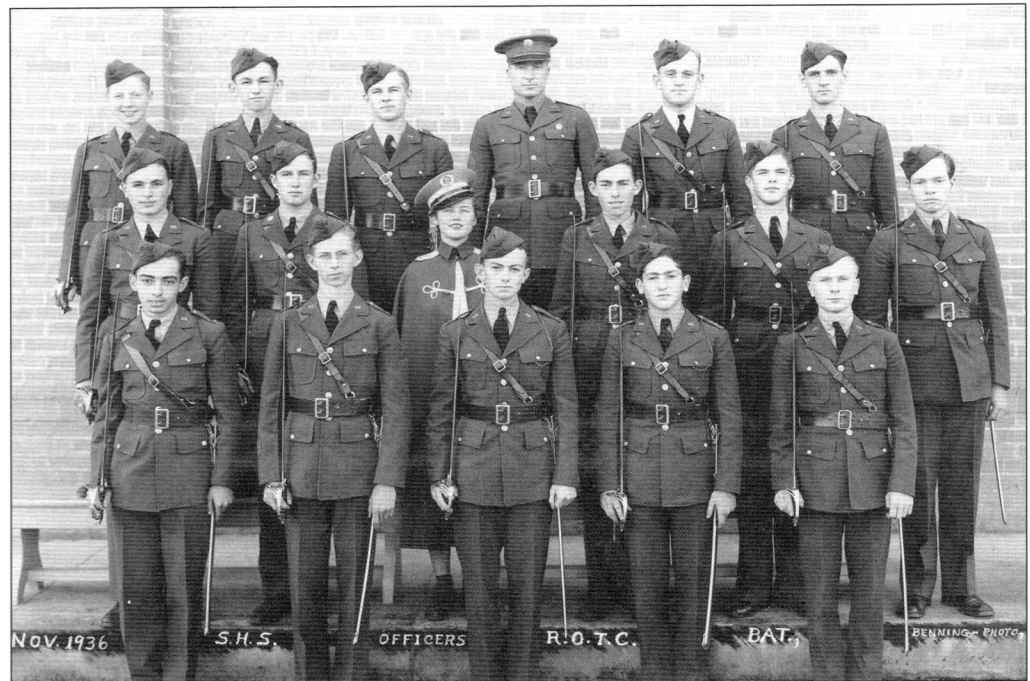

Pictured in 1936 are ROTC battalion officers of Sacramento High School. Notice the only female officer in the center. It was uncommon for women to hold any official military position prior to World War II.

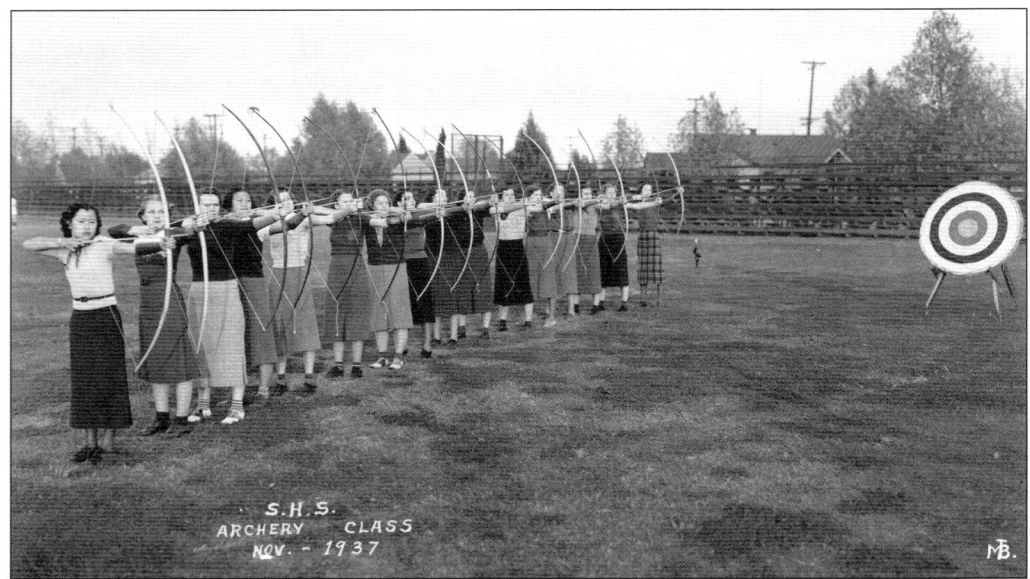

Physical education at Sacramento High School included archery. This is the girls' archery class of winter 1937. Notice that the girls are dressed in their school clothes.

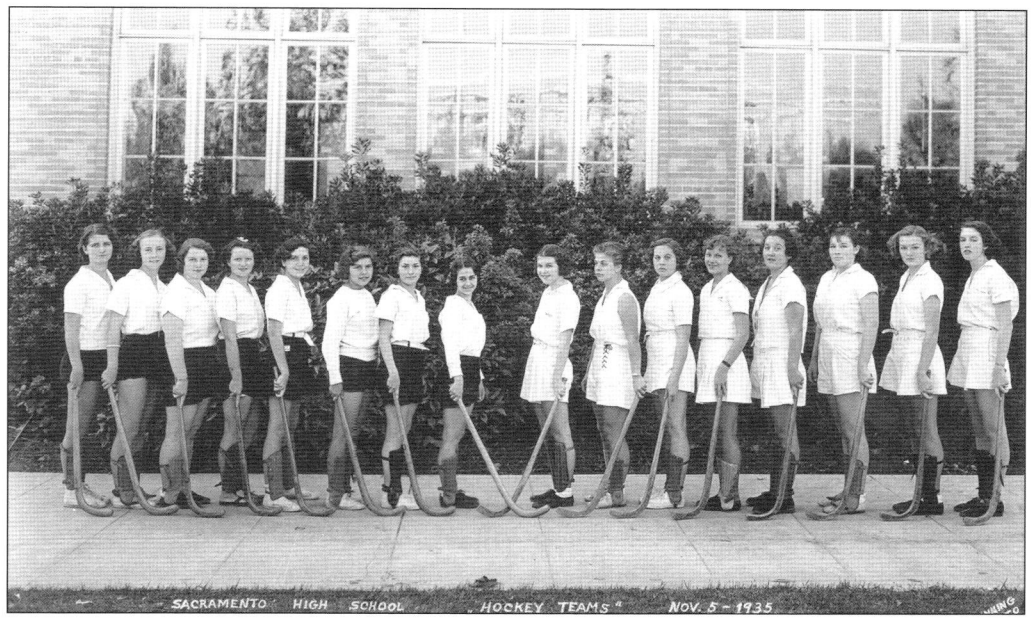

Sacramento High School pioneered in women's physical education. This photograph from winter 1935 shows the Sacramento High School girls' hockey team—Sacramento's first female hockey team.

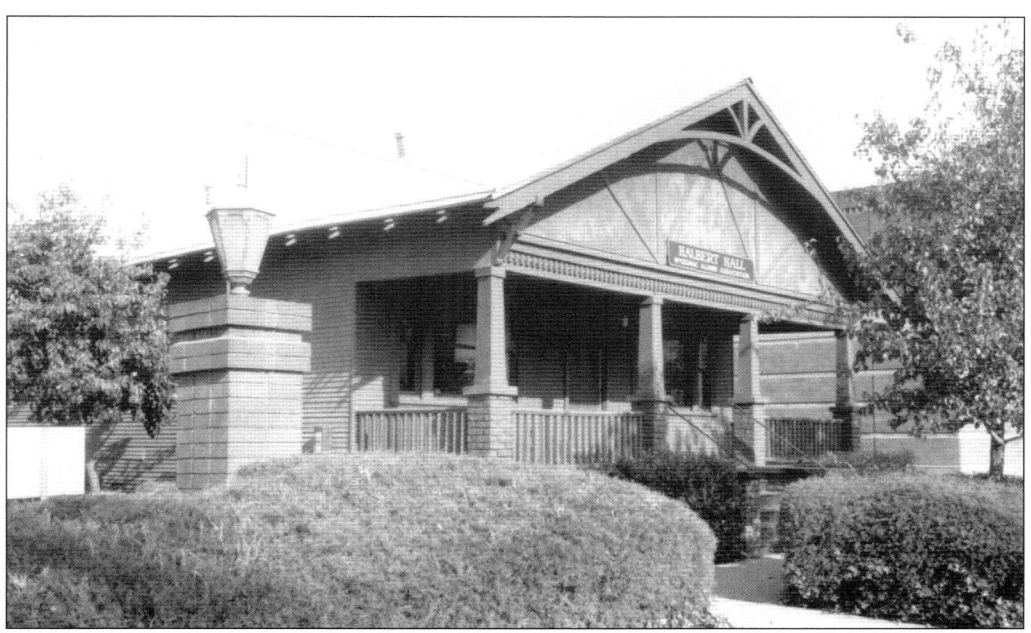

Halbert Hall is the alumni building for the McGeorge School of Law and is shown here in a 1984 photo. (Photo courtesy of OHP.)

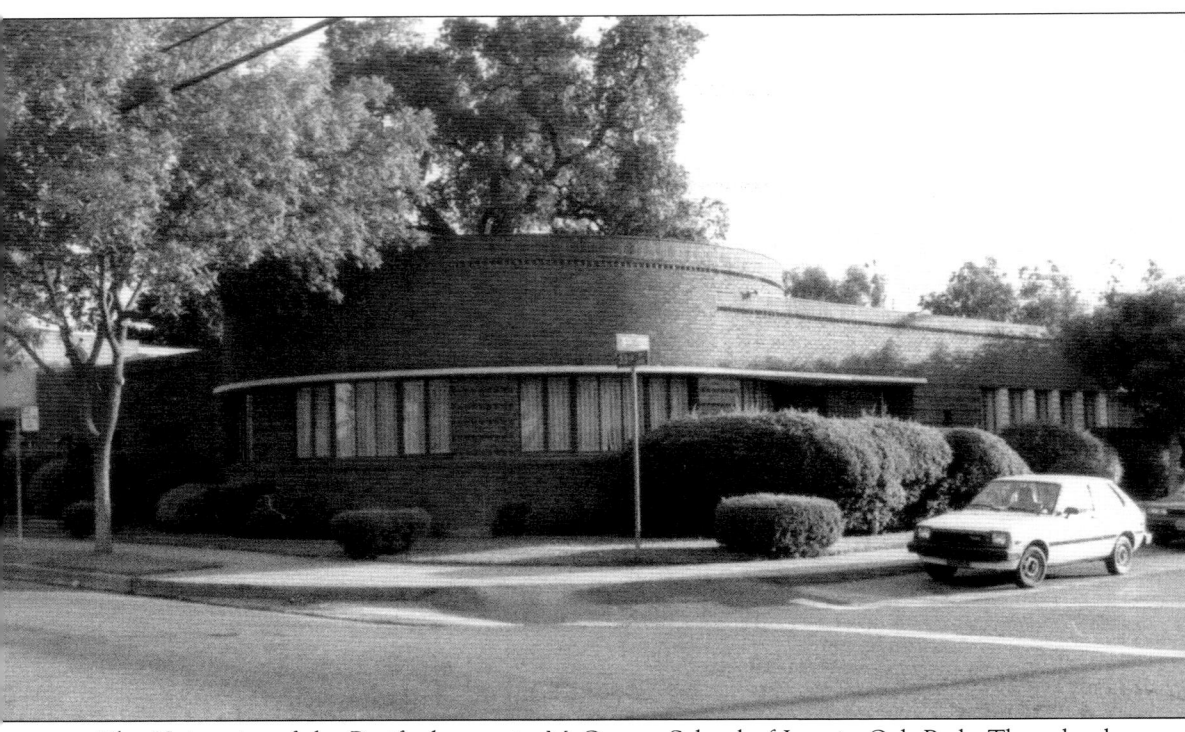
The University of the Pacific houses its McGeorge School of Law in Oak Park. The school, shown here in 1984, has become one of the premier law schools on the Pacific Coast. (Photo courtesy of OHP.)

Eight

MINISTERS AND MINISTRIES
By Marcelo Zamarripa

Churches have played a key role in the development of cities throughout the course of history. Accessibility to churches was important to new immigrants because churches served as a gathering place as well as a place of worship. In the early development of Oak Park, the role of churches was just as important. The earliest immigrants to arrive in Oak Park were European, so it was understandable that one of the earliest churches to be erected was the First English Evangelical Lutheran Church. Organized in 1890 at a "Fireman's Hall" in Sacramento, Oak Park residents traveled to First English until 1923, when the church permanently moved to Oak Park at the corner of Fourth Avenue and Thirty-ninth Street. In 1945 First English purchased a house near the church, which was dedicated in 1946 as a parish house. Another house on Thirty-ninth Street, purchased in 1949, was dedicated as a parsonage. In 1953 the church raised $33,000 over a three-year period, which helped put up more buildings and increase the size of the church. At its inception, First English was all white. When Rev. Morgan Edwards began his pastorate in 1952, the first black members were welcomed into the church, which made First English a unique congregation within the community. Throughout the years, First English has played a key role in Oak Park and has been involved in the Oak Park Neighborhood council and the Project Area Committee.

As the Oak Park community became more diverse with the arrival of the Irish, Italians, and African Americans, more churches were built to accommodate these varied religious needs. One of the earliest black churches to be established in Oak Park was the Shiloh Baptist church in 1856, founded by Rev. Charles Satchel, who served as the church's first pastor from 1856 to 1859. The first meetings of the church were held at a Chinese Christian Chapel in Sacramento, until the Shiloh congregation purchased its first building for $800 in 1856 on Fifth Street. It was destroyed by fire in 1861. At the time of the fire, the Shiloh congregation totaled 40 people. After the fire, the church was able to build a new brick building for $2,500.

From 1891 to 1931, Shiloh Baptist underwent some major changes. It was incorporated in 1898, suffered another fire in 1905, built three new structures, and had three different pastors. At the time of the Great Depression, the membership of Shiloh had dramatically decreased to around 50 churchgoers. However, with the arrival of the Rev. J.T. Muse in 1934, the church was able to rebound and had 800 people attending by the time Muse left in 1947. Some of the accomplishments Shiloh has achieved in its 140 years are the founding of seven churches and a ministry of 26 pastors.

Other churches developed in the same era in Oak Park had a similar impact on their congregations. The old Immaculate Conception Church served the Irish Catholic community both spiritually and educationally. The Oak Park Methodist Church still serves the Oak Park community as the center for Celebration Arts, an organization that celebrates dance, the arts, and drama. Kyles Temple A.M.E. Zion Church has been in existence for 85 years and still does its part in uplifting the community. Almost 120 years later, the churches in the Oak Park region are still doing what they set out to do at their inception. Their longevity has created stability in the community, and their continued emphasis on living the Gospel, as expressed most fully by St. HOPE, is at the heart of the future of Oak Park.

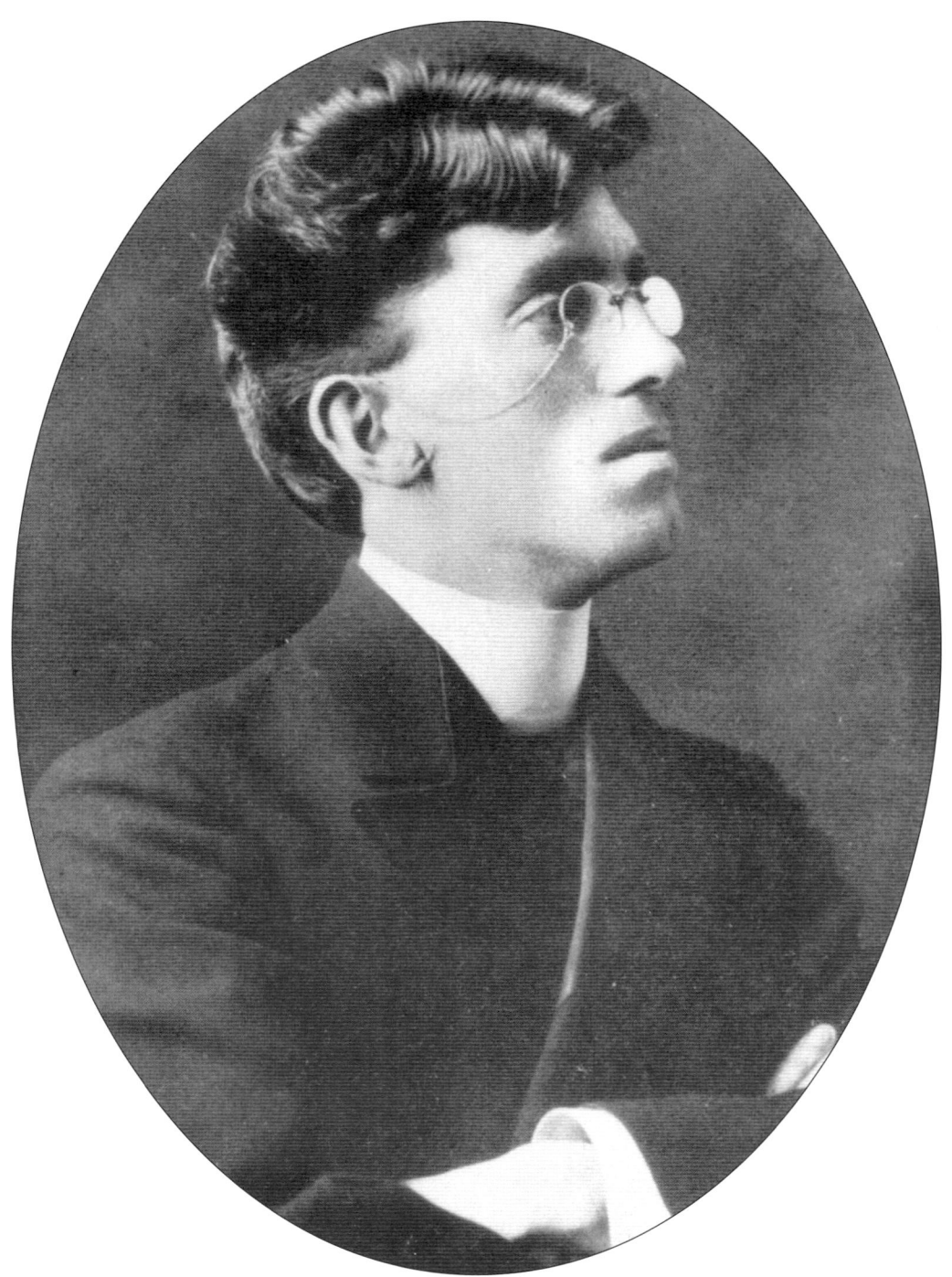
Rev. William Francis Ellis, shown in this c. 1910 photo, was a Catholic priest at the old Immaculate Conception Church in Oak Park. Reverend Ellis also instructed Irish schoolchildren in the church's parochial school.

Fr. John Ellis and Fr. William Ellis (seated), shown in this c. 1920 photo, were Catholic priests at the Irish-dominated old Immaculate Conception Church.

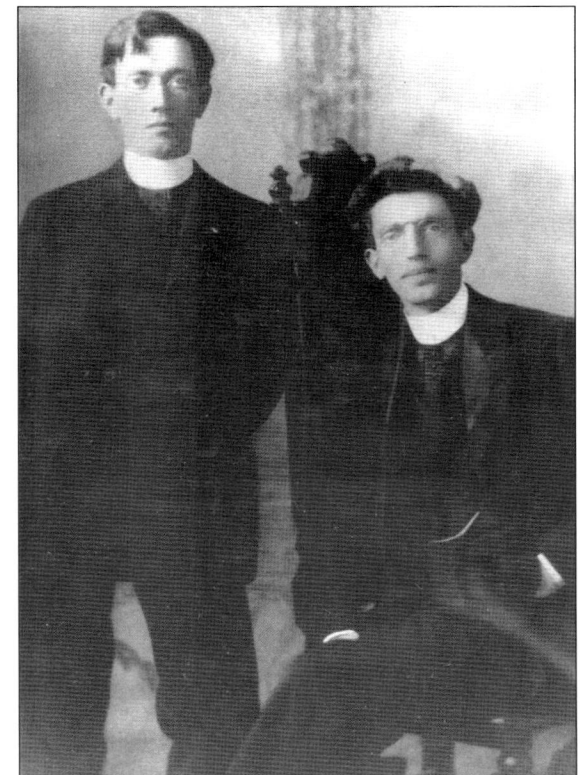

Irish students pose in this c. 1909 photo in front of the old Immaculate Conception Church located on Thirty-second Street in Oak Park. Fr. William Ellis is standing in the doorway.

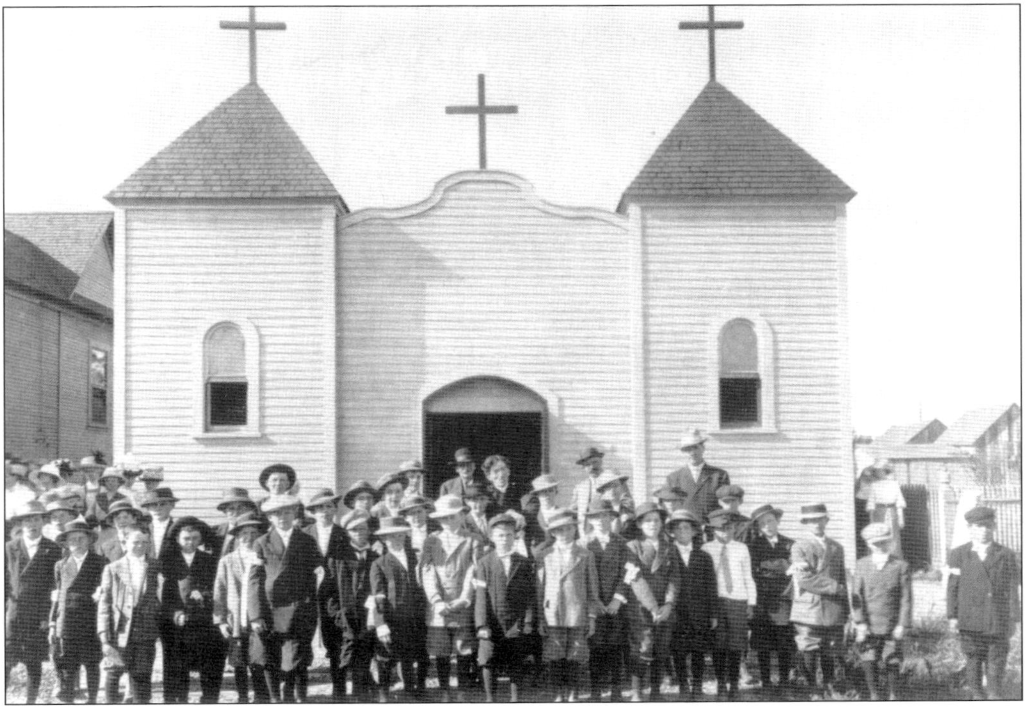

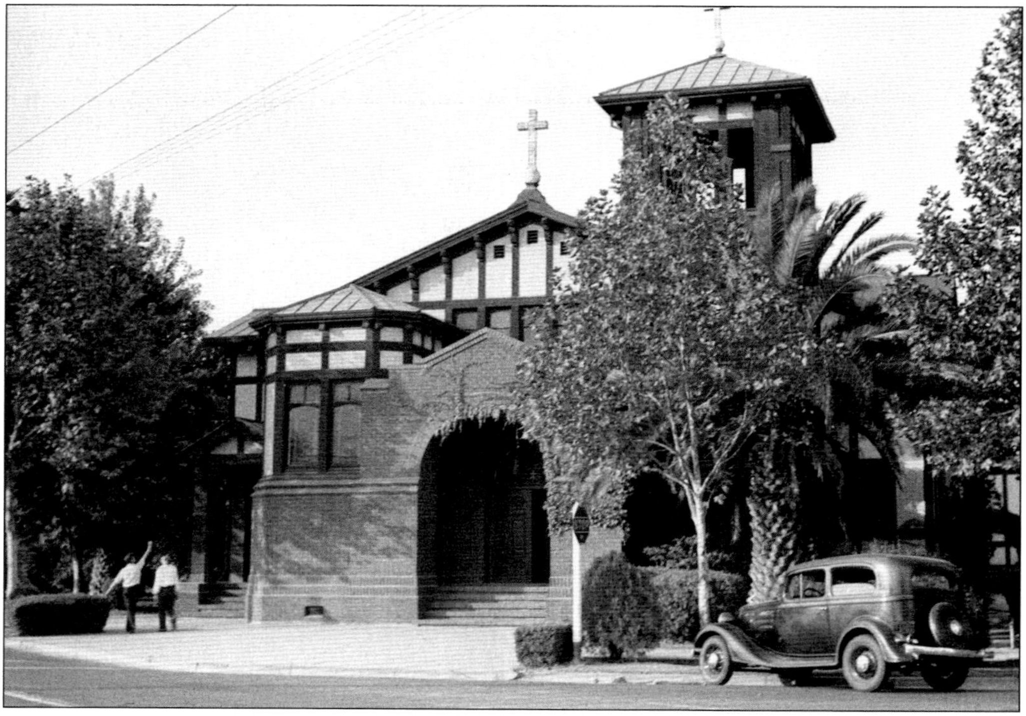

Located at 2549 Thirty-second Street, Immaculate Conception Catholic Church still serves its parish today. The impressive architecture, as shown in this c. 1935 photo, demonstrates the success of the parish.

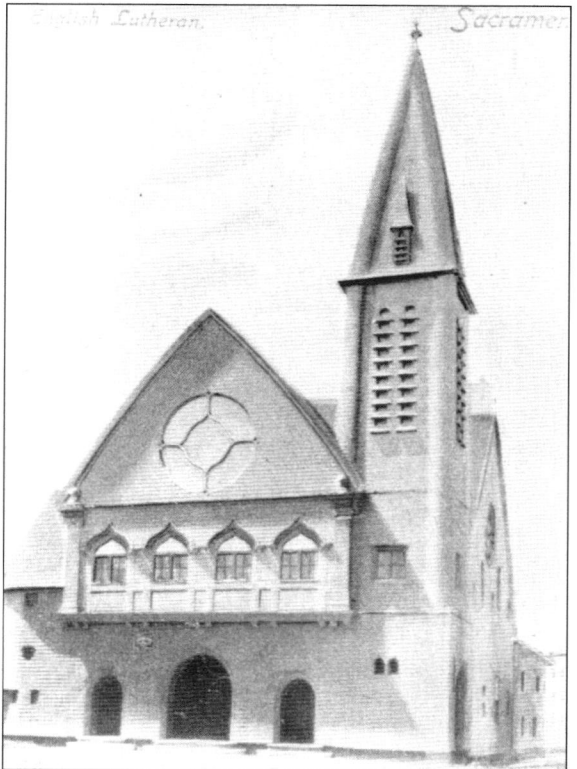

First English Evangelical Lutheran Church was founded at this site on Sixteenth Street between J and K Streets in Sacramento, shown in this c. 1893 photo. The congregation moved to Oak Park in 1923 where its church still stands on Thirty-ninth Street.

Rev. J. Gordon McPherson served as pastor of Shiloh Baptist Church and as the founder of the *Sacramento Forum*.

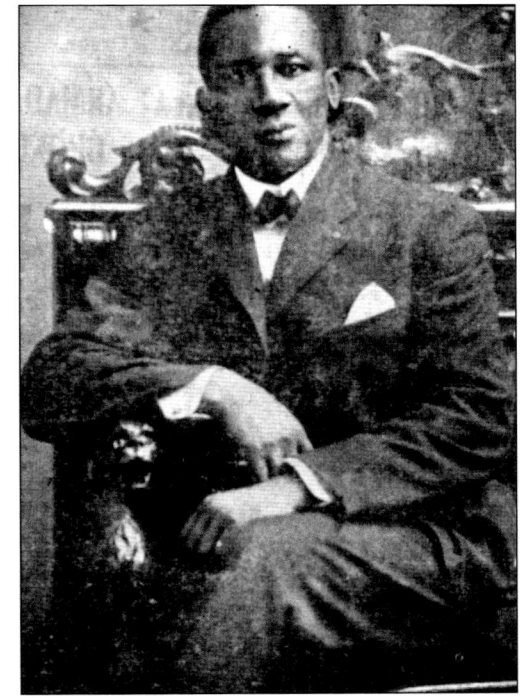

The Shiloh Baptist Church choir prepares for services in the 1920. From left to right are (top row) Mr. Kindle, Mr. Larue, and Mr. O. Blakey; (middle row) Mrs. Barber, Mrs. Netta Sparks, Mrs. Pauline Smith, Mrs. Blakey, and Mrs. Kindle; (bottom row) John Smith, three unidentified people, and Mr. Julius Harris, a visiting minister.

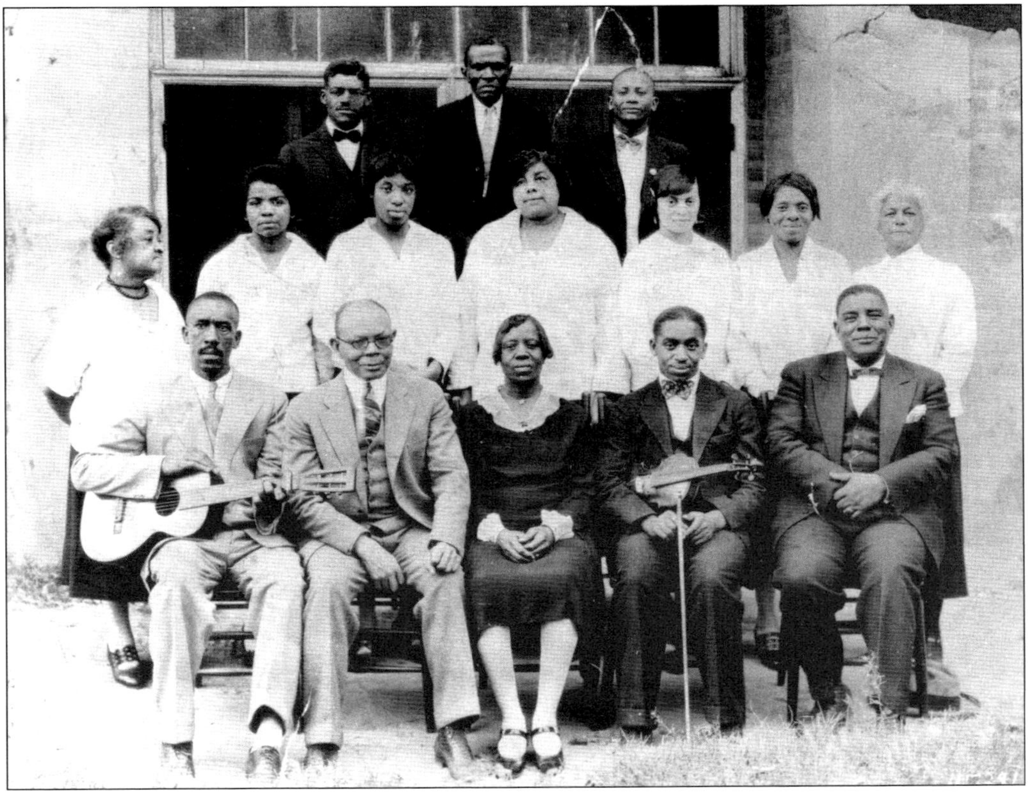

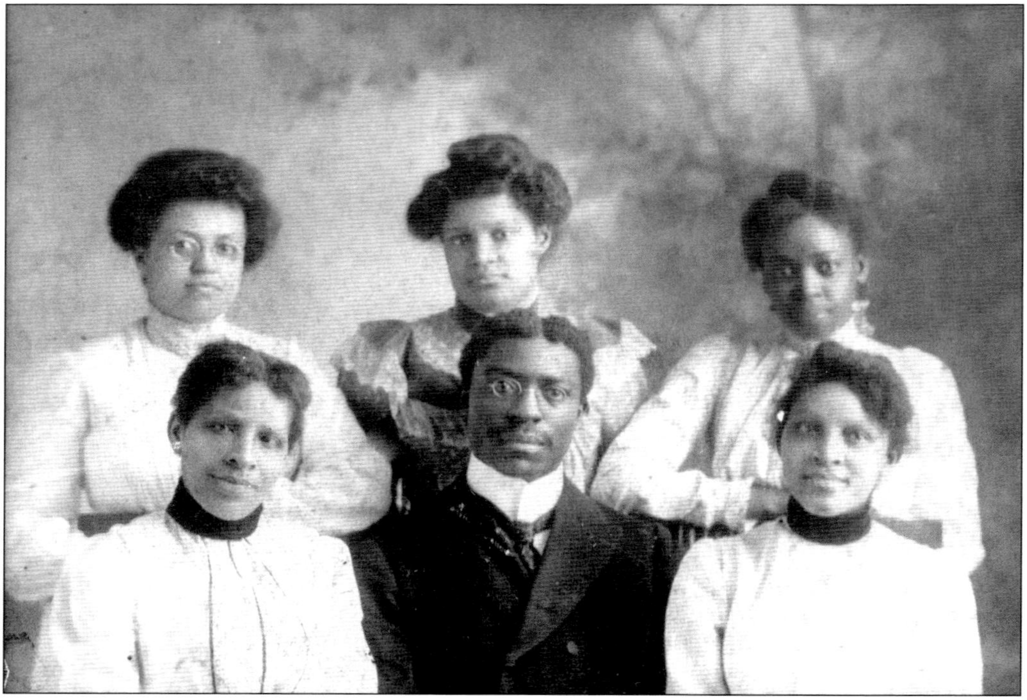

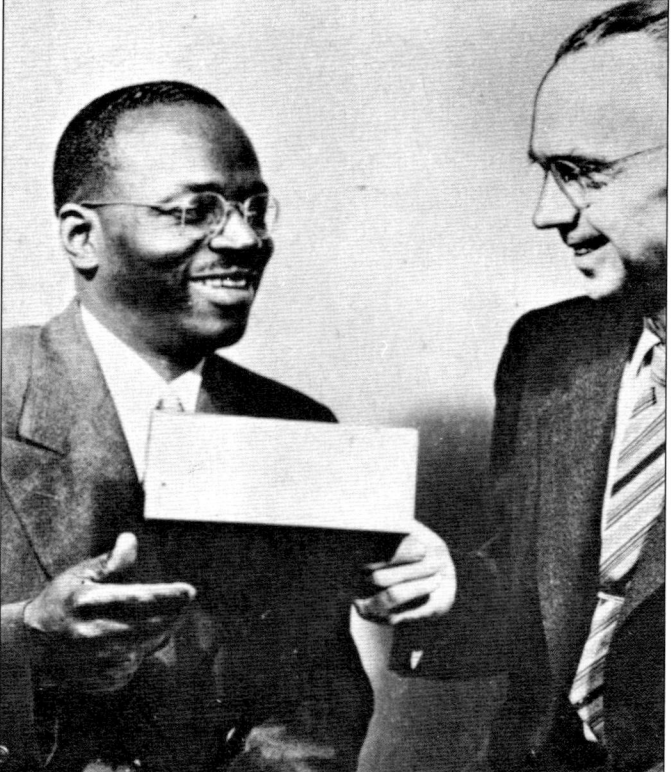

This undated photo depicts members of the Shiloh Baptist Church choir. Seated, from left to right, are Lucy Ray, Reverend McPherson (minister of Shiloh Baptist Church), and Maude Ray. Standing are two unidentified people and Maude Russell.

Rev. Joseph Williams accepts the deed for Shiloh Baptist property at Sixth and P Streets in this c. 1949 photo. Before the deed was accepted, Shiloh had paid off its previous debts and celebrated by having a parade in Oak Park.

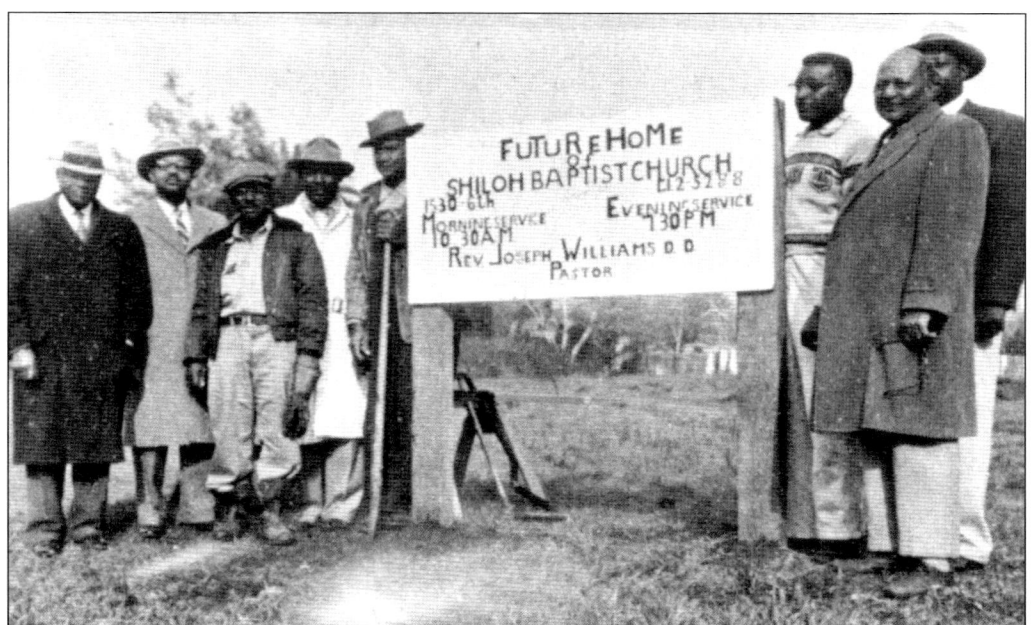

Workers stand around a sign erected at the new site of Shiloh Baptist Church in Oak Park in this c. 1949 photo. The new site was located at the corner of Sixth and P Streets.

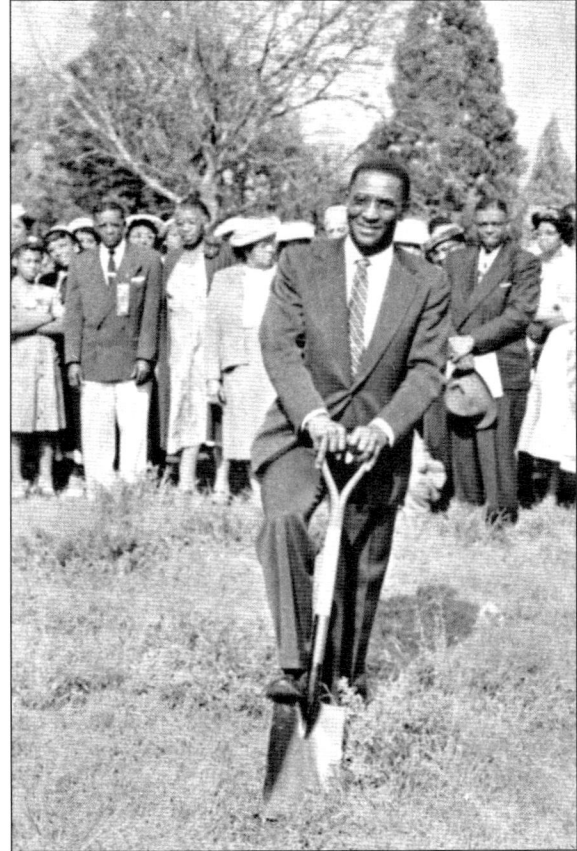

Rev. Willie Cooke breaks ground c. 1958 as the pastor for Shiloh Baptist Church. The new building stood at 3565 Ninth Avenue in Oak Park and was developed by James C. Dodd & Associates, Inc., a locally owned African-American firm.

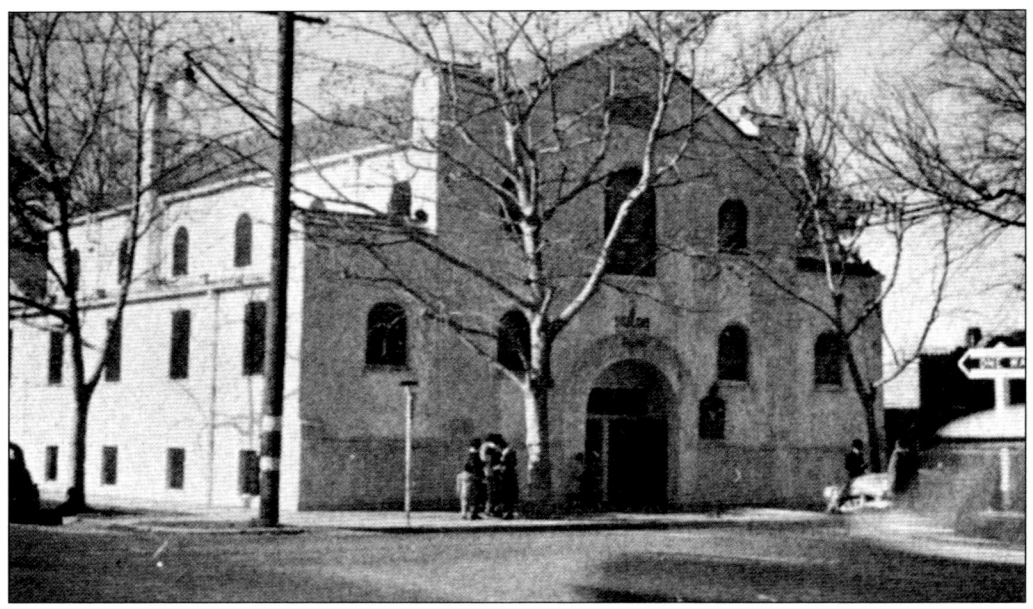

This exterior view of Shiloh Baptist Church in 1958 depicts its simple yet functional architecture.

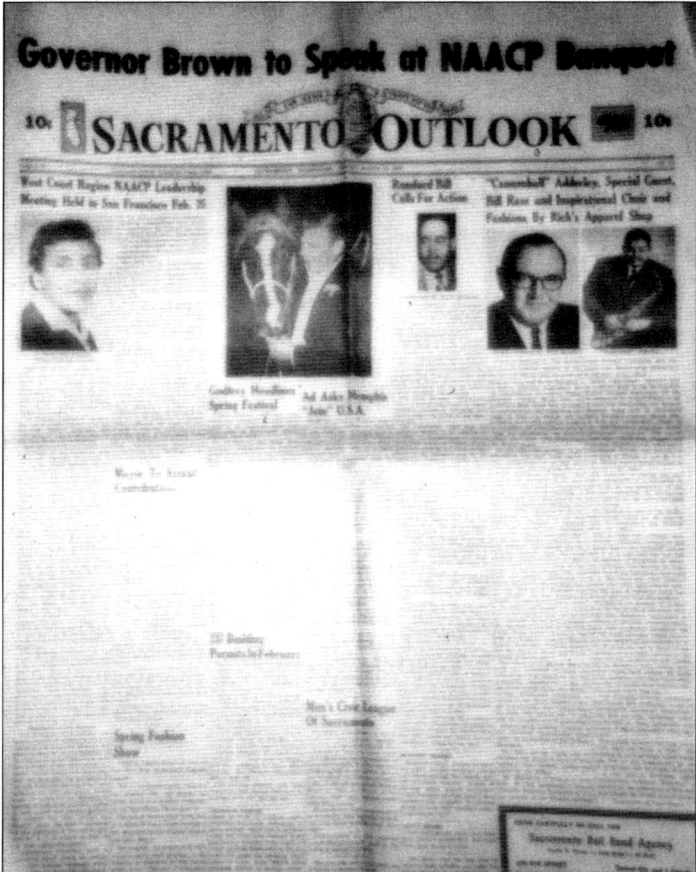

The *Sacramento Outlook* newspaper, Sacramento's third black newspaper, was founded by Shiloh's Rev. J.T. Muse in 1942.

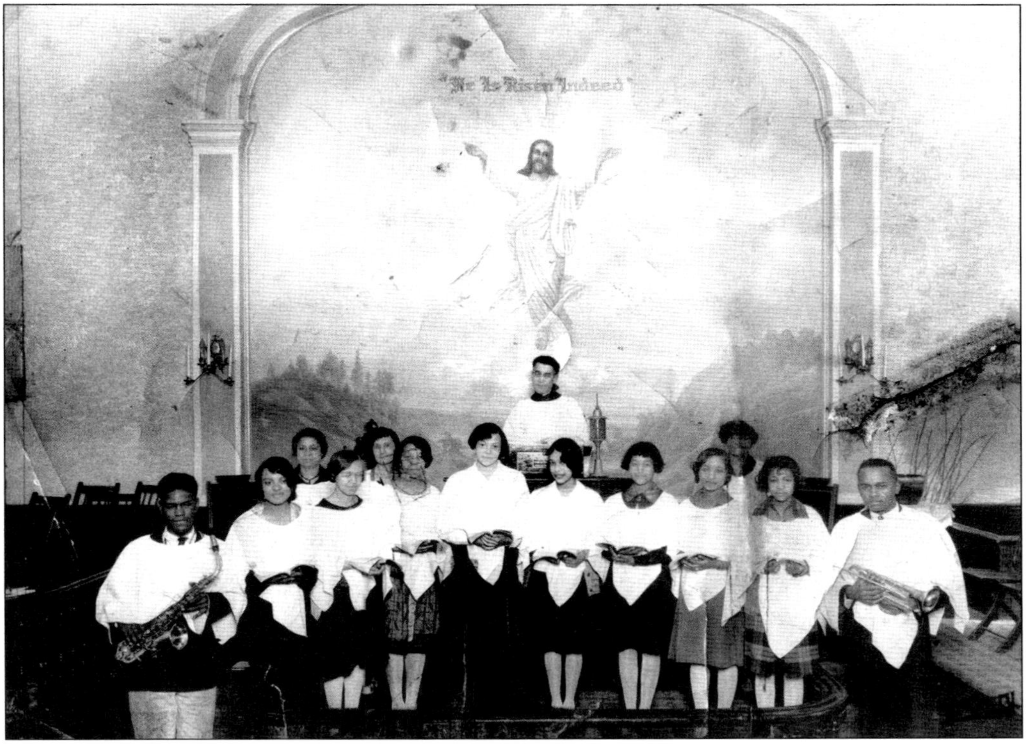

Members of the St. Andrews A.M.E. Church choir on Seventh Avenue prepare for services, c. 1925.

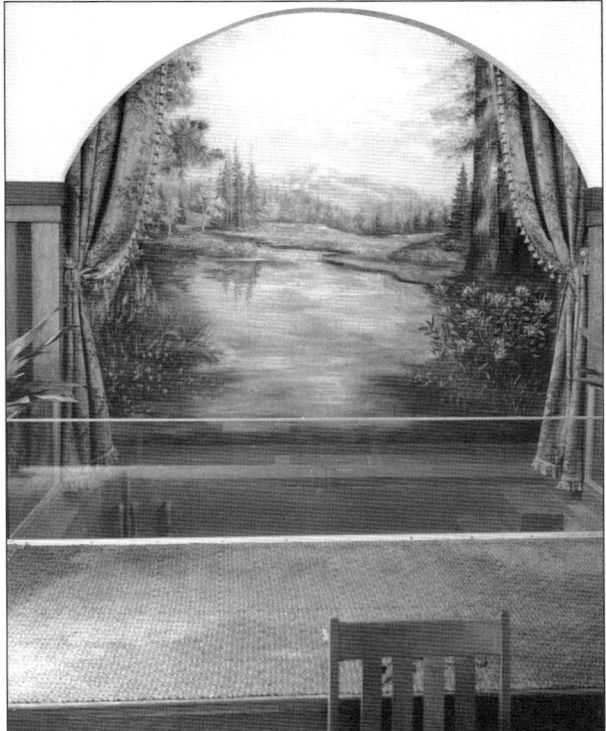

Kyles Temple A.M.E. Church was founded in Oak Park in 1918. This is a recent yet undated photograph.

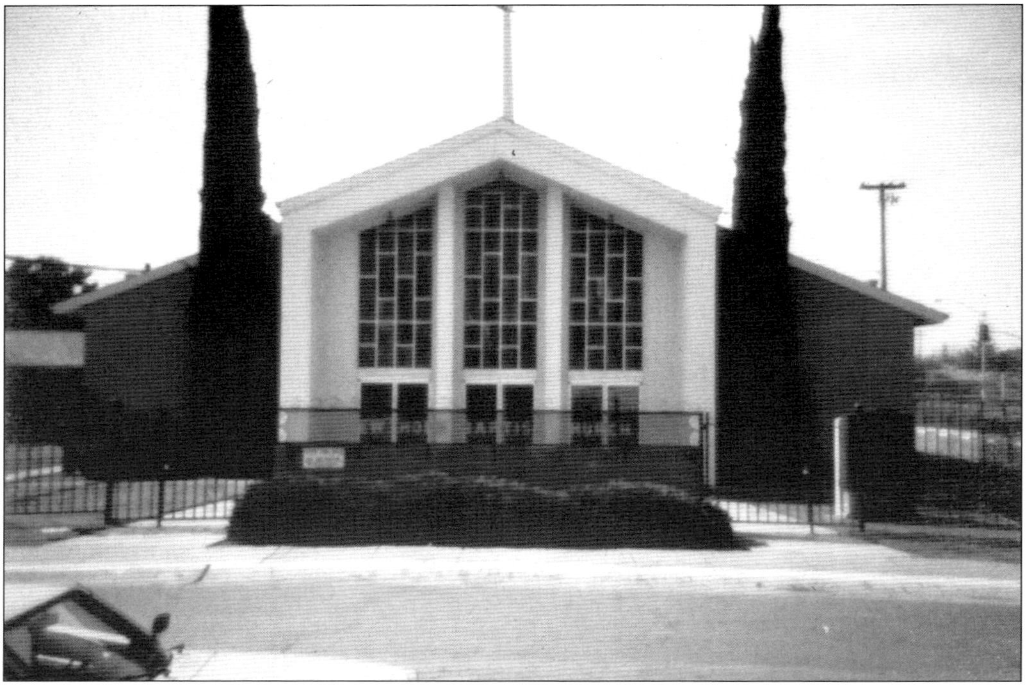

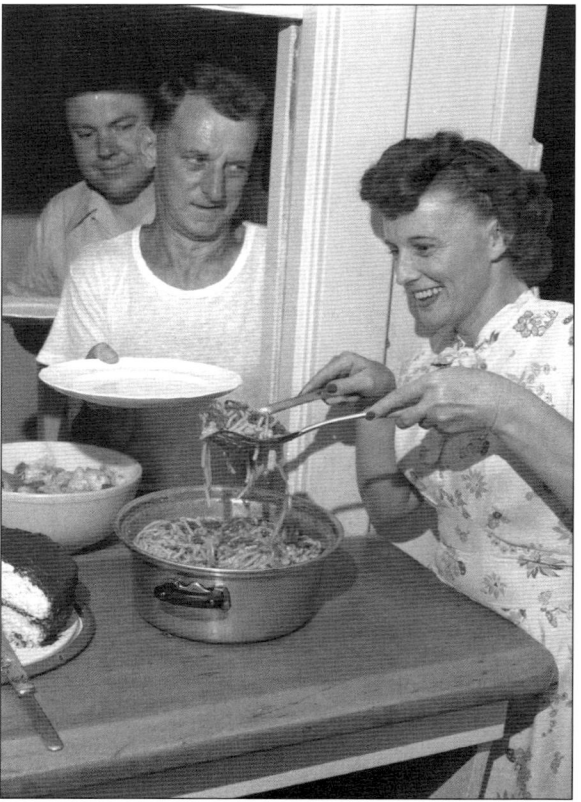

As part of its expanding ministry, Shiloh Baptist Church founded New Hope Church in 1932.

In an expression of faith-based community service, an unidentified woman serves food at the Oak Park Church of Christ potluck dinner, c. 1955.

Members of the Oak Park Church of Christ join forces to paint the exterior of the building, c. 1955.

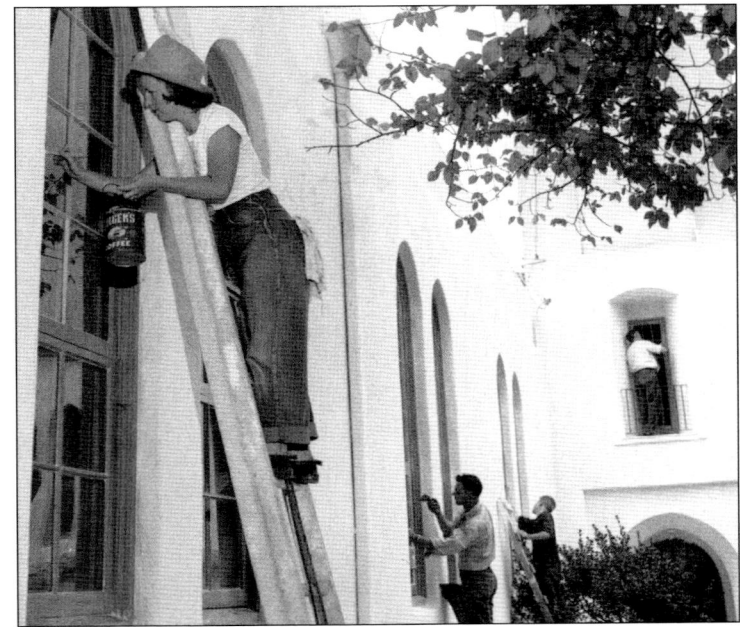

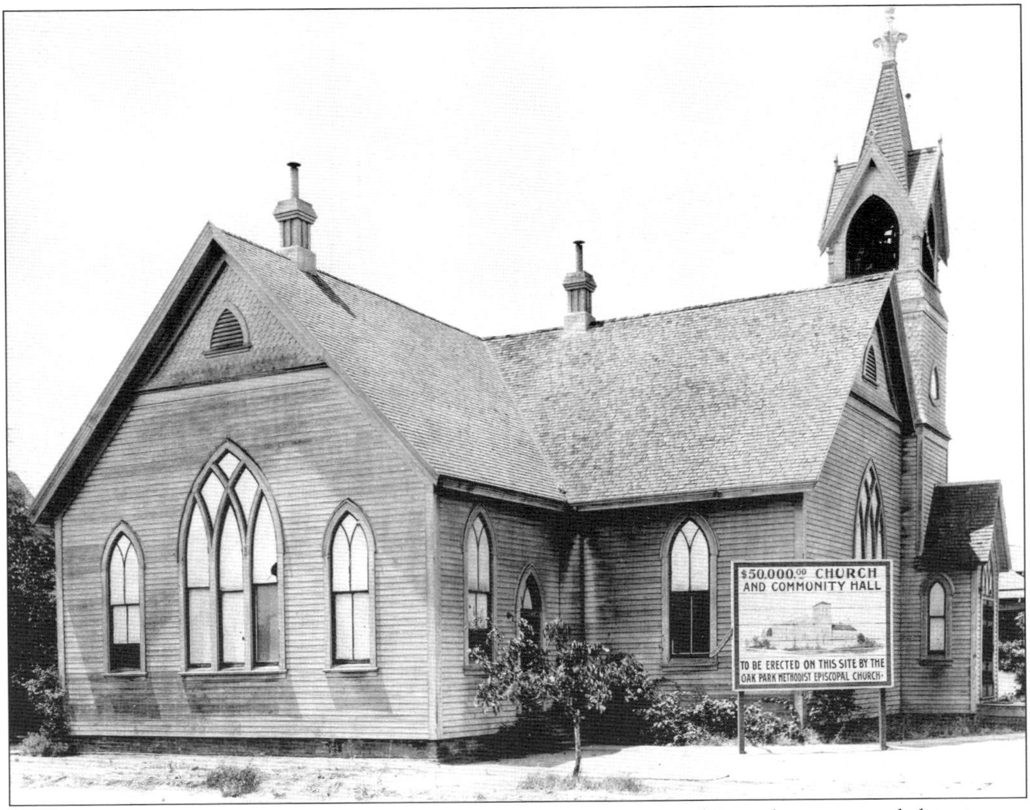

Oak Park Methodist Episcopal Church at Thirty-sixth Street and Broadway erected this sign to announce the building of a new church and community hall.

105

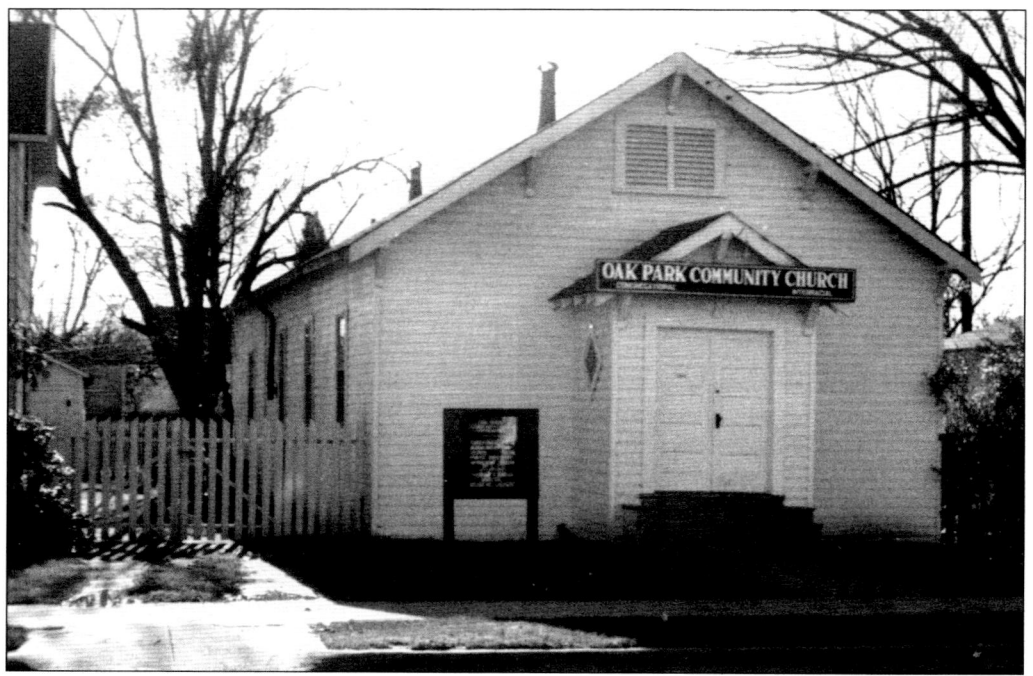

Oak Park Community Church has been a mainstay in Oak Park for many years. This humble building reflects the working-class character of the community.

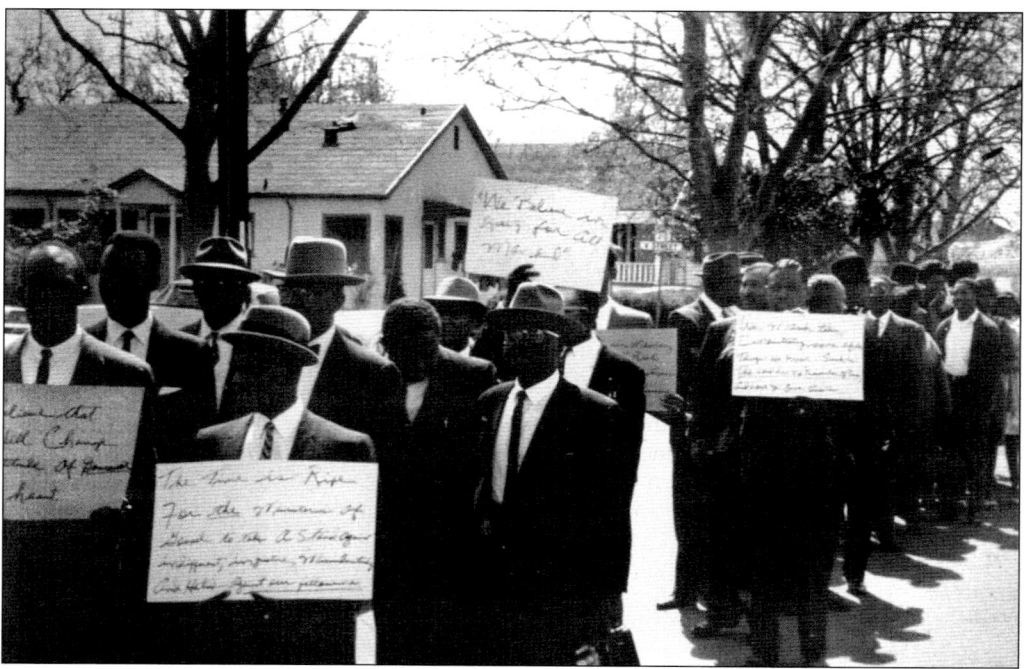

Participants in the 1963 Minister's March from Southside Park to the Capitol in support of Dr. Martin Luther King's voting rights effort in Selma, Alabama, included ministers from Oak Park.

Nine

IN CASE OF EMERGENCY
BY LAWRENCE ADAMS

The rapid growth of Oak Park at the turn of the 20th century created a demand for protective city services such as fire and police. On the evening of November 5, 1905, Sacramento fire commissioner A.A. Turple gathered a large delegation of Oak Park residents at Red Men's Hall for the purpose of organizing a volunteer fire department to meet one essential need of the new community. At the meeting D.W. Taylor was elected temporary chairman, W.H. Collins was temporary secretary, and the other residents in attendance signed up as volunteer firemen. The department again met on November 10 to appoint people to a number of permanent positions. J. Latourette was elected president, W.W. Greer vice president, and W.H. Collins secretary and treasurer. Also at the meeting, the fire commission elected Charles A. Fical chief engineer, and he appointed D.W. Taylor assistant chief and C.W. Todd foreman.

From its founding, the volunteers found themselves battling fires not only in Oak Park, but also in Sacramento. A unique cooperative relationship developed between the two departments that helped ease the merger that came with annexation. This relationship was further strengthened by the cooperation of the Sacramento Police Department, which assisted with fire fighting when called upon.

Over the years the equipment used by Oak Park fire fighters has changed with technological innovations. In 1904 equipment consisted of hand-pulled carts, which were later replaced with a one-horse powered wagon. Several years later, a special tax was levied on the residents of Oak Park that allowed the fire commission to purchase up-to-date equipment such as a chemical horse-drawn wagon and, perhaps more important, a station from which to base operations. This original fire station on Cypress Avenue (renamed Fourth Avenue) was soon supplemented by an additional station. Likewise, as the 20th century progressed, these early chemical and steam powered wagons were replaced by modern ladder trucks.

The police department differed a great deal from the other city services for the Oak Park District. Initially a sheriff kept the peace; after annexation, the city took responsibility for patrolling Oak Park. The Sacramento Police Department opened its first substation in Oak Park at the old corporation yard on Thirty-second Street between S and T Streets in 1925. The station was equipped with two patrols cars, a sergeant, and two patrolmen. This new substation was designed to handle the rapidly growing district of Oak Park.

Unlike the fire department, the police department did not have a firm community base in the neighborhood, which eventually led to a type of disassociation between the residents of Oak Park and the police force. This problem was compounded with the ever-changing cultural and ethnic makeup of the residents of Oak Park. This contributed to an adversarial relationship between the police and local residents, never more evident than during the turbulent decade of the 1960s.

During the 1960s, Oak Park witnessed emotional and oftentimes violent social unrest, as minority residents clashed with police officers. The most violent confrontations to take place are commonly referred to by residents as "The Oak Park Riots." To address the combative relationship between residents and police, the police implemented a community-relations program and opened a storefront community office on Thirty-fifth Street. The office was intended to be a place where community leaders and residents could address certain issues, which would result in ending the antagonistic relationship with police.

Much of the cause of the riots can be traced to the policing policies of the city of Sacramento, particularly the removal of police from foot patrol with the coming of the automobile. Today the Sacramento Police Department, like departments throughout the country, is returning to the foot patrol through a community-oriented policing policy. Police are returning to the streets and are getting to know their constituents. The policy has been highly effective in breaking down the barriers between citizens and those who are employed to protect them.

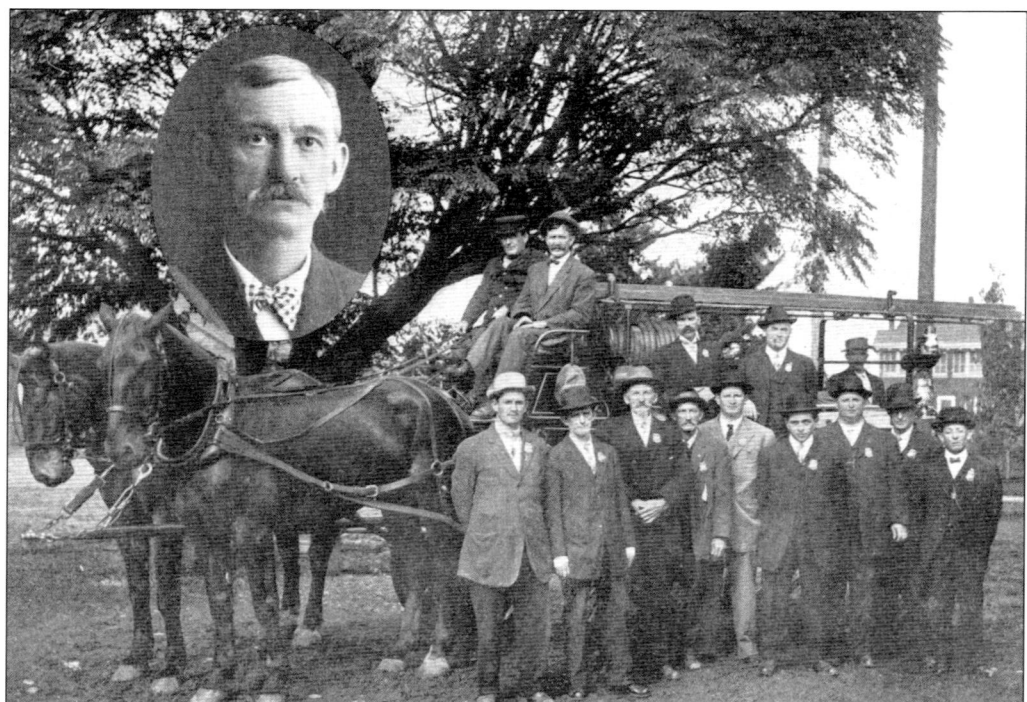

This photograph shows the original 1899 Oak Park Fire Department and volunteers, standing in front of their two-horse drawn water carriage. In the top left hand corner is C.W. Todd, president of the department.

This is a photo montage of the 1899 City of Sacramento Fire Department headed by Chief Henry H. Guthrie. Both the Oak Park and Sacramento Fire Departments assisted each other when fires grew beyond their control.

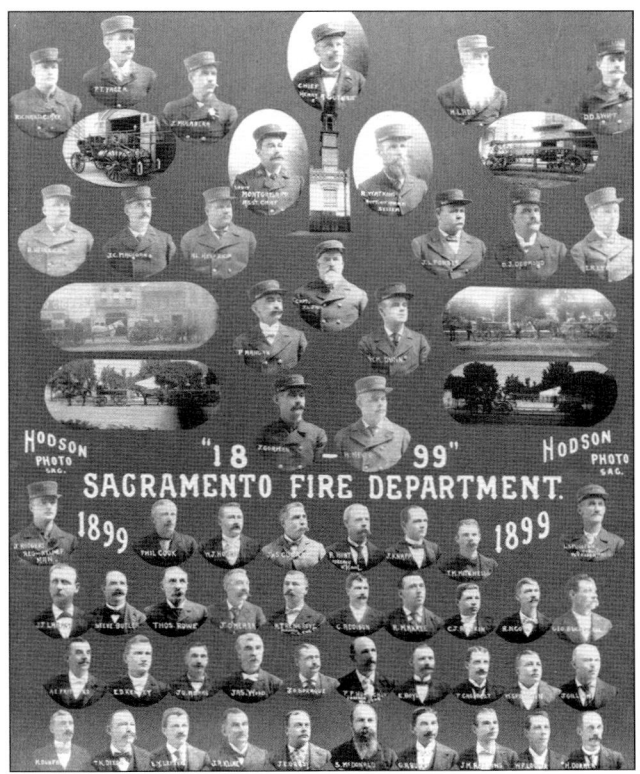

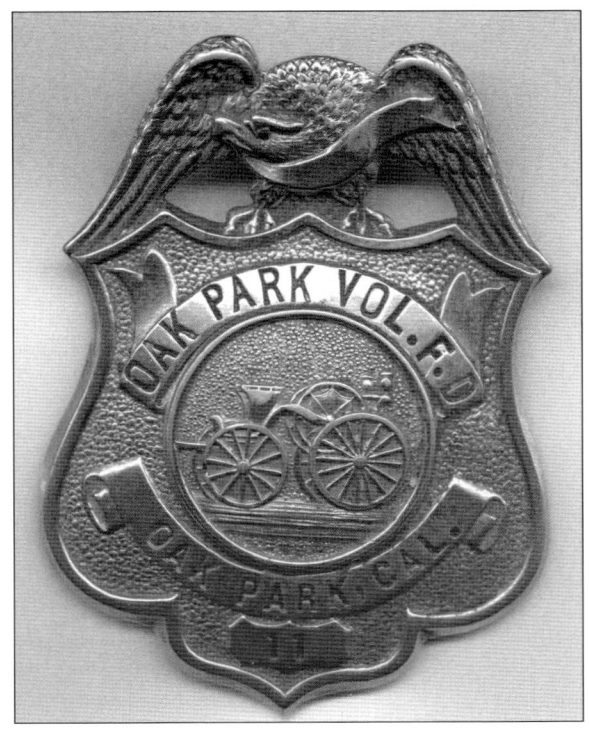

Prior to 1911, the Oak Park Fire Department was entirely separate from the Sacramento Fire Department. This badge was worn by members of the Oak Park Fire Department.

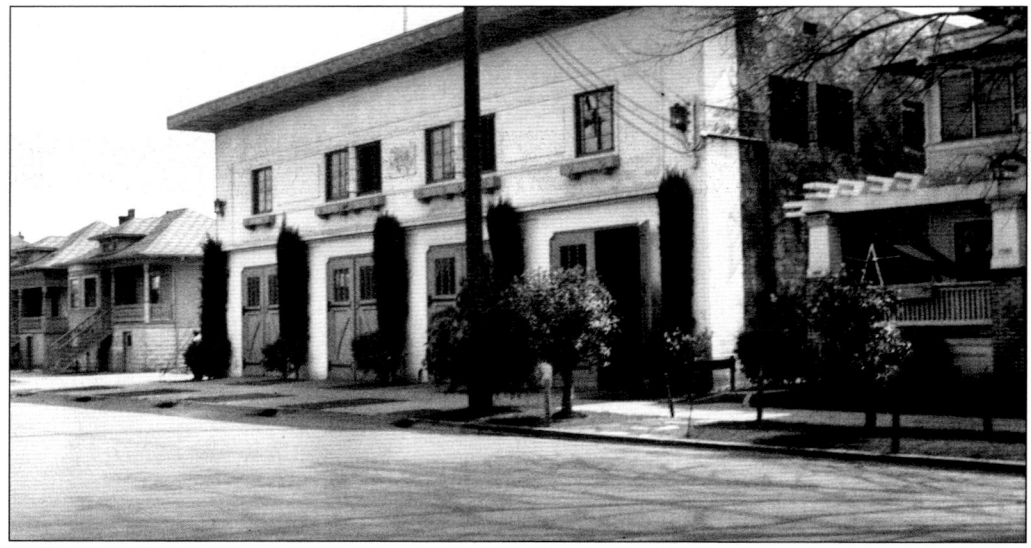

Built in 1915, Fire Station Engine No. 6 was the largest station in Sacramento and the second largest station on the West Coast. The station was located at 3414 Cypress Street.

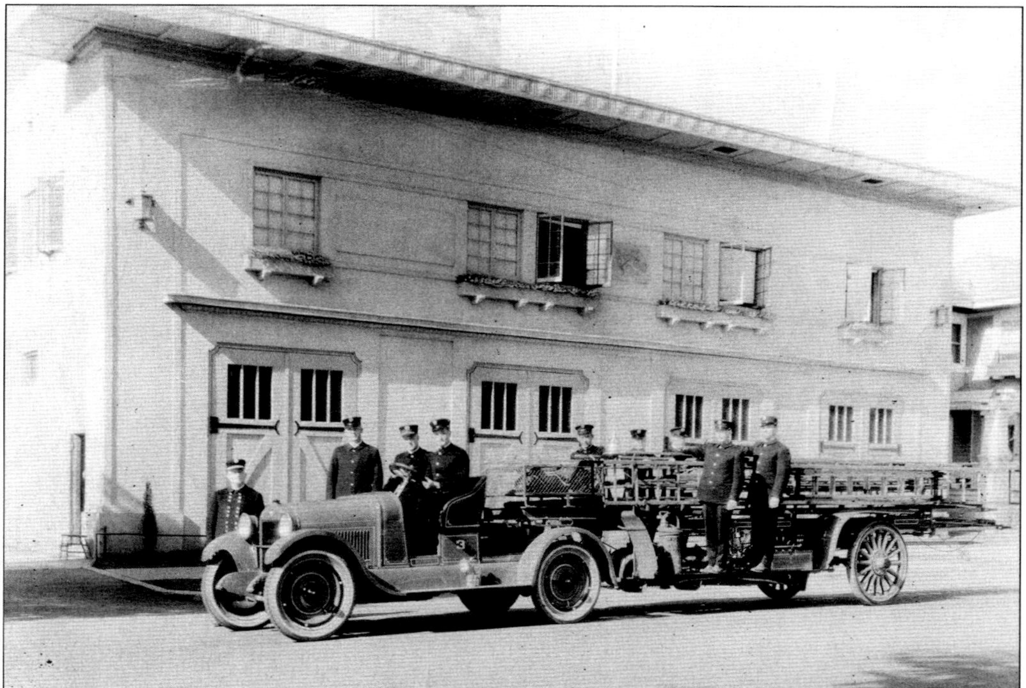

Firefighters of Station No.6 in Oak Park pose c. 1925 alongside their new fire engine in front of the firehouse.

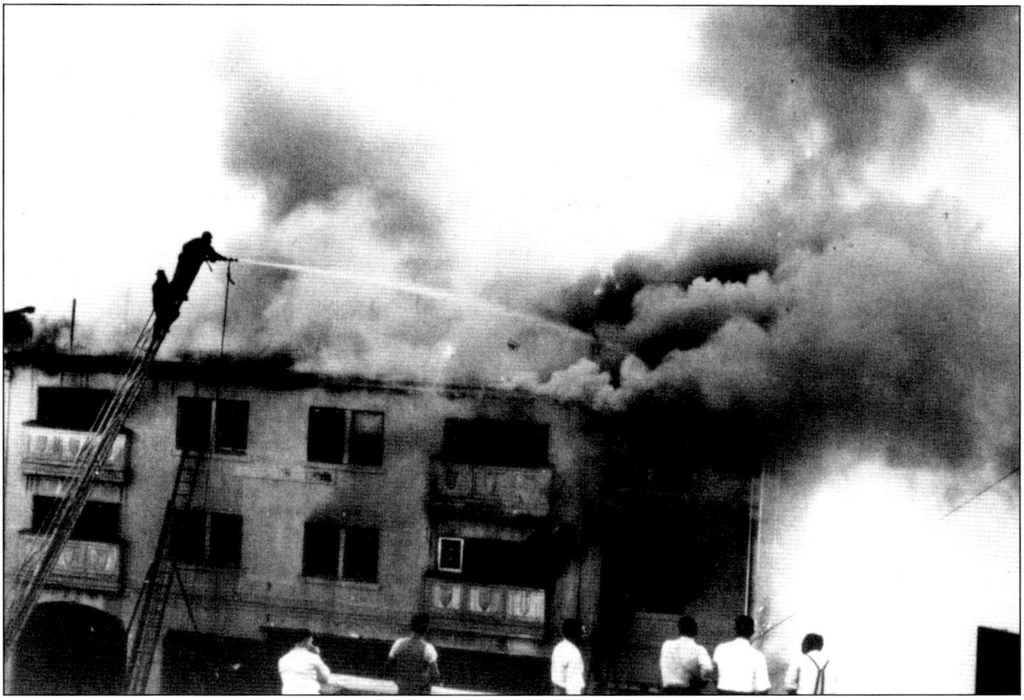

Members of Station No. 6 along with other stations throughout the city attempt to save the Boones Furniture warehouse, the Eagles Hall, and the Mithias Building on July 17, 1944.

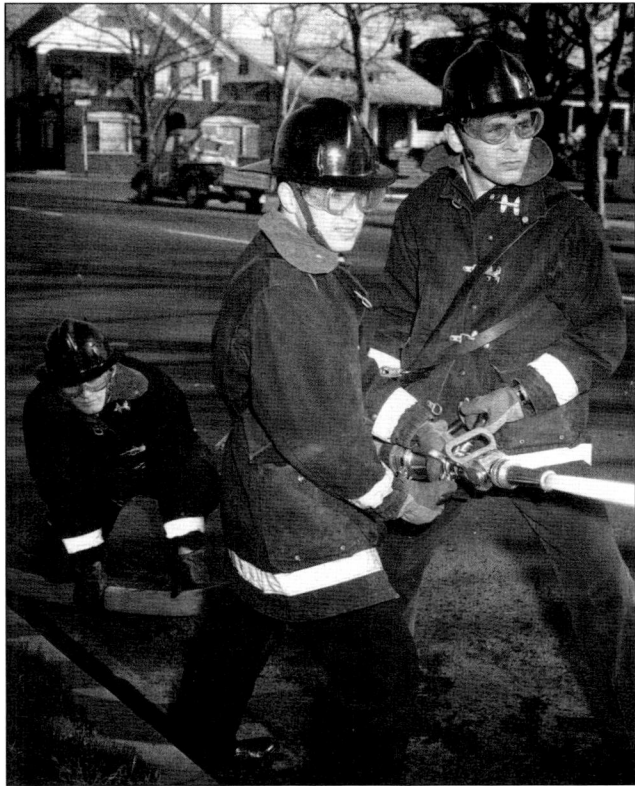

Firefighters man the water hose to extinguish a fire off of Fourth Avenue in Oak Park, c. 1960.

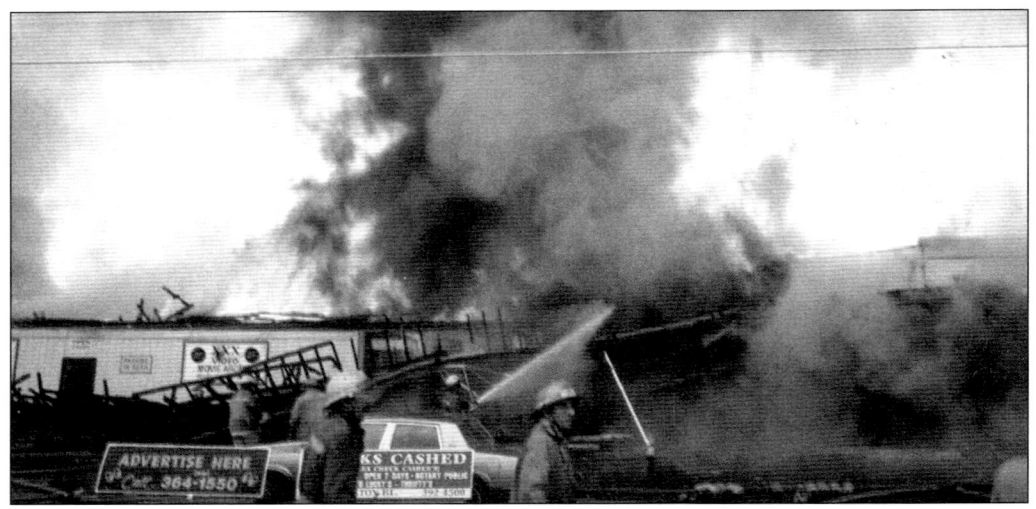

A three-alarm fire erupted c. 1980 at a shopping plaza located at Stockton Boulevard and Fruitridge Road.

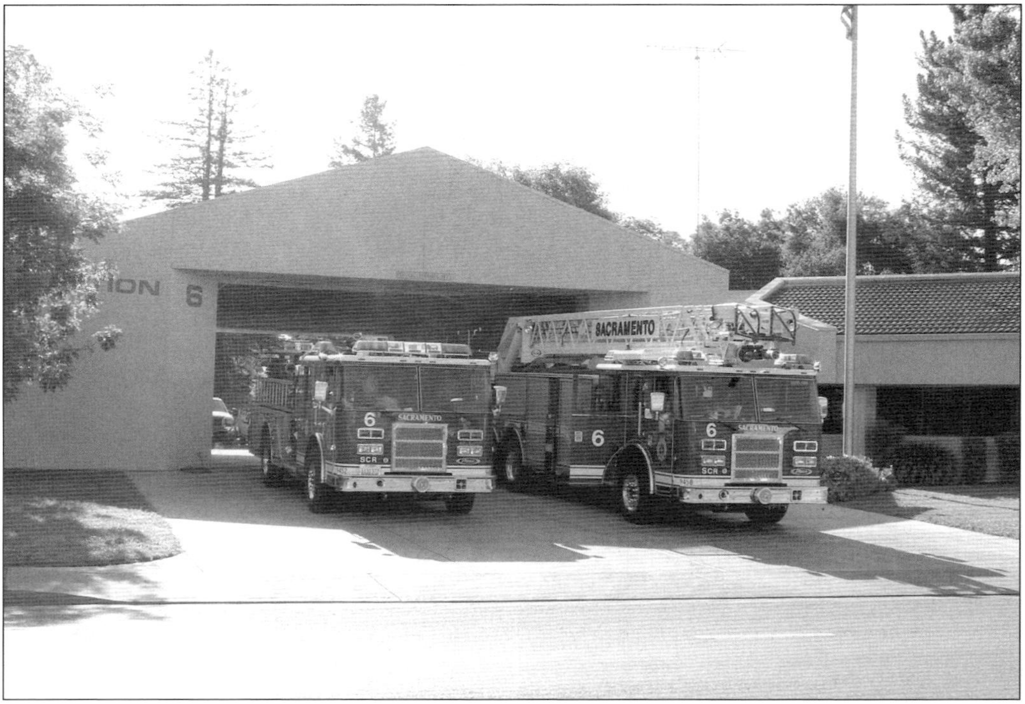

Oak Park Fire Station No. 6, originally on Fourth Avenue in 1977, relocated to its current location on Martin Luther King Boulevard. (Photo by Gabe Aeschliman, 2004.)

A police officer models the uniform of a typical Oak Park police officer, c. 1915.

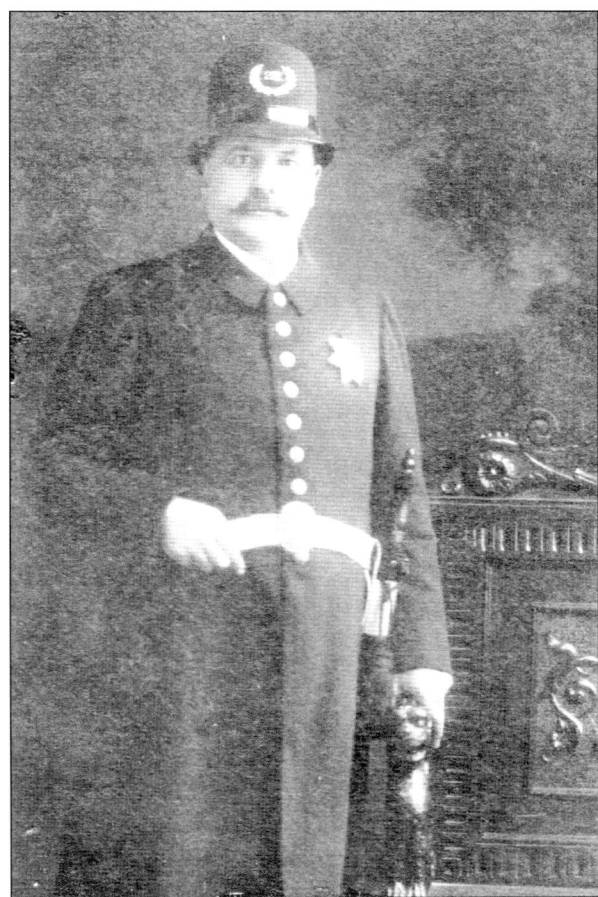

Paddy wagons like this were used c. 1920 to round up unruly citizens in Oak Park, most frequently for public intoxication.

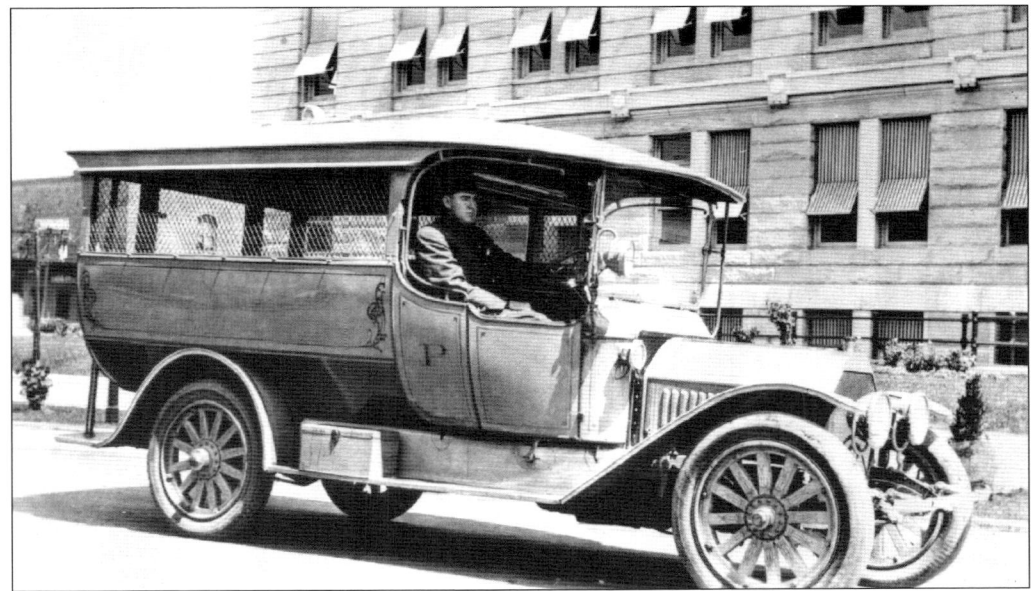

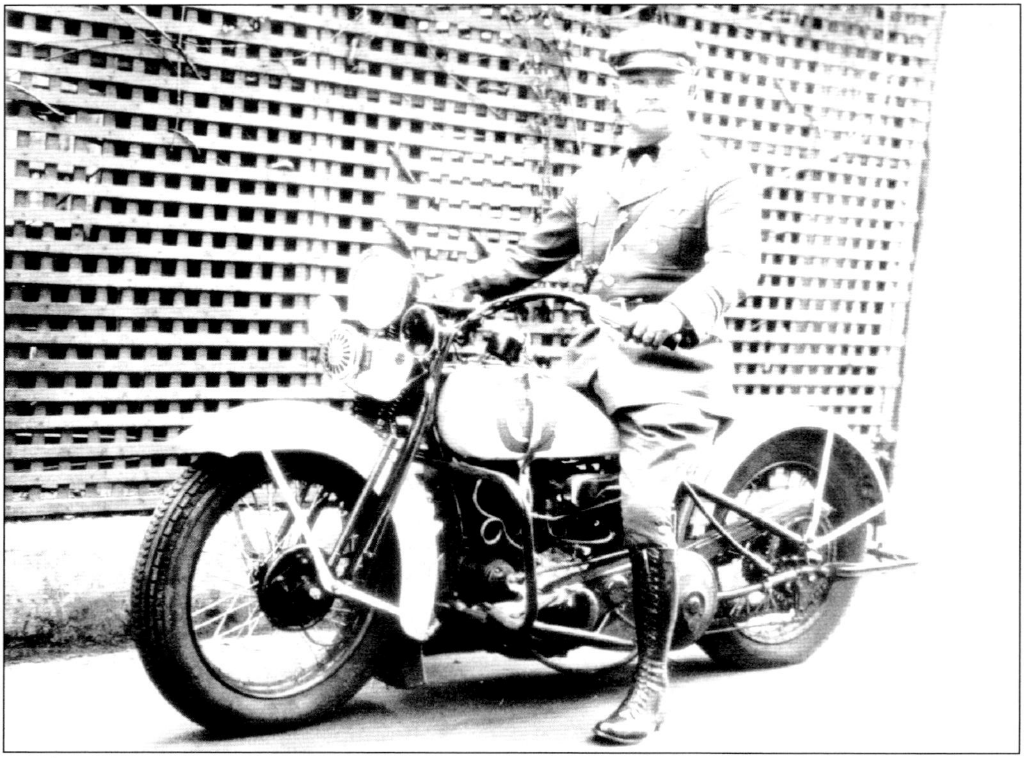

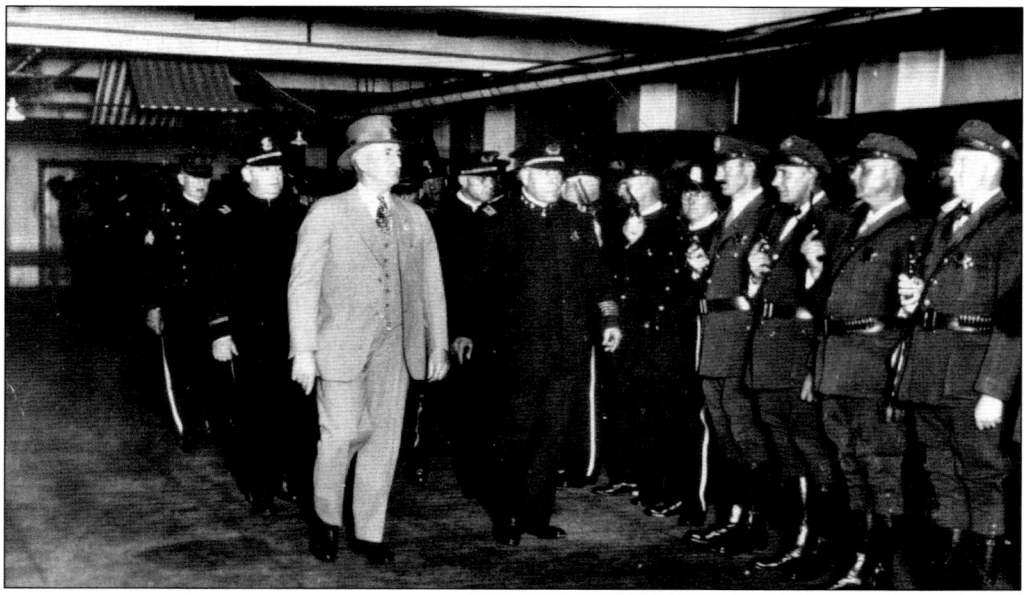

Frank Boniface, a traffic officer who patrolled the Oak Park Neighborhood, poses on his motorcycle, c. 1930.

Sacramento police line up for the annual inspection of officers in the Hall of Justice basement locker room in 1928. Upon completion of the inspection, several of these officers went on patrol in Oak Park.

On June 15, 1969, Oak Park erupted in racial violence when police officers clashed with residents in Oak Park. The Sacramento Police Department reported that the bullet holes in the windshield of this patrol car were caused by residents firing upon them.

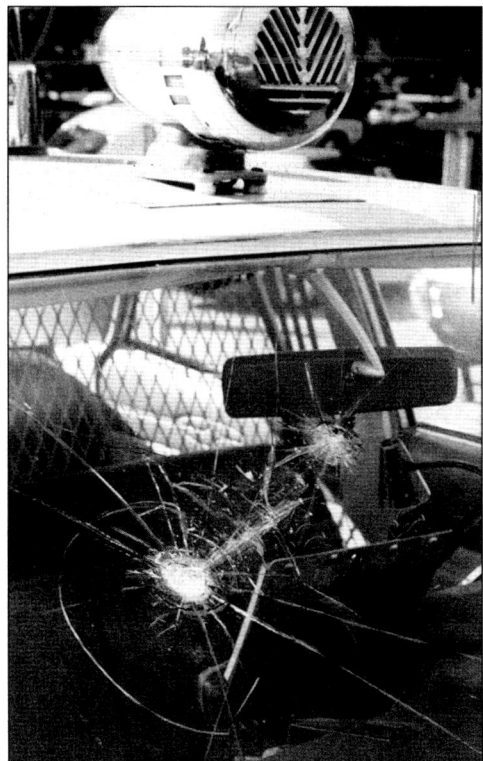

These are some of the weapons confiscated from the Black Panther Headquarters on Thirty-fifth Avenue by the police following the aftermath of the Oak Park Riots in 1969.

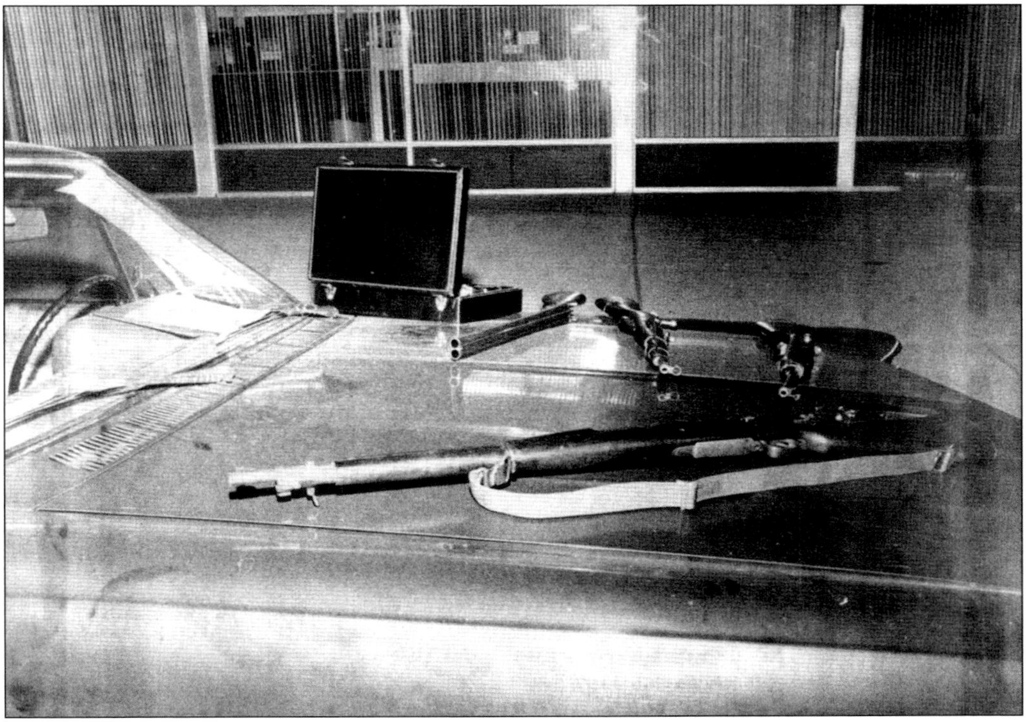

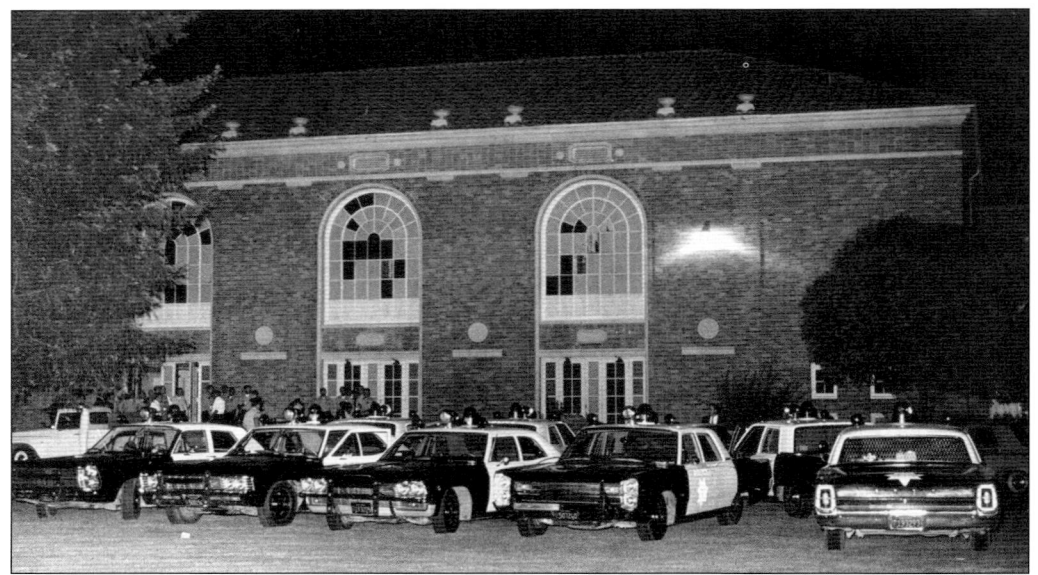
During the Oak Park Riots, police set up an emergency headquarters at Sacramento High School June 15–16, 1969.

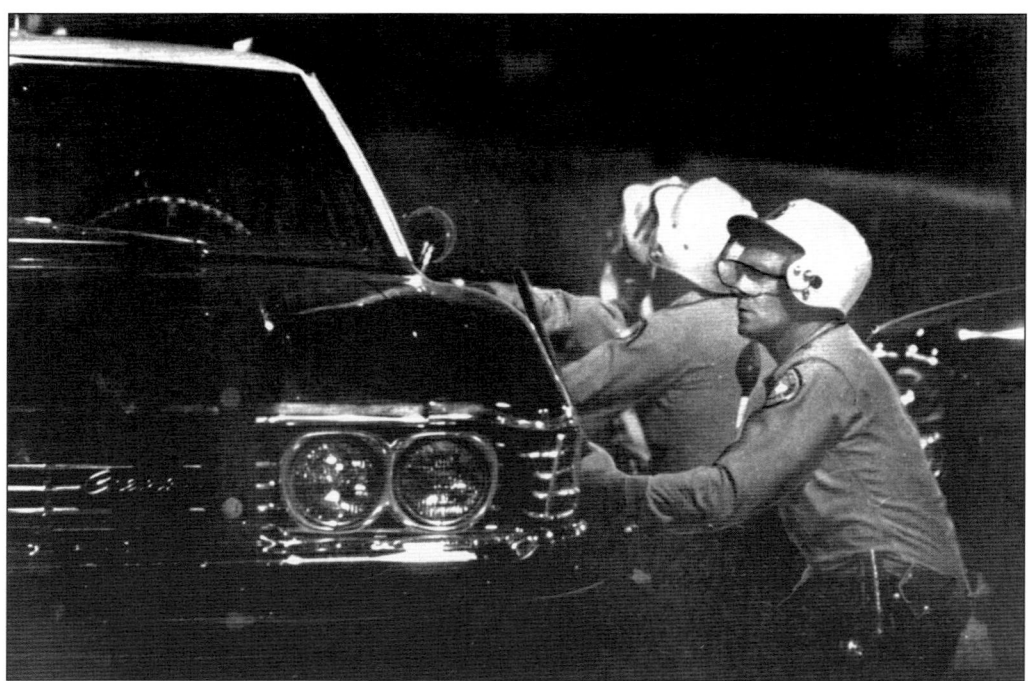
Sacramento police officers crouch behind a squad car for protection during some volatile moments during the Oak Park Riots in 1969.

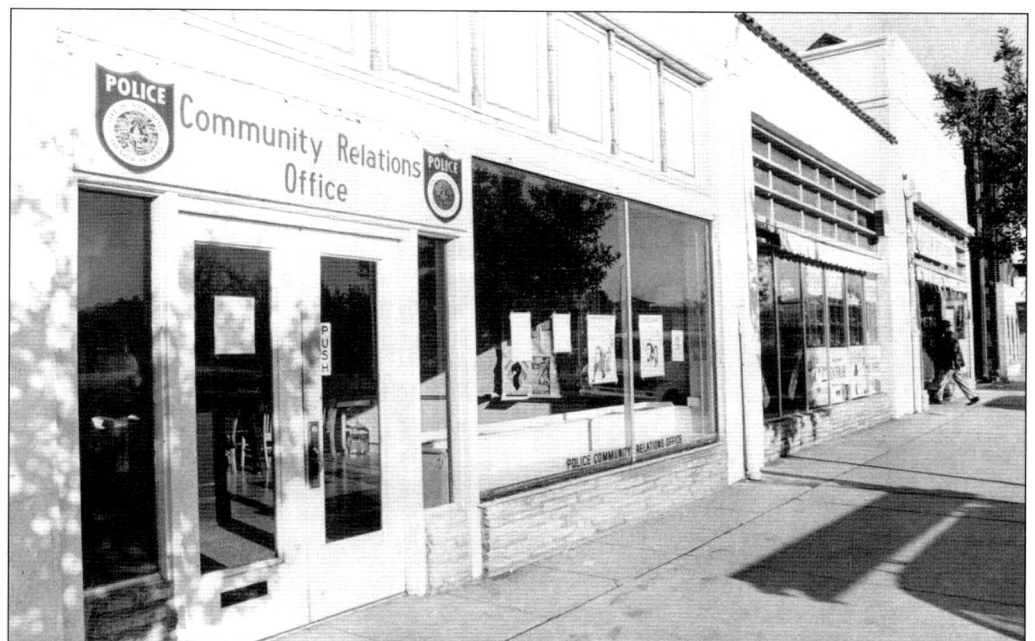

In 1968 the Sacramento Police Department opened its storefront community-relations office in Oak Park on Thirty-fifth Street. The office was designed as a meeting place for community residents and police officers to discuss mutual concerns.

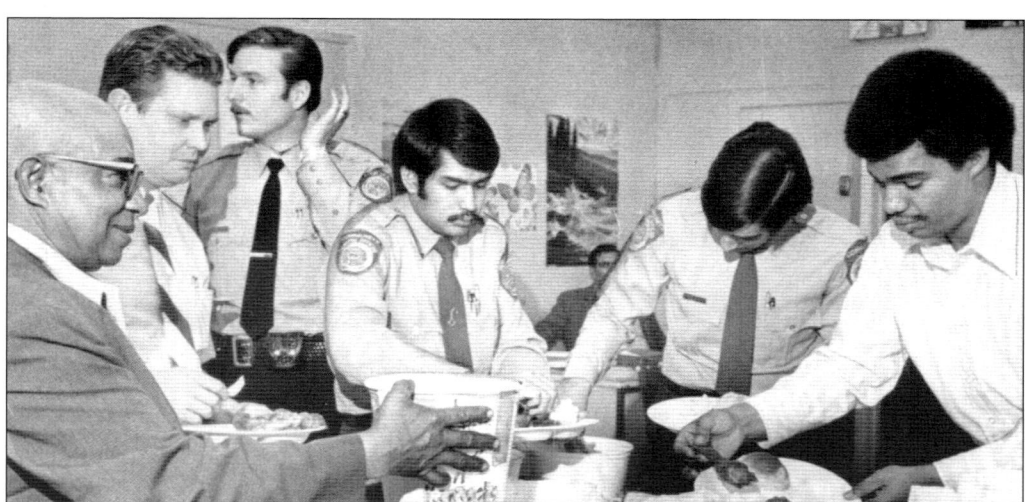

Cleveland Jackson (left), the president of the Oak Park Public Relation Council, handed out dinners at the community relation office. He promised to provide dinners every time a new police officer began a new patrol in the neighborhood.

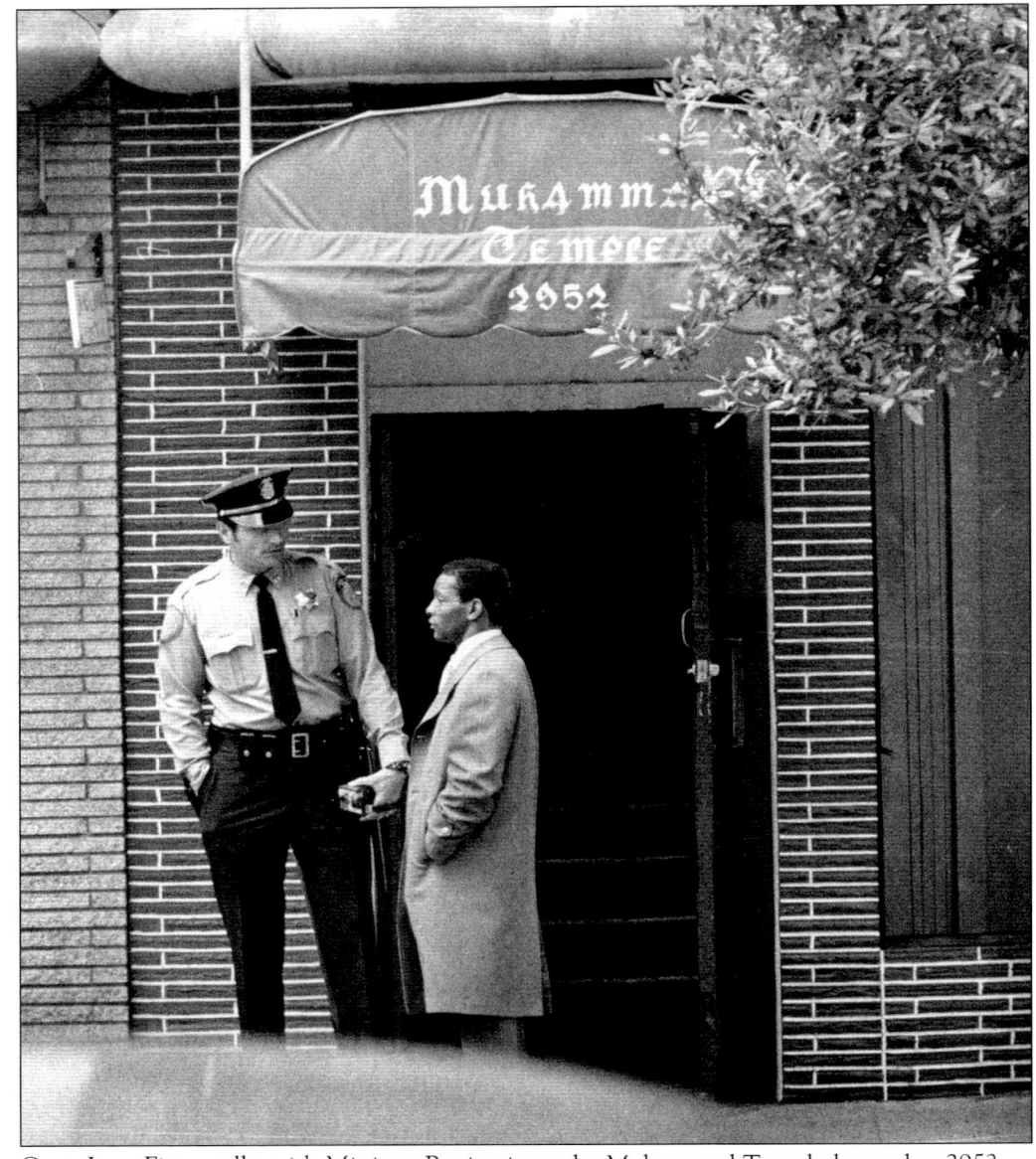
Capt. Jerry Finny talks with Minister Benjamin at the Muhammad Temple located at 2952 Thirty-fifth Avenue in Oak Park in 1974.

Ten

Revitalization and Rebirth

By Gabe Aeschliman

Nearly 100 years after the formation of the Oak Park suburb, a growing group of community members has begun a revitalization effort that substantially improves upon previous urban renewal programs. Instead of handing down a program from federal, state, or city government, the people of Oak Park have initiated their own program led by native son and former Phoenix Suns star Kevin Johnson. Unlike most successful residents who escape the inner city, Kevin Johnson has not turned his back on the community in which he was raised. What he started as an after-school program for 30 students has grown into a complete urban renewal program.

The St. HOPE corporation, an outgrowth of St. HOPE Academy founded in 1989 by Johnson, has grown into a multi-faceted organization focused on economic, social, and intellectual redevelopment. The organization is comprised of smaller sub-groups that focus on a specific area of redevelopment. The St. HOPE Development Company restores historic Oak Park structures, providing new infrastructure to attract new businesses. In 2003 the "40 Acres" complex, which contains a bookstore, art gallery, theater, barbershop, and Starbucks Coffee House, opened in restored historic buildings. The St. HOPE public schools attempt to rehabilitate education in Oak Park. After a bruising battle with the California Teachers Union, in 2003 St. HOPE obtained a charter for Oak Park's only high school that was suffering from poor student performance. Finally, the Neighborhood Corps engage committed young people to take an interest in the Oak Park community.

St. HOPE has achieved much success in rehabilitating the wounded Oak Park area due primarily to its grassroots organizational style. The group argues their biggest fear is gentrification of the fragile community. They do not want to price poor people out of the area like so many revitalization efforts before them. They want to "give a voice to the community" and provide a higher quality of living for current residents. Through education and economic advancement, St. HOPE has provided Oak Park with hope that has been nonexistent for the latter portion of the 20th century. With this mentality and support from both inside and outside Oak Park, St. HOPE is well equipped with the tools for success.

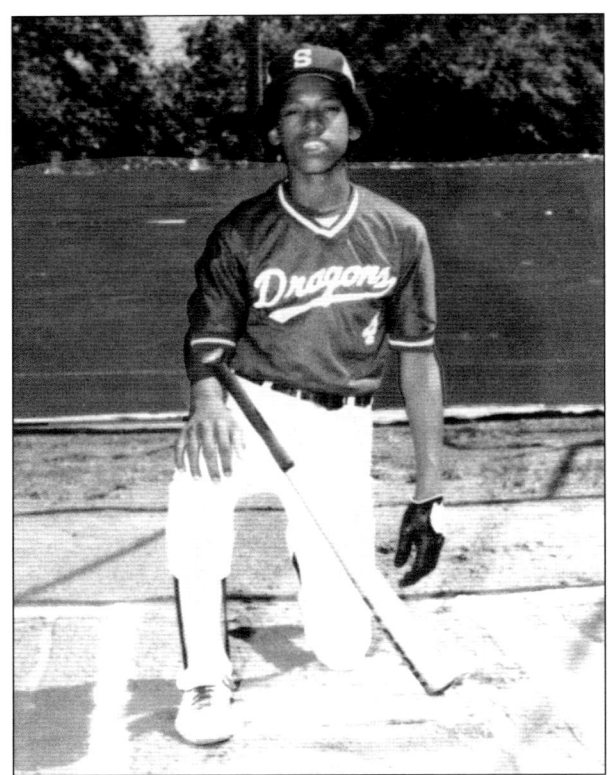

Kevin Johnson, founder of St. HOPE Foundation, grew up in Oak Park. Although best known for his basketball career with the Phoenix Suns, he is shown here as a member of the Dragon's baseball team in his freshman year at Sacramento High School, 1980. (Photo courtesy of St. HOPE.)

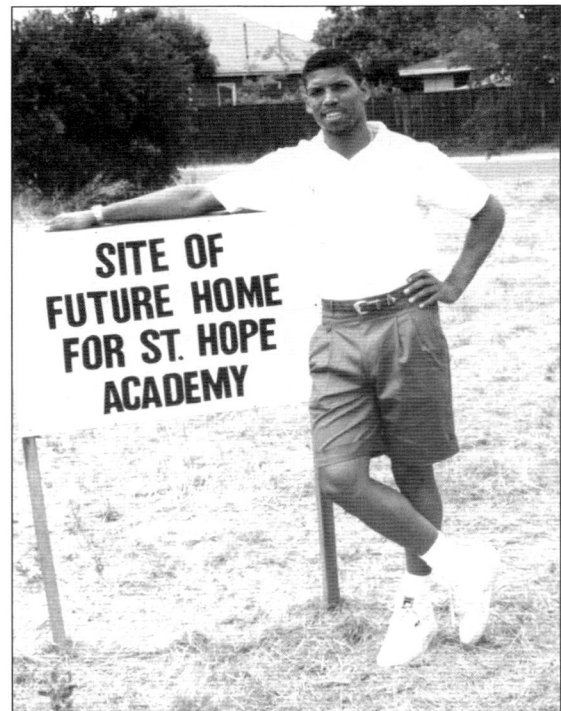

Kevin Johnson poses at the future location of the St. HOPE Academy. Completed in 1989, the academy was St. HOPE'S first project. (Photo by Bill Jones, courtesy of St. HOPE.)

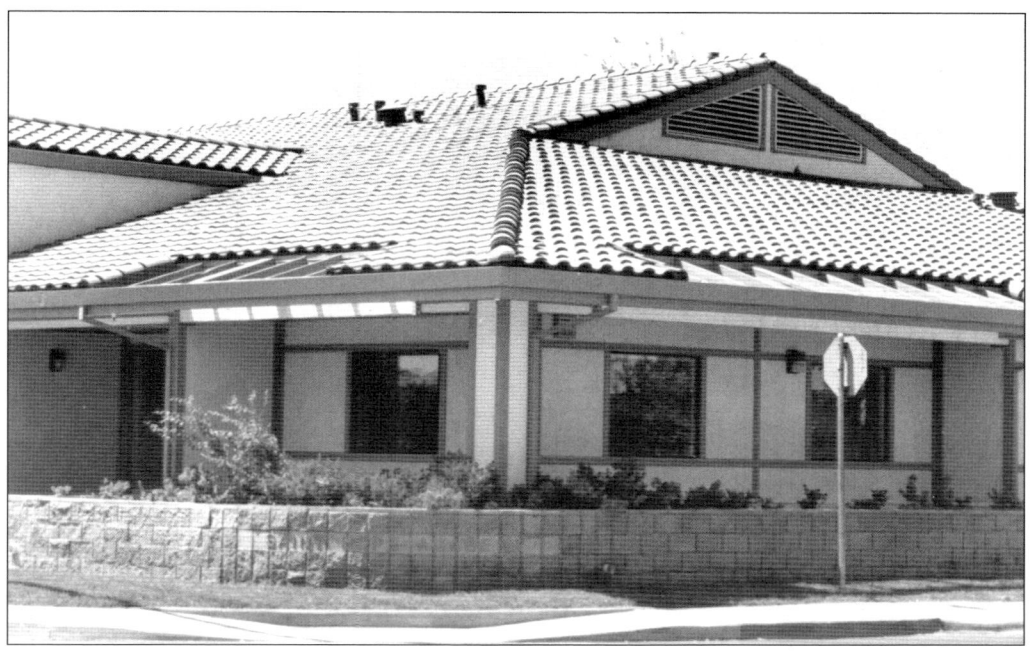

The St. HOPE Academy, shown in this c. 1990 photo, offers support programs for young Oak Park residents. The after-school program attempts to hedge off potential problems facing inner-city children. (Photo courtesy of St. HOPE.)

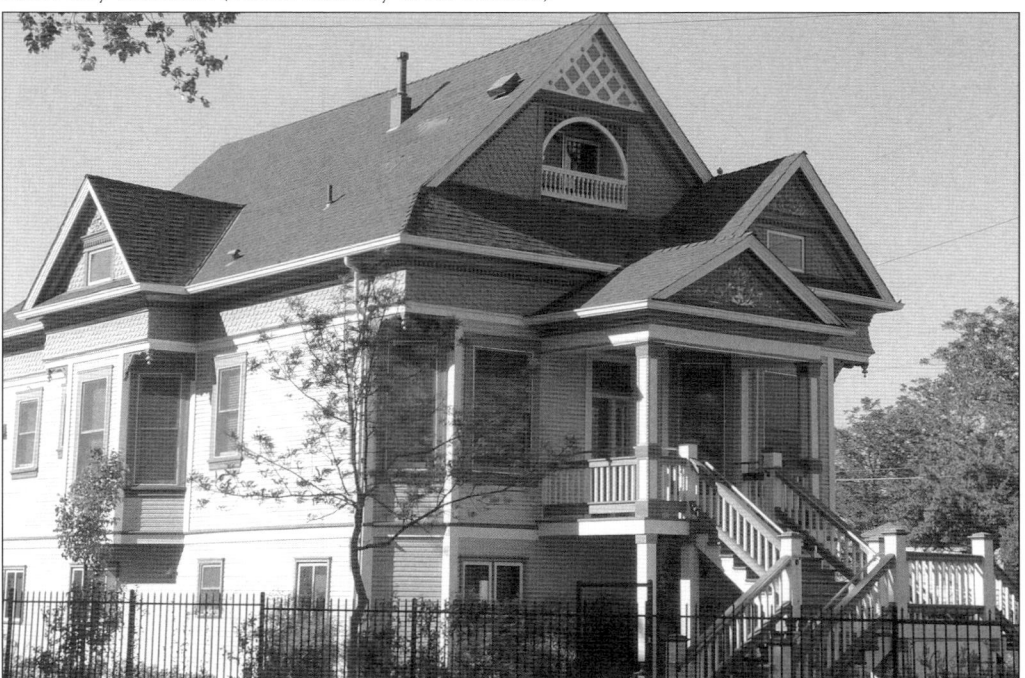

Renovation of this 1885 residence (above) was the first project for the St. HOPE Development Company in 2001. After completion of a parking lot nearby, the historic house is planned to provide space for professional businesses. (Photo by Gabe Aeschliman, 2004.)

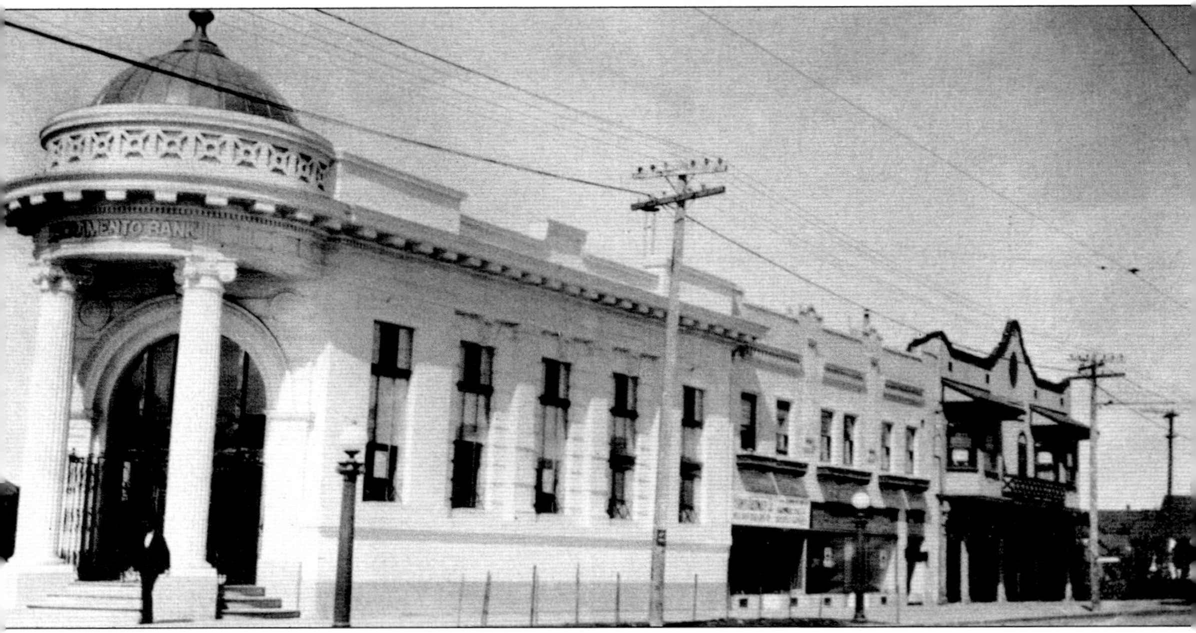

These two photos show the transformation of the 1915 Sacramento Bank to the current U.S. Bank. The St. HOPE Development Company took care to keep most of the original structure intact. The opening of the U.S. Bank in 1995 provided Oak Park with a much-needed second banking firm. This project marked St. HOPE's first business partnership. (Bottom photograph by Gabe Aeschliman, 2004.)

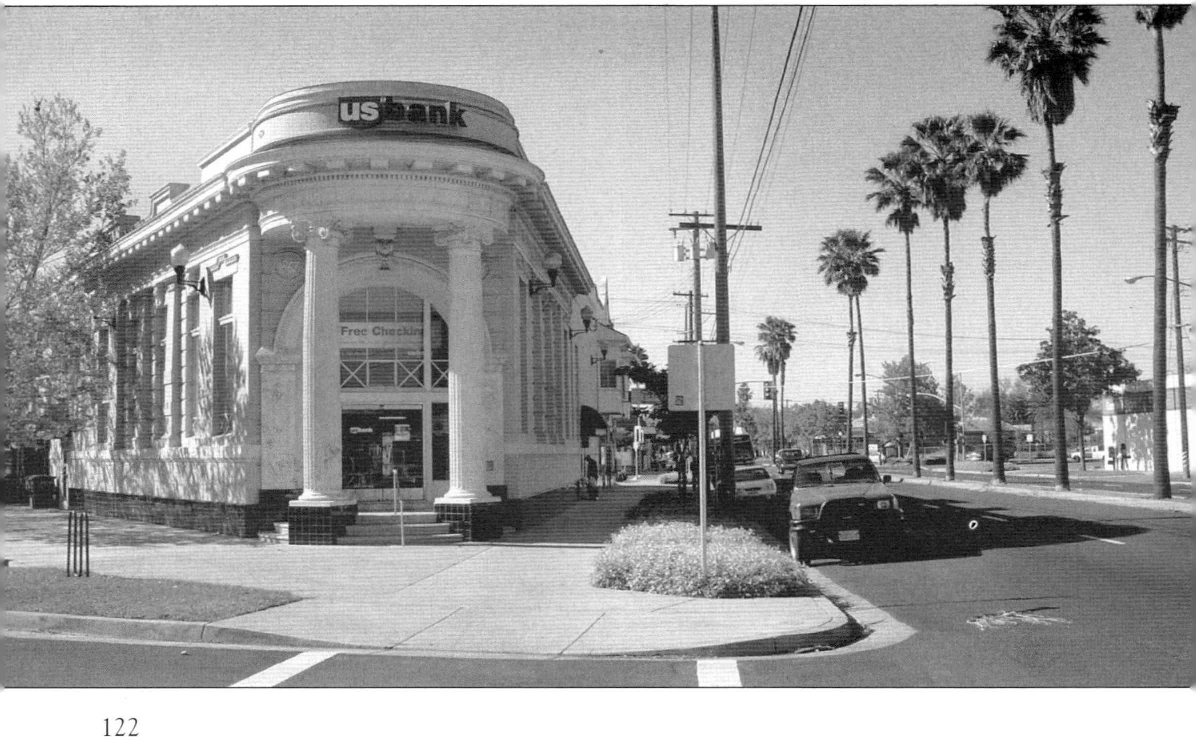

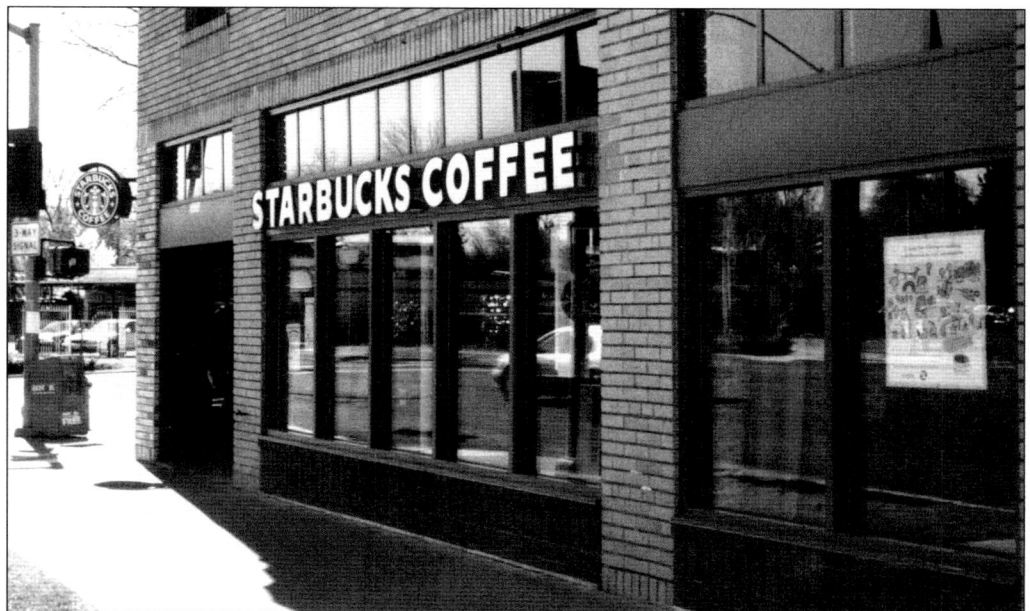

In 2003 St. HOPE renovated the Woodruff Hotel and contracted with the Mondavi Center to bring art performances to Oak Park. The hotel also became the location of the largest Starbucks coffeehouse in Sacramento. (Photo by Gabe Aeschliman, 2004.)

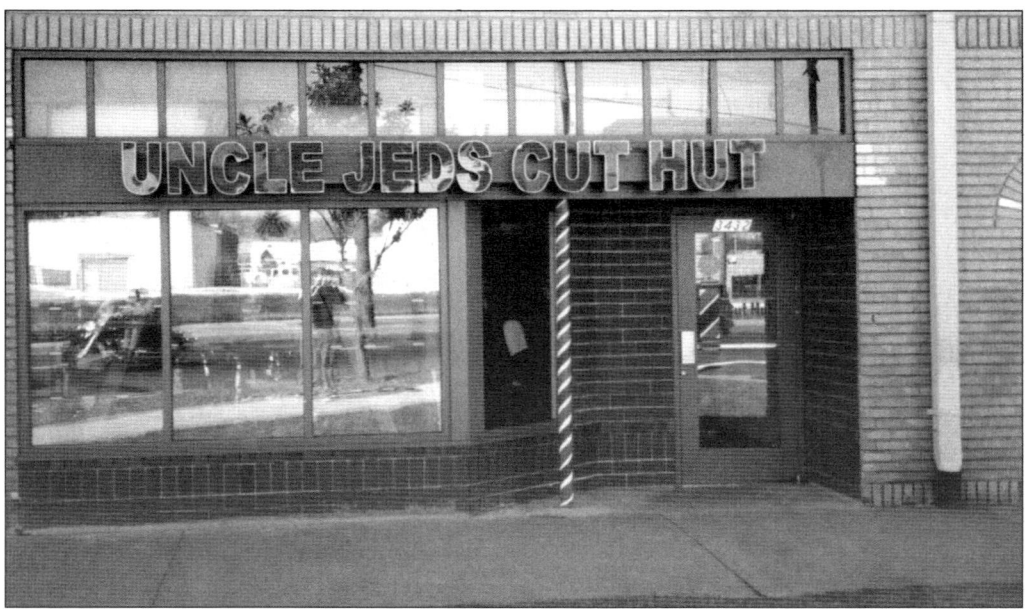

Uncle Jed's Cut Hut is more than a place to get a haircut. The business is reminiscent of the traditional African-American barbershop, offering a forum for discussion on various topics such as art, music, politics, and sports. (Photo by Gabe Aeschliman, 2004.)

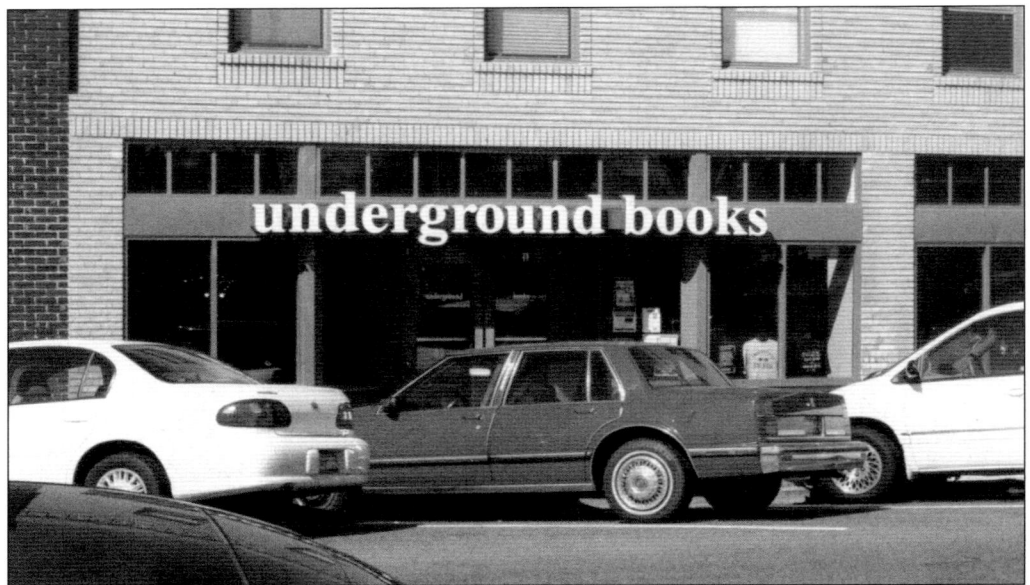

Underground Books drew its name from the underground African-American culture, which, until recently, went widely unrecognized by American society. This bookstore offers Oak Park residents a place to purchase and read ethnic and popular books. (Photo by Gabe Aeschliman, 2004.)

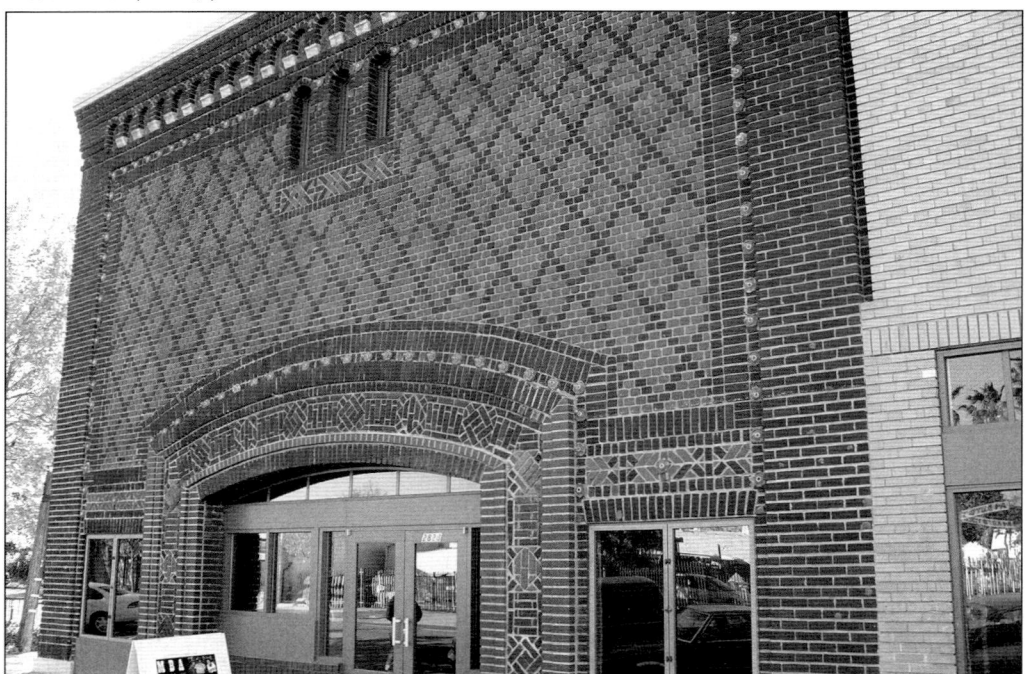

The Guild Theater was originally erected as a movie house called the Victor Theater in 1915, later changing its name to the Oak Park theater in the mid-1900s. The theater fell into disrepair and was under two feet of water when St. HOPE began renovation. Now seating 200, the Guild Theater hosts a variety of multicultural events. (Photo courtesy of St. HOPE.)

This picture depicts the 2003 Neighborhood Corps, which Kevin Johnson described as the most critical component of the St. HOPE program. Hood Corps provides those involved with leadership skills, while also providing a number of services for the neighborhood and the St. HOPE organization. (Photo courtesy of St. HOPE.)

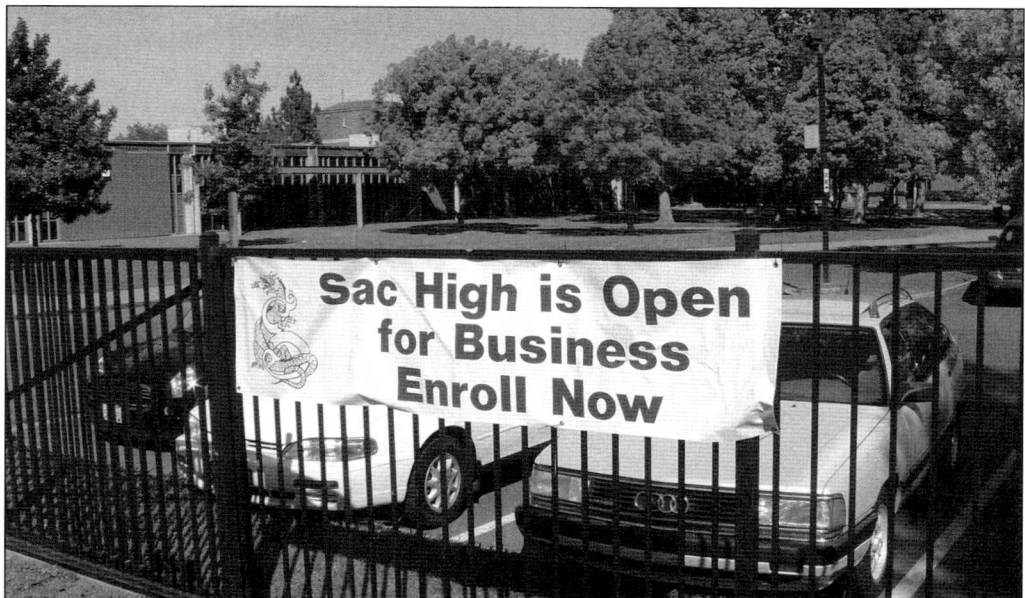

The battle for the charter of Sacramento High School in 2003 was the biggest obstacle St. HOPE faced since its creation in 1989. St. HOPE won the struggle and opened the charter school's doors in September 2003. (Photo courtesy of St. HOPE.)

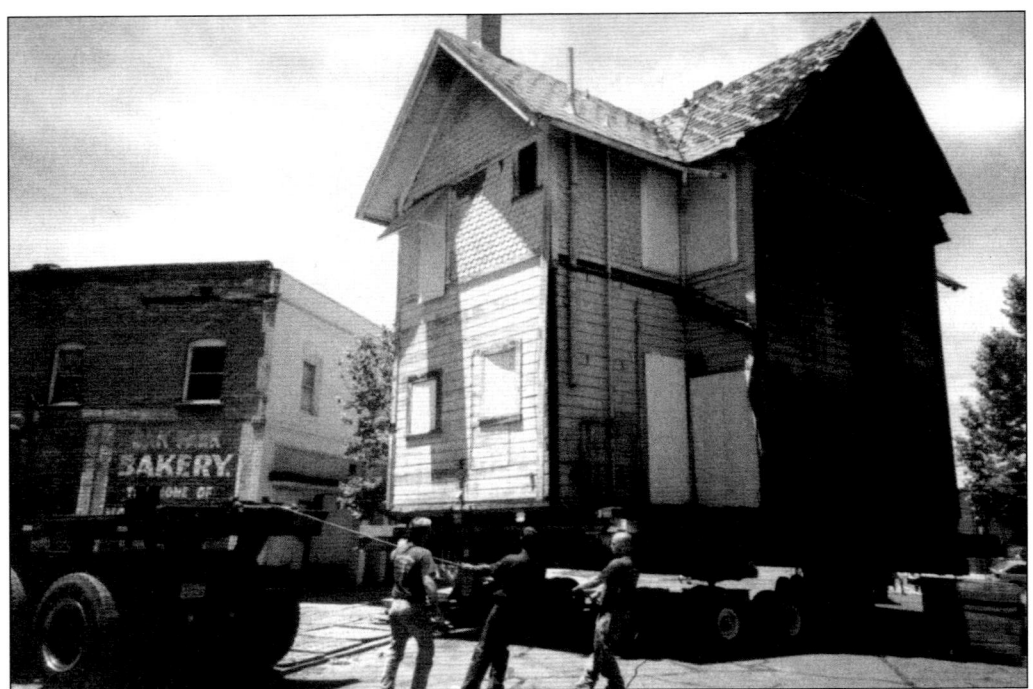

The St. HOPE Development Company moved this late 19th-century Victorian home next to the 40 Acres project. Once owned by Joseph Lewis, developer of the Victor Theater, this home is believed to be the oldest residence in Oak Park. (Photo courtesy of St. HOPE.)

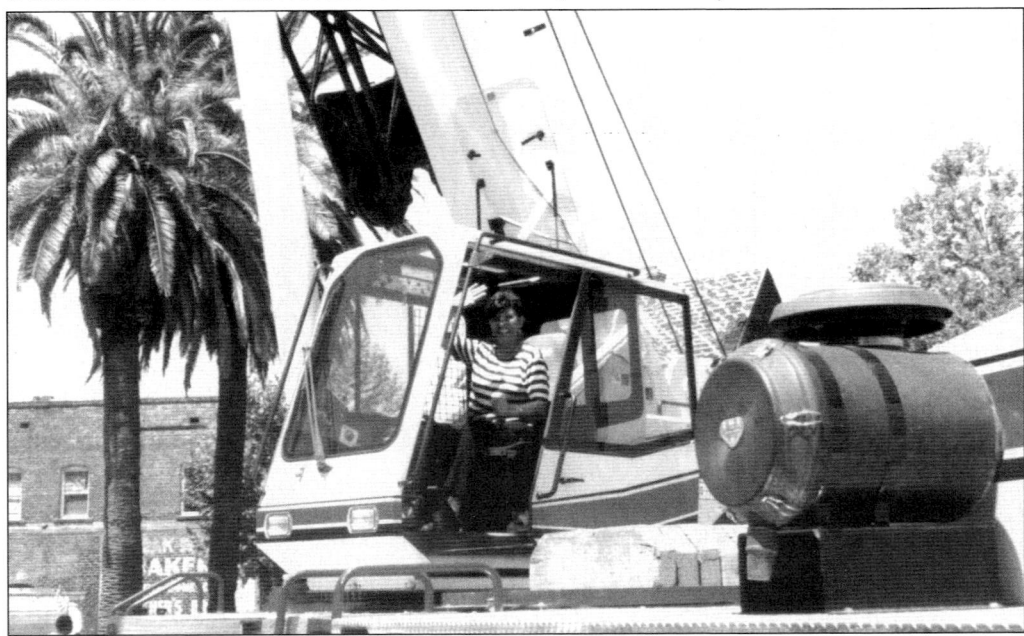

Georgia West, known affectionately as "Mother Rose," is program director of the St. HOPE Foundation. She poses here for a picture during the movement of the 19th-century Victorian home in 2000. (Photo courtesy of St. HOPE.)

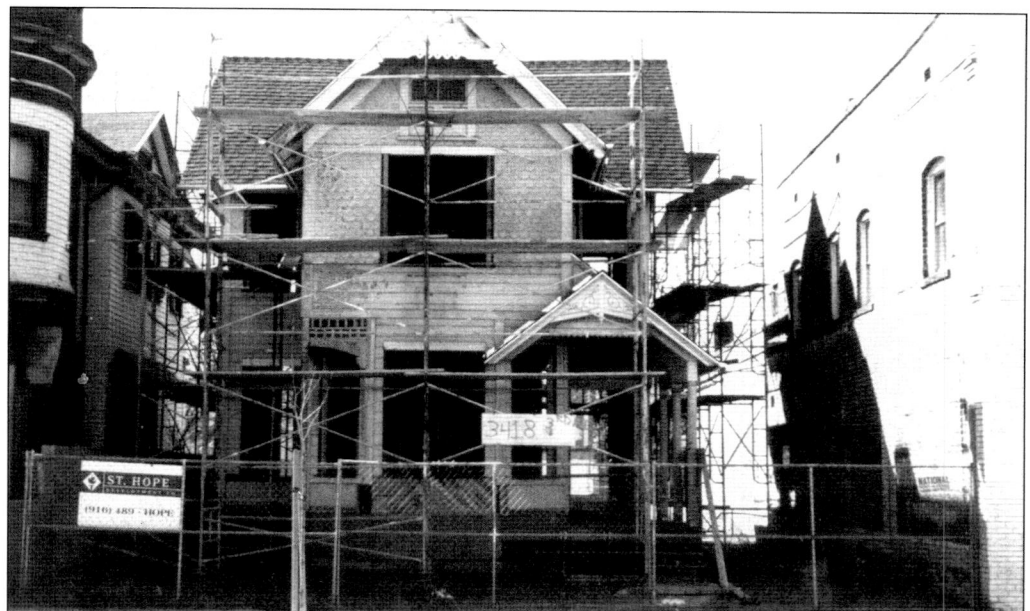

Much like the 1885 Victorian project, this one-time residence is planned to be converted into a professional building that will house the Sacramento Philharmonic Orchestra, again trying to revitalize the once prosperous business district. The building is planned to be completed by 2006. (Photo by Gabe Aeschliman, 2004.)

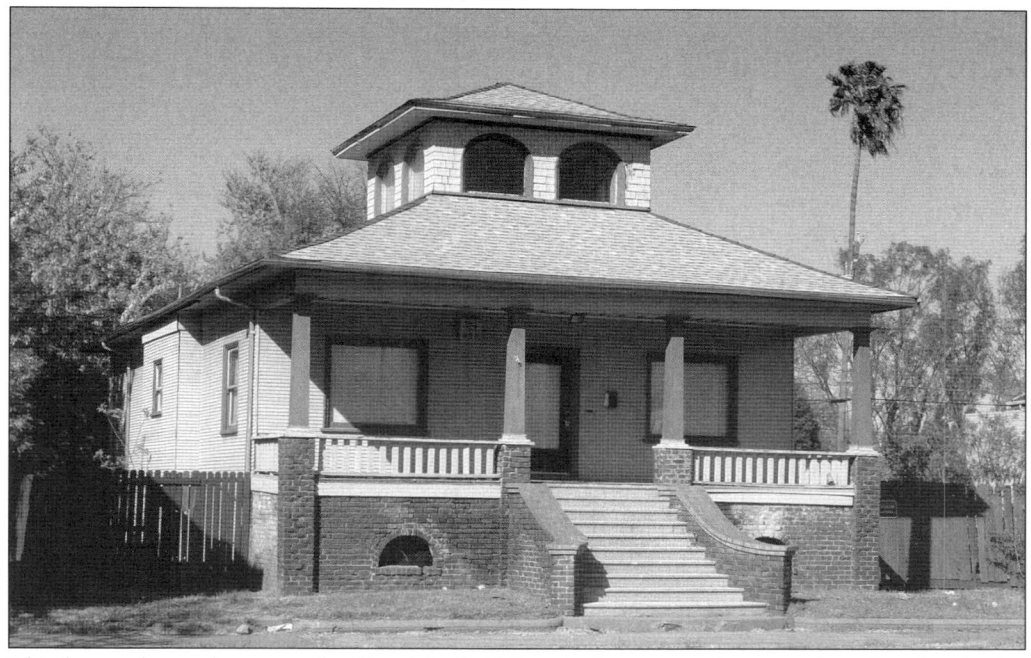

This home, located next to the Gosticks Building, is the current home and studio of artist-in-residence Milton Bowens. In 2004 St. HOPE planned to develop a preschool that focuses on special needs such as autism. This location is planned to serve 100 children. (Photo by Gabe Aeschliman, 2004.)

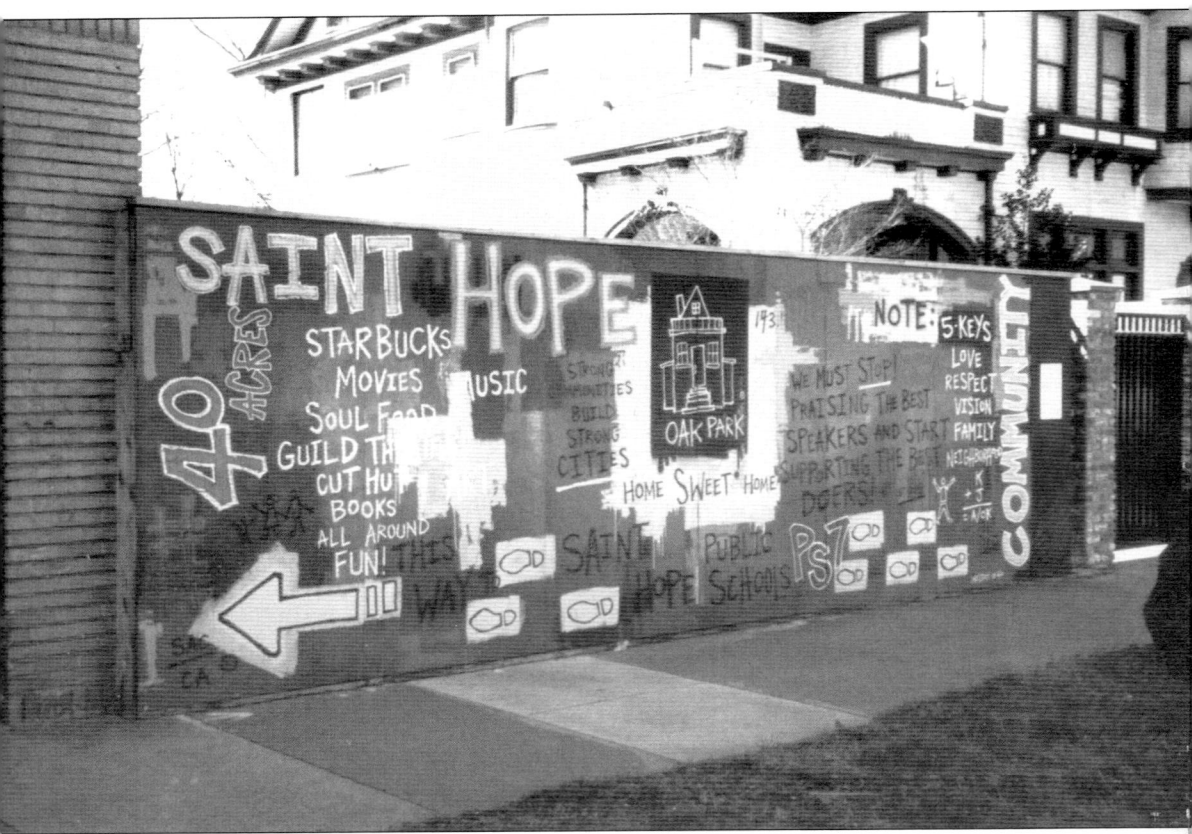

This mural, created by resident artist Milton Bowens, provided a temporary construction barricade for a future 40 Acres restaurant patio. The quotation on the right side of the mural states, "We must Stop! praising the best speakers and start supporting the best doers." This is the essence of St. HOPE. (Photo by Gabe Aeschliman, 2004.)